PERILOUS INTERVENTIONS

More Advance Praise for *Perilous Interventions*

'This is an outstanding book on the side effects of interventionism, written in extremely elegant prose and with maximal clarity. It documents how people find arguments couched in moralistic terms to intervene in complex systems they don't understand. These interventions trigger endless chains of unintended consequences—consequences for the victims, but none for the interventionists, allowing them to repeat the mistake again and again. Puri, as an insider, outlines the principles and legal mechanisms, then runs through the events of the past few years since the Iraq invasion; all of his chapters are models of concision, presenting the story of Ukraine, Syria, Libya and Yemen, among others, as standalone briefings to the uninitiated. It was high time that somebody in international affairs approached the problem of "iatrogenics", that is, harm done by the healer. This book should be mandatory reading for every student and practitioner of foreign affairs.' —Nassim Nicholas Taleb, risk specialist and bestselling author of *The Black Swan* and *Antifragile*

'As the world copes with the unending political tragedy in the Middle East, Hardeep Singh Puri offers a trenchant critique of the Western use of military force and the abuse of the United Nations Security Council that are now widely seen as contributing to the regional crises. The severe judgements of Puri, who served as India's envoy to the United Nations in both Geneva and New York, do not stem from the traditional Indian obsession with the principles of territorial sovereignty and non-intervention. They emerge from Puri's first-hand experience at the UN Security Council during 2011–12, when India served as a non-permanent member and was eager to establish its credentials as a responsible global power. Puri's call for military prudence and revitalization of multilateralism are also shaped by India's failed intervention in Sri Lanka's ethnic crisis. *Perilous Interventions* captures an important moment in India's international experience and is a major contribution to the current international debate on when, where and how to use military force.' —C. Raja Mohan, director, Carnegie India

'In *Perilous Interventions*, Hardeep Singh Puri takes a forensic swipe at the United Nations Security Council, forcefully arguing that if it continues to function as it presently does it will further discredit the cause of peace and security. Since his posting as a young diplomat in the Sri Lankan Tamil war, Puri has had a ring-side seat on numerous faulty interventions and knows why they went wrong. He ended up at the heart of the Security Council and its ill-fated decisions on Libya and Syria where it was "clear as daylight" that arming rebels would create unprecedented chaos. He describes whimsical decision making without thinking through consequences and asks poignantly why governments pursue policies which are against their own interests. Puri's is a robust, refreshing and experienced voice explaining what many of us are wondering every day: how it was ever possible that terror could have such a grip on global politics. The insight is chilling and brilliant. His view is all the more important because it doesn't come from the safe talking shops of the Washington Beltway, London's Whitehall or a European Union committee. This is the eye of how and why things fall apart when run by an old-guard global system that has not been reformed for more than seventy years.' —Humphrey Hawksley, author and former foreign correspondent for BBC

'Hardeep Singh Puri's *Perilous Interventions* opens a welcome window into the closed-off inner sanctum of multilateral diplomacy, the United Nations Security Council. The look is a privileged one—both because Puri, a former Indian ambassador, was a member of the Council himself at a critical intervention-minded moment and because he wields a pen that cuts through institutional self-regard and obfuscating UN speak to reveal how the panel can end up undermining the very thing it is charged with insuring: international peace and security.' —Warren Hoge, former *New York Times* UN correspondent

'As the saying goes, everyone has twenty-twenty hindsight. That saying certainly is applicable to events that took place in the United Nations Security Council in 2011 and 2012 regarding Libya and Syria—events which ultimately led to what Hardeep Singh Puri describes as "the mess that the world finds itself in". That mess includes the catastrophic consequences of the intervention in Libya and, even worse, the protracted war in Syria, with over 300,000 dead and over four million of its citizens displaced. Perhaps even more significant is the rapid and related rise of the ISIS as a new brand of militant terrorism. But it turns out that Puri has no need to invoke hindsight vision: he demonstrably got it dead right during his two-year participation in the Security Council regarding the future consequences of actions (and inactions) on the part of the Council (and, unilaterally, on the part of some of its permanent members) in both instances. He provides us with an insider's view, having been a direct participant in the events described so chillingly in this narrative. It is a must read for anyone trying to decipher the mysterious process of decision making in the Security Council.' —Gert Rosenthal, former permanent representative of Guatemala to the United Nations

'This remarkable account of the UN Security Council's role in the Libyan intervention and its continued difficulties in Syria provides a very valuable insider's perspective. As India's permanent representative to the UN, and with extensive experience in multilateral diplomacy, Hardeep Singh Puri probes beneath the broad public declarations (protection of civilians) to examine the underlying motives of the principal actors, especially the US, UK and France. His account of the ambivalence of the US, still reeling from inaction in Rwanda fifteen years earlier but feeling propelled to act, leaves the reader with an acute sense of uncertainty as to how the US will respond to ongoing crises in Syria, Yemen and Libya. This is a must-read account for anyone who wants to probe beneath the conventional narrative to understand how the Security Council actually decided and acted in Libya and its longer-term consequences.' —John L. Hirsch, former US ambassador to Sierra Leone

'Hardeep Singh Puri is a rare diplomat—a real political thinker who is not afraid to write fiercely and challenge stale assumptions. I may not agree with everything he says, but by the bottom of the first page, all I wanted to do was to keep reading. Just like when I used to interact with him when he was on the UN Security Council, every thought is engaging, intelligent and provocative in equal measure.' —Dr Simon Adams, executive director, Global Centre for the Responsibility to Protect

Perilous Interventions is an important work of scholarship of the world order and the institution which was supposed to maintain it, the United Nations Security Council. Clearly, as Puri tells it, the world order is frayed and the UNSC is no longer in a position to honestly exercise the enormous powers that were given to it by the UN Charter in the wake of the Second World War. The UNSC was the realpolitik part of the idealistic UN system. Unfortunately, what Puri tells us is that realpolitik has gone haywire and little or nothing is left of the ideals for which all the nations of the world agreed to sign the UN Charter.' —Dr Manoj Joshi, distinguished fellow, Observer Research Foundation

'Hardeep Singh Puri brilliantly depicts a new trend of world powers unleashing their vision and interests on the rest of the world. We are privileged to a front-row view of what took place at the ever-secretive horse-shoe table of the UN Security Council directly after the Arab Spring. The action (and inaction) recounted sheds new light on this turning point for the Middle East and the world as a whole. A must read for neophytes, seasoned diplomats and anyone who is seriously interested in the future of the UN.' —Jimena Leiva-Roesch, senior policy analyst, International Peace Institute

'With his extensive diplomatic experience and inimitable eloquence, Hardeep Singh Puri tackles the central dilemmas confronting the United Nations Security Council as it struggles with new and persisting challenges to world peace. At a time of geopolitical redistribution of international influence and emerging multipolarity, Ambassador Puri exposes ill-conceived military strategies and questions both the morality and the effectiveness of interventionist ideologies. The analysis and insights emanating from his personal involvement in the Security Council's deliberations are required reading for all who are ready to learn from the misconceptions of the first years of the twenty-first century in order to allow the United Nations to fulfil its mission more responsibly and effectively in the decades ahead.' —Antonio Patriota, permanent representative of Brazil to the United Nations and former foreign minister

'A distinguished professional diplomat from India offers a unique window into the geopolitical cockpit of the United Nations Security Council during two tumultuous years in Libya, Syria and elsewhere. The book provides a necessary corrective to the dominant narrative of the three Western permanent members and cautions that when you destroy a state, the gates to every corner of hell are opened. Those wishing to avoid repeating the tragic perilous interventions of recent history had better read this book.' —Ramesh Thakur, former assistant secretary-general of the UN

'When Hardeep was on the Council, I used to say that speaking after him was like playing the harmonica after a full symphony orchestra. He is as forceful and analytical in this book as he was then.' —Vitaly Churkin, permanent representative of Russia to the UN

'Hardeep Singh Puri's voice is one the whole world should heed. His message to the global North is that coercive military intervention has been, as often as not, catastrophically counterproductive—even when conducted for the highest-minded of stated reasons: to halt feared mass atrocity crimes. But he also tells the global South not to abandon the principle of the Responsibility to Protect but rather to *reinforce* it—by demanding that it be given military application only after the most rigorous prudential debate in the Security Council, and with mandates strictly monitored to ensure no overreach. This is an authoritative and informed insider's account, and it makes compelling reading.' —Gareth Evans, chancellor of the Australian National University, former Australian foreign minister, president emeritus of the International Crisis Group, and co-chair of the International Commission on Intervention and State Sovereignty

PERILOUS INTERVENTIONS

The Security Council and the Politics of Chaos

HARDEEP SINGH PURI

HarperCollins *Publishers* India

First published in India in 2016 by
HarperCollins *Publishers* India

Copyright © Hardeep Singh Puri 2016

P-ISBN: 978-93-5177-759-5
E-ISBN: 978-93-5177-760-1

2 4 6 8 10 9 7 5 3

HarperCollins *Publishers*
A-75, Sector 57, Noida, Uttar Pradesh 201301, India
1 London Bridge Street, London, SE1 9GF, United Kingdom
Hazelton Lanes, 55 Avenue Road, Suite 2900, Toronto, Ontario M5R 3L2
and 1995 Markham Road, Scarborough, Ontario M1B 5M8, Canada
25 Ryde Road, Pymble, Sydney, NSW 2073, Australia
195 Broadway, New York, NY 10007, USA

Typeset in 12/15 Adobe Garamond Pro at
SÜRYA, New Delhi

Printed and bound at
Thomson Press (India) Ltd.

For my granddaughter Amaya Zai,
in the hope that her generation will be dealt a better hand

CONTENTS

FOREWORD
Reforming the UN No Longer an Option

Hardeep Singh Puri's *Perilous Interventions* comes at a pivotal moment for the United Nations (UN) and the global system at large: a time of great potential, but also, to borrow a word from its title, a time of great peril and uncertainty.

Seventy years ago, when the UN Charter affirmed our collective determination to save succeeding generations from the scourge of war, the founding fathers probably did not anticipate the drastic changes we are witnessing today—changes that compounded the threats, challenges and risks to our collective security. From rampant poverty—with the frustration and anger it creates—to the mutating threat of violent extremism and terrorism; from the double-edged sword of new technologies to the existential risks posted by climate change and natural disasters. These are challenges that are transnational, enormous, complex and deeply interconnected. They are challenges that no one country or even a group of countries can single-handedly overcome. As a result, the world has no option but to look at the UN and rethink the virtues of multilateralism.

At its essence, this is the fundamental message of this book. By taking a series of case studies of how the Security Council operated during critical moments in recent history, how the behaviour of member states affected our peace and security landscape and how intervention was too often the answer over preventive diplomacy and mediation, it reveals how severely we, as an international community, need to do some soul-searching, to think back to why the UN was set up in the first place and to rethink how the existing structures—above all, the Security Council—need to be adapted in order to suit the challenges of today.

Reforming the UN is no longer an option—it is a prerequisite for a sustainable global order. The reviews of peacekeeping operations, the peace-building architecture and the status of the implementation of the women, peace and security agendas are significant inputs in this debate. The recommendations they present go a distance in bridging the gap between what the organization is expected to achieve and what it is actually accomplishing on the ground. But meaningful reform at the UN is a deeply political issue, one that requires vision and boldness. Among these issues, I believe that reforming the Security Council should be a priority.

On the one hand, there is a need to strengthen the Security Council by ensuring better representation for developing countries, in both the permanent and non-permanent categories. On the other hand, and while the circumstances might not yet be fully ripe for drastically changing the way the veto power is applied, the five permanent members should consider voluntarily refraining from using the veto if a measure brought to the Council garners the support of the rest of the membership of the Council. In other words, if fourteen of the fifteen members of the Security Council vote for a resolution, this expression of global will should not be so easily dismissed, in particular in the case of resolutions dealing with war crimes, crimes against humanity, genocide and cessation of hostilities between belligerent parties. Without some kind of change to the Security Council, there is little hope that the multilateral apparatus can better serve our world today. At the end of the day, it is the fulcrum of international decision making and the only forum where force can be legitimately authorized.

Reform, however, is needed in other fora. The General Assembly—where all 193 member states have an equal voice—needs to be empowered in order to have its share in the responsibility for the maintenance of international peace and security. UNGA Resolution 377A, also known as 'Uniting for Peace', should be revisited and revitalized. This is another way to allow the organization to act in case the Security Council fails to do so, as a result of lack of unanimity amongst its five permanent members. In this regard, I would highlight that the 2015 resolution, titled 'Revitalizing the Work of the General Assembly', is a step in the right direction. For the first time since the establishment of the UN, there is a clear call for transparency in the process of selection of the secretary-general. Strengthening the General Assembly and its decision-making process will lead thereby to a more representative and democratic UN system.

The recommendations put forward by last year's series of review processes present the potential for extremely important reforms. I would like to commend the emphasis placed by the High-Level Independent Panel on UN Peace Operations on the 'primacy of politics'. As we discussed in the Arab High-Level Workshop, organized by the Cairo Center for Conflict Resolution and Peacekeeping in Africa in March 2016, this should mean a shift from 'conflict management' to 'conflict resolution' as the guiding rationale for all UN peacekeeping and special political missions. Failure to do so would result in protracted conflict, as we saw in Palestine and as we see today in Syria, to which a chapter is devoted in this book.

I would also like to highlight the emphasis placed by the reviews on partnerships, especially between the UN and regional organizations. On the one hand, the partnership between the UN and the African Union must enter a new phase towards a strategic partnership, where the UN supports African plans, most notably Agenda 2063 and its leading initiative to silence the guns by 2020. On the other hand, the UN and the League of Arab States should seek to explore avenues for further cooperation and coordination. Partnerships with regional organizations provide an important lifeline for the multilateral system's continued relevance and effectiveness: the tools, legitimacy and local knowledge they can provide are invaluable.

The failures in international diplomacy that this book catalogues are a clarion call for the need for change, in our existing structures and our collective behaviour and attitudes as a community of states. Its author has the unique ability to claim that he was right from day one: India's position on Libyan intervention in 2011 was cautious and sober. It reflects a style of prudent and seasoned diplomacy that I came to know well as Egypt's ambassador to India from 1983 to 1986. More importantly, the author's arguments are based on years of first-hand expertise in a multi-decade career as a professional diplomat, one whom I came to know well over the years from his earliest days in Geneva, throughout my decade-long tenure as Egypt's foreign minister and subsequently secretary-general of the Arab League, to our multiple interactions with the International Peace Institute (IPI) sessions in Salzburg, Vienna and New York and, more recently, in his capacity as secretary-general of IPI's Independent Commission on Multilateralism. I hope that this book's message is heard, internalized and acted upon.

Cairo
June 2016
Amre Moussa
Former Secretary-General of the League of Arab States,
Foreign Minister of Egypt, Permanent Representative of Egypt
to the UN, and Ambassador of Egypt to India

INTRODUCTION

The idea of this book took shape when India served its seventh term as an elected non-permanent member of the United Nations Security Council (UNSC) in 2011–12.[1] I was excited with the prospect of representing India on the all-powerful Council, tasked to prevent conflicts and to make, keep and build peace in some of the world's most troubled countries and regions. As early as March 2011, however, this excitement started wearing off, and I started getting the feeling, initially faint and then more strongly, that we were participants in a live, telescoped in time, theatrical sequel to Barbara Tuchman's *The March of Folly*.[2] As I saw the Libyan and Syrian crises unfold, I had the same sense that Tuchman evoked: of decision makers acting against their own interest. In doing so, they did not weigh the consequences carefully, shut out sound advice and better judgement because they seemed inconvenient, and ignored perfectly feasible alternatives.

Most professional diplomats shed their innocence before they arrive at the horse-shoe table around which the Security Council meets. In the real world of foreign and security policy, decision makers are invariably confronted by cruel choices that are equally problematic and come in various shades of 'lousy'. Practitioners are acutely conscious that it is only diplomacy's outward packaging that is couched in a commitment to a higher moral purpose. The shameless pursuit of narrowly defined interests is most often the

1

motivation and seldom raises eyebrows in the world of multilateral diplomacy. Few play hardball and some acquiesce easily. The surprising part, however, is that diplomats with the benefit of a reasonably good education and the widest experience and exposure get so easily co-opted to act against the best interest of their own countries in a short-, medium- or long-term time frame. And they do so in spite of enough precedent to show that the arming of rebels and the use of force will have devastating consequences. They set aside their better judgement to serve their masters in the fulfilment of a supposedly higher moral cause. Instead of solving existing problems, they end up creating an entirely new set of problems.

Prior to 2011, I used to say that very little is known about the Security Council to people outside the charmed circle at the apex of multilateral diplomacy. After the experience of two years on the Council, I have good reason now to believe that very little is known about the Security Council even within the charmed circle, should that be defined in terms of the 193 member states. Still less—and that does not amount to very much—is known about how the Council actually functions. It conducts most of its decision making in closed sessions, not open even to other member states, let alone the press. Much of what appears in the press is based on briefings, what is on the record, or on the background provided by those members who naturally want to put a spin on its proceedings. In this, the five permanent members—the United States, Russia, France, the United Kingdom and China—have a natural advantage. Only three of them actually utilize that leverage. The mainstream narrative in the Western press, by and large, is shaped by the US, the UK and France.

The uninitiated have every right to ask: why is it important to know how the Security Council arrives at its decisions? The simple reason is it is the only global body which has the authority to make a determination whether there exists a threat to international peace and security. Having made that determination, it alone can authorize measures to deal with that threat. This means that other than in self-defence, countries can legitimately wage war only with the authorization of the Council. But to get a reasonably good picture of the mess we are in and to understand the legality of conflicts, one only has to look around the world and ask the question: how many and which one of these raging wars is in self-defence and/or has been authorized by the Security Council?

The motivation to write this book came from a desire to tell the outside world how decision making took place within the Security Council in 2011–12 in relation to the momentous developments in Libya and Syria. This analysis is based on my own participation in the Council and other verifiable information in the public domain. I also presided over the Council in August 2011 and November 2012, when Libya and Syria loomed large on the agenda. The desire to bring this into the public domain is itself anchored in the deep belief that if the Council is allowed to function as it presently does, it will only bring further discredit to the cause of peace and security.

My target audience, therefore, consists of those in the multilateral system who do not pay sufficient attention to what goes on inside the Council and those who uncritically accept the fanciful justifications that are offered—'weapons of mass destruction' (WMD) in Iraq in 2003 and 'protection of civilians' in Libya in 2011. My intention is also to look beyond policymakers and strategic communities to drive home the realization among ordinary, well-meaning people that the use of force, whether authorized by the Council or not, should be resorted to only as a final desperate measure. 'We, the peoples' constitute an essential but often overlooked core of the UN Charter. They have an enduring interest in the affairs of war and peace because they are deeply affected by them.

The use of force, with or without Security Council authorization, has invariably had unintended consequences. In most cases, the consequences have been disastrous. The one exception often cited is the 1999 intervention in Kosovo, where the North Atlantic Treaty Organization (NATO) carried out air strikes without Security Council authorization and succeeded in halting the ethnic cleansing of the Albanian population. When a doctor makes a mistake in diagnosing a patient's ailment and prescribing a course for treatment, there is often a remedy available, at least till the patient is alive. Even thereafter, medical practitioners can be sued for malpractice. The problems resulting from a bridge or building that falls, whether due to an engineer's blunder or substandard civil works, can be similarly addressed. Issues of international peace and security, however, pose an entirely different dilemma.

Consequences of mistakes are of a far more serious and permanent nature. Those responsible for these decisions have by and large sought refuge behind the shield of 'collective responsibility' and 'noble intent', such as the need for the elimination of WMDs and the protection of civilians. Rectifying these mistakes presents a nearly impossible challenge. For decisions involving the use of force with the Council's authorization, responsibility would clearly lie with decision makers in national capitals and their representatives in the Council implementing those instructions. The use of force without the Council's authorization falls in an entirely different category. This book introduces the concept of 'perilous intervention' to define this phenomenon.

Perilous Interventions

What is a perilous intervention? A perilous intervention is about whimsical and reflexive decision making, and about taking decisions with far-reaching consequences without thinking through their consequences. It is about the urge to intervene, about the 'use of force' and about 'all means necessary', often to achieve a 'regime change', even when that is not the explicitly stated objective. Interventionist mindsets invariably seek destabilization to settle scores, with or without the use of force. This has been, is and always will be perilous.

It essentially involves succumbing to short-term pressures. Its stated intentions are always laudable and noble: to promote, protect and advance peace and security and human rights, and to save populations from intended mass atrocities by tyrannical rulers. The action is undertaken without weighing the pros and cons, or understanding the underlying social and cultural forces and political dynamics at work, based on either an incomplete or a self-serving analysis and disregard of wise counsel.

Policymakers do not prepare or provide for the prevention or neutralization of the profound, intended or unintended, direct or collateral, and short- or long-term consequences, loss and damage. Such damage is witnessed across the board in the developmental, social, ecological and health sectors. It exacerbates the already fragile peace, security and human rights situation not only in the countries that are the targets of intervention but also in faraway ones that are the perpetrators.

Also, perilous interventions are costly. Billions of dollars in precious resources are spent on military operations and occupation. In addition to the billions of dollars lost in the destruction, degradation and disruption of infrastructure and essential services, 'development' itself is set back decades. The air, water and soil are polluted and poisoned. All these further require huge investments to rebuild the revenue-generating assets which are also damaged in these interventions. The human cost is immeasurably high as hundreds of thousands are killed in air attacks, military interventions and post-occupation operations, many more than those liberated from the despots.

In the case of Iraq, Libya and Syria, millions have been internally displaced, at the same time producing the biggest desperate migration crisis since the Second World War. Sectarian—the Shia–Sunni—and internecine rivalries and attacks have taken a daily toll: 100 deaths a day in Iraq alone, not to speak of those in Libya and Syria.

The consequences listed above stem from policy mistakes based on wrong and simplistic assumptions and double standards: 'Your terrorist is my freedom fighter unless he turns his guns on me.' They are also the by-products of distinctions made between 'moderate' fighters and rebels and violent extremists, and arming them conveniently and indiscriminately with arsenals and equipment to engineer regime change. Advocates of intervention commit the cardinal error of subjectively equating human rights violations with mass atrocities. Human rights violations take place in all countries. There are prescribed remedies at the national level. Where violations are of an egregious nature, the international community provides for a naming and shaming mechanism through the human rights institutional architecture in Geneva.

Popularly accepted definitions of mass atrocities, however, cover genocide, ethnic cleansing, war crimes and crimes against humanity. Subjective labelling also places governments confronting destabilization challenges from an armed insurrection at a disadvantage. Be that as it may, when a legitimate government adopts force to fend off rebels armed by foreign governments, deploys guerrilla tactics, razes neighbourhoods and cities down and uses civilians as human shields, it cannot but be labelled as genocide perpetrated by the defending government. A legitimate government cannot commit mass atrocities just because it is confronted by a terror threat. The response itself has to be anchored in the values of a civilized society which places a premium on human rights and humanitarian approaches.

The Vicious Cycle of Perilous Interventions

This perilous brand of intervention has set in motion a vicious cycle of terrorism and chaos that is explained through the following matrix. The diagram illustrates the vortex of motivations for the interventions and their resulting consequences. The desire for geopolitical domination, unseating undesirable or inconvenient regimes and establishing dependent ones in their place constitutes a familiar pattern. Yet, the desired results are rarely achieved, as seen in Afghanistan and Iraq. Instead, it has invariably led to the rise of terrorists and non-state military actors, creating a new set of rivals altogether.

It was clear as daylight even in 2003 that international military intervention and the arming of rebels, individually and the two together, would create unprecedented chaos and result in the unravelling of countries. Many wise and prescient policymakers and strategic thinkers advocated caution and were ignored. In retrospect, it has been established beyond doubt that these have been primarily responsible for the mess that the world finds itself in. Along with the military action in Iraq, the mishandling of Libya and Syria has made a seminal contribution to the rise of a phenomenon like the ISIS (Islamic State of Iraq and Syria, alternatively translated as Islamic State of Iraq and the Levant or Islamic State of Iraq and al-Sham).

This, in turn, has provided motivation for the militarization of strategic thinking and the urge to intervene, which have been presented as inevitable in the context of the menace of terrorism. There have also been latent attempts to regain domestic popularity through the display of military machismo by securing existing and new markets for weapons, testing weapons, refurbishing US–NATO military presence and alliances, arming rebels and the like. This has led to an exacerbation of the Sunni–Shia divide and a virulent ideology of jihad against the West and other moderate

Muslim and non-Muslim states. The Westphalian concept[3] of state sovereignty that was the basis of the post-war global architecture has been turned on its head and the concept of a caliphate has taken shape in the form of a trans-border Islamic takeover of all states, with people pouring in from the West to join the cause. The Shia–Sunni rivalry has led to bloodshed within and among Islamic neighbours, further exacerbating chaos, destabilization and radicalization in the region.

Where regime change has been effected, weak or splintered governments have been held hostage by subregional or sectarian militias and violent extremists and terrorists. The state and its institutions have broken down, replaced by a reign of terror. Instability in a region so rich in natural resources has also prompted swift action on the part of the West to secure its economic interests, including control over major trade/strategic routes. Finally, there has been the motivation for protecting human rights, which brings into picture the doctrine of Responsibility to Protect (R2P) in a bid to prevent genocide, protect populations, especially women and children, and secure access for humanitarian support.

Interventions with any of these foregoing motivations have more often than not resulted in development being set back at least twenty years in these countries. The migration crisis being witnessed today is the biggest since the Second World War. It has upset delicate social, ethnic, tribal and sectarian balances and the secular ethos often maintained by authoritarian regimes. Terrorist outfits have gained a firmer foothold, unleashing a vicious cycle of use of force and arming of rebels, destabilization of national and international order, terrorism and chaos, and a perennial threat to global peace and security.

INTENDED & UNINTENDED CONSEQUENCES OF INTERVENTIONS

Domination of new regime partial – New regime unstable & threatened by local / sectarian forces – Unravelling of nation – Radicalization & terror – Non-state actors gain ground.

Disintegration of state & local institutions – Undoing of social & sectarian balance – Irreparable damage to infrastructure, heritage & habitat.

Consolidation of old & new rivalries: state & non-state – High economic costs for intervening powers – Ideological trans-border coalitions formed – Inflow of sympathizers.

Peace & security of targeted & intervening countries compromised – Mass atrocities & terror attacks – Acute health & migration crises.

POLICY MOTIVATIONS FOR INTERVENTIONS

Counter political rivals; back allies – Regime change in conflict zone – Establish democratic & dependent regimes – Gain strategic depth & legitimacy.

Military intervention deemed indispensable – Mobilize military alliances (NATO / Russian-led) – Military-industrial complexes – Secure new market for weapons – Arm rebels.

Control over natural resources in conflict zone – Control over trading & strategic routes – Corporate interests.

Concerns about WMDs & conflict spillover (real or imagined) – Counter threats in countries of origin – Prevent attacks on Western / intervening countries.

Responsibility to Protect invoked – Prevent mass atrocities – Ensure democracy & accountability – Secure humanitarian support.

VICIOUS CYCLE OF PERILOUS INTERVENTIONS

- PHYSICAL, POLITICAL, CULTURAL AND ECOLOGICAL DAMAGE
- HIGH COSTS TO INTERVENING POWERS
- PERVERSE IMPACTS OF REGIME CHANGE
- PEACE, SECURITY AND RzP OBJECTIVES COMPROMISED
- GEOPOLITICAL DOMINATION OVER COUNTRIES AND REGIONS
- THE HUMAN RIGHTS AND HUMANITARIAN PROJECT
- MILITARIZATION OF STRATEGIC THINKING AS THE URGE TO INTERVENE
- MAINTAINING PEACE AND SECURITY
- ECONOMIC INTERESTS

Understanding the Motivations

Two questions need to be asked. First, why do governments pursue policies which are counterproductive and against their own best interest? Do they do so out of sheer incompetence or as part of a larger game plan? Sometimes it is difficult to tell. Second, why do countries—and not just the rich and powerful ones—interfere in the affairs of other countries through the arming of rebels, use of force and regime change? Do they do so drawing inspiration from Rudyard Kipling and his theory of the white man's burden, or because of economic interests and strategic objectives?

Each case and each situation is sui generis. The answer or the explanation must necessarily distinguish between the empirically verifiable facts and the conspiracy theories that periodically surface and eventually turn out to be not entirely bizarre.

When Benjamin Netanyahu assumed office in Israel in 1996, the Institute for Advanced Strategic and Political Studies (IASPS) based in that country presented a report[4] on a 'New Israeli Strategy'. This suggested, among other things, the need for Israel to shape its strategic environment and transcend the Arab-Israeli conflict through some key policy changes. To achieve this end, it was important to remove Saddam Hussein from power in Iraq, which would ensure the weakening of Syria and blocking of its regional aspirations. The Institute's 'Study Group on a New Israeli Strategy Toward 2000' had thus put forward twenty years ago, almost prophetically, key strategic moves that required Israel to work closely with Turkey and Jordan to 'contain, destabilize and roll back some of its most dangerous threats' in the region.

Even though traces of this kind of thinking had resonated in the mainstream discourse in the last decade, I came across this study well after the manuscript of this book was prepared for publication. I had covered Netanyahu's dangling the 'regime change' carrot in Chapter 1, based on his statements on record in the US, well before I saw this study.

The powerful influence exercised by think tanks, particularly those situated in close proximity to the seat of power, should not be underestimated. In a scintillating analysis of the Obama doctrine which appeared in the April 2016 issue of the *Atlantic*,[5] Jeffrey Goldberg, author and national correspondent for the *Atlantic*, observed that for Obama, 'August 30, 2013 was his liberation day', as he 'defied' the US's foreign policy 'playbook' and its 'high-maintenance allies in the Middle East'. He 'resented' the domineering of military commands and the 'widely held' belief that Washington's think tanks answered to 'their Arab and pro-Israel funders'. Moreover, he also spoke up against demands for military action from 'free riders', to which, there was a reaction from the US's European allies and Saudi Arabia.

In 2015, four years after a West-led intervention left Gaddafi's Libya unravelled, 3,000 emails from then Secretary of State Hillary Clinton's private email server were released. One of them, sent by her close confidant, Sidney Blumenthal, drew attention to the 143 tonnes of gold accumulated by the Muammar Gaddafi government with the intent of using it as a pan-African currency, which would in turn have provided the francophone African countries with 'an alternative to the French franc'.[6] It further revealed factors that could have motivated France to attack Libya, which included, among other things, greater access to Libya's share of oil production, increased French influence in North Africa, and an opportunity for the French military to reassert its position in the world. Communications from Hillary Clinton's private email server do not, however, form the basis of the analysis of the use of force in Libya, both in the run-up to its authorization in Resolution 1973 in March 2011 and in its implementation in the following months, in Chapter 3.

Telephone conversations between Gaddafi and former British prime minister Tony Blair from early 2011 reveal that the Libyan leader pleaded desperately for the West to avoid a military intervention and regime change in his country. He is quoted as saying, while referring to the al-Qaeda, 'They have managed to get arms and terrify people. People can't leave their homes ... It's a jihad situation. They have arms and are terrorizing people in the streets.' His warning was blatantly ignored and was followed by air strikes led by NATO, the US and France that eventually overthrew Gaddafi's government. Soon after, most of Libya was conquered by jihadi groups linked to the al-Qaeda, some of which helped the Central Intelligence Agency (CIA) 'run guns from Benghazi to fellow jihadis in Syria'.[7] In fact, Hillary Clinton's declassified emails also disclosed that her right-hand man had informed her that 'radical/terrorist groups such as the Libyan Fighting groups and AQIM [al-Qaeda in the Islamic Maghreb] are infiltrating the NTC [National Transitional Council] and its military command'.

The ongoing Sunni–Shia animosity has been effectively captured by cartographer M.R. Izady's assessment as being less about who the rightful successor to Muhammad was and more about who was 'going to control something more concrete right now: oil'.[8] Almost all the fossil fuels in the Persian Gulf 'are located underneath Shiites ... even in Sunni Saudi Arabia, where the major oil fields are in the Eastern Province, which has a majority Shiite population'.[9] This could provide an insight into the behaviour of and some part of the explanation for actions by some of the Sunni Gulf monarchies in Saudi Arabia, Bahrain, Oman, the United Arab Emirates and Qatar. But again, as in the case of Hillary Clinton's emails, that is not the basis of the analysis in the chapters on developments in Libya, Syria and Yemen. These chapters are anchored in the decision-making processes of the Security Council in which I participated and witnessed how a reluctant US was persuaded to fight someone else's 'shitty war', in American permanent representative (PR)[10] Susan Rice's words to French counterpart Gerard Araud on 15 March 2011. This comment was well known among permanent representatives in the Council then. Araud has now gone public.[11]

Sectarian venom is spreading across the Middle East. The Saudi war in Yemen in March 2015 and the execution of Sheikh Nimr al-Nimr, an outspoken Shia cleric from the predominantly Sunni kingdom's oil-rich Eastern Province, in January 2016 have crossed all red lines. The Sheikh unequivocally condemned violence and yet he was executed as a terrorist. That forty-three Sunni jihadis were simultaneously put to death for the bloody crimes of which they were convicted more than a decade ago is seen by many Saudi Shias—an estimated three million people—as a cover for a political assassination they regard as a declaration of war. With the price of oil hitting historic lows, alarm bells in the House of Saud are ringing.

The geopolitical dynamics and desire for regional and subregional domination may provide a better, at least a fuller, explanation of what is happening and is painted with a broad brush as 'sectarian'. What is often forgotten is that Alawites in Syria are regarded as heretics by the Shia and that Iran's rivalry with Saudi Arabia may have an explanation tucked away in the history of the Iran–Iraq war. That might also explain the paranoia that the House of Saud displays in its dealings with the Houthis, followers of the Zaidi branch of Shia Islam, which constitutes 40 per cent of Yemen's population.

The Scope of This Book

In 2003, I was India's PR to the United Nations in Geneva and did not have the benefit and privilege of a ringside seat in the Security Council in New York. I do not, for that very reason, cover its decision making in Iraq. In any case, a sceptical Council had then refused to be persuaded by the specious and flimsy evidence of the existence of chemical weapons, and the military action without Council authorization has been sufficiently documented in terms of its lack of justification.

My intention originally was to produce a clinical analysis limited only to the decision making leading to military action in Libya in 2011. The situation in Libya, however, then played into the evolving mess in Syria. Council inaction in Syria and the opening up of sectarian fault lines constituted not only an unprecedented threat to peace and security but also a potential flashpoint between the US and Russia, even though Moscow and Washington might still not necessarily see the evolving mess through a Cold War prism. Therefore, Syria had to be covered.

One may reasonably ask: why write a book on the crises five years after they started? The answer is that it is always a good idea to allow a little time to lapse between the unfolding of developments and the writing of an account about them. The passage of time invariably helps make the narrative more objective and reduce, if not altogether eliminate, the subjective element. Since several of the actors within the Council were and continue to be close friends, the delay was also intended to allow the passion of interventionists to cool off with the unfolding of consequences.

Chapter 1 discusses the origin and functioning of the dreadful by-product of military interventions in Iraq, Libya and Syria: the ISIS, whose members were incubated in jails under the rule of the despots in these countries; what the rise of this organization means for the international community; and the reasons for both young men and women joining the cause of the so-called caliphate in large numbers from across the world.

Chapter 2 reflects on the Arab Spring and how the widespread discontent manifest in the self-immolation of Mohamed Bouazizi, a young fruit vendor in Tunisia, resonated throughout the region, creating a ripple of similar events in neighbouring countries through the few months that followed. These nations were also home to victims of repressive regimes curtailing civil liberties. While the Arab Spring in its nascent stage received tremendous applause from the rest of the world for attempting to voice dissent, the narrative changed drastically after the entrenched regimes decided to use brutal force against protesters, who were at first peaceful and unarmed. In retrospect, the mainstream Western narrative of the Arab Spring was also somewhat contrived. The arming of rebels by some of the Gulf states and the West, and military intervention—first in Libya, resulting in a regime change, and then unsuccessfully in Syria—laid the basis and created the conditions for a full-blown civil war, with Iran and Russia supporting Bashar al-Assad, and the West, Saudi Arabia, Turkey and the Gulf states bent on seeking the ouster of the Assad regime.

Chapter 3 outlines the Libyan and Western responses to the alleged worsening of the internal political situation owing to the nature of Gaddafi's rule, ill-treatment of the Libyan people and eventually the brutal repression of dissent. While the international media, after the outbreak of protests, demonized Gaddafi, the West simultaneously intervened militarily in Libya following authorization for the use of force by the Security Council ostensibly for the protection of civilians. The chapter traces the events that led to the passing of Security Council Resolutions 1970 and 1973, shedding light on some of the formal and informal exchanges that took place between Council members; how France struck a deal with the National Transitional Council (NTC)[12] in Libya through clandestine meetings arranged by French public intellectual Bernard-Henri Levy; and the lobbying that was going on within the Council for the authorization of a no-fly zone.[13]

In 2011, the *New York Times* published a front-page article declaring: 'US Tactics in Libya May Be a Model for Other Efforts'. Fast forward five years:

> When you destroy a state, the gates to every corner of hell are opened—no frontiers, no police, no law, no education, no infrastructure, no government, a Hobbesian war of all against all. After Iraq, one might have thought Western policymakers would have paused before turning Libya into a 1,000 km breach in the previously reasonably solid southern Mediterranean border through which refugees and jihadis now pour or export weapons and Islamist ideology.[14]

The *New York Times* itself acknowledged its flip-flop in a two-part coverage in February 2016 by Scott Shane and Jo Becker. Glenn Greenwald, writing on Libya in the *Intercept* on 27 January 2016, said:[15]

> The immediate aftermath of the NATO bombing of Libya was a time of high gloating. Just as Iraq war advocates pointed to the capture and killing of Saddam as proof that their war was a success, Libya war advocates pointed to the capture and brutal killing of Gaddafi as proof of their vindication ... 'We came, we saw, he died,' Clinton said on '60 Minutes'.

He then went on to say:

> Just as there was no al-Qaeda to attack in Iraq until the US bombed its government, there was no ISIS in Libya until NATO bombed it. Now the US is about to seize on the effects of its own bombing campaign in Libya to justify an entirely new bombing campaign in that same country.

This chapter on Libya also details how decision making in Washington was fractured and there was a sizeable feeling that Washington was being taken for a ride, even if the others were not exactly 'free riders'.

Chapter 4 on Syria traces the history of the region since the drawing of 'a line in the sand' by British civil servant Sir Mark Sykes and Francois Georges-Picot of France that divided the Middle East along artificial imperial lines, with no consideration for ethnic, religious or economic divisions. These botched-up divisions have manifested themselves in present-day Syria, which has become a quagmire as a result of the numerous factions getting involved in the conflict with the backing of various international players. With the rise of ISIS, Syria has turned into the world's most dangerous conflict zone, continuously threatening international peace and security.

The chapter then focuses on the Security Council's inaction in Syria following the Libyan experience. The three easy steps for regime change witnessed in the Libyan case—a Council resolution, arming of rebels and military action by NATO—could not be replicated in Syria. Manipulation of Council authorization in the Libyan case, lack of appetite for intervention in Washington, and Russian interest allowed for just one easy and messy step: the arming of rebels. Without doubt, Assad, like his father Hafez, has been bad news for his own people. But celebrating and encouraging an uprising against a nasty authoritarian ruler is, as experience has shown in Iraq in 2003, Libya in 2011 and Syria from 2011 to date, the easier part. Statesmanship demands calling a halt to the chaos and helping restore legitimate state authority in all three countries.

Syria and Yemen, covered in the next chapter, perhaps provide material for a classic case study of how the health of civilian populations is impacted by armed conflict. A report[16] prepared by members of the Syrian American Medical Society presents astonishing figures that illustrate how the health care system in Syria has disintegrated since the beginning of the conflict. The deliberate targeting of 'medics and healthcare infrastructure, the exodus of physicians and nurses, the shortage of medical supplies and medications, and the disruption of medical education and training' have all contributed to the severity of the public health crisis.

Chapter 5 deals with the political turmoil in Yemen, the Sunni-majority neighbour of Saudi Arabia, which also houses a significant percentage of Shias, including the long-rebelling Houthis. Peter Maurer, president of the International Committee of the Red Cross, has observed that he had witnessed more damage in Yemen in five months than what Syria had sustained in four years.[17] No mean feat, achieved by the other elephant in the room, Saudi Arabia. In a statement on 8 January 2016, Ban Ki-moon, the UN secretary-general, said he was particularly concerned about reports of intense air strikes on civilian buildings in Sana'a, the capital city. The use of cluster munitions in populated areas may amount to a war crime due to its indiscriminate nature, the statement said.

Chapter 6 attempts to explore the situation in Ukraine. With the Security Council already discredited, President Vladimir Putin of Russia did not think it necessary even to make a reference to it before acting on Crimea. Legally, the Russian overreach was in clear violation of Ukraine's sovereignty. Politically, it was projected as mere preservation of Russia's strategic interests.

Chapter 7 covers Sri Lanka. It has been included because its ethnic crisis and the civil war that followed were exacerbated by the arming of rebels. India's policy towards Sri Lanka changed dramatically from Indira Gandhi's government to that of her son, Rajiv, who sought course correction but paid for it with his life. India's decision to intervene in Sri Lanka, initially through the arming of rebels and subsequently as an impartial mediator, left both the Sinhalese majority and Tamil minority in Sri Lanka and the Tamils in India largely dissatisfied.

Chapter 8 deals with the plight of migrants fleeing the ongoing, and in many cases worsening, conflicts in their countries. It is instructive to compare the conditions that prevailed in these countries before the regime changes that were attempted by Western policies with the situation today. This chapter gives an overview of everyday life as it was under the erstwhile oppressor, and how it has changed, arguably for the worse, leaving them uncertain and insecure and forcing them to flee their war-torn countries. It is a sad reflection on how the international community reacts to perceived threats to international peace and security. The rallying around Syria did not take place until migrants started arriving in Europe. The world's conscience was stirred by images of a lifeless infant boy lying face down in the sands of the Greek island of Kos. His body had washed ashore after he drowned along with several members of his family in their desperate attempt to flee Syria. However, the humanitarian tragedy epitomized by three-year-old Aylan Kurdi soon became a bargaining chip in the hands of certain regional powers bent on making amends for past wrongs or attaining geopolitical gains that had until then proven elusive through conventional means.

The final chapter reflects on the evolution of the doctrine of Responsibility to Protect (R2P)[18] and seeks to re-evaluate its relevance. Given recent experiences, it has been suggested that it would be wise to consider integrating R2P with the concept of Responsibility while Protecting (RwP),[19] first floated by Brazilian president Dilma Rousseff in a speech to the UN General Assembly (UNGA) in September 2011. While RwP has gained some, but limited, traction, even its proponents would agree that the 'doctrine' needs to be developed. Each case of 'intervention' is distinct and sui generis. It becomes complex when accompanied by its even more problematic proxy on the ground, the arming of rebels. The two together have produced widespread chaos and disorder.

Conclusion

It may still be politically incorrect to say that life under Saddam Hussein was better, or that Gaddafi embodied the Libyan state, which has unravelled without hope in the absence of his iron-fisted rule. The objective reality is that the al-Qaeda and ISIS could not have come into existence without powerful state sponsors, among them the countries that sought and worked for Saddam's and Gaddafi's ousters. Unless all concerned agree that ISIS constitutes a greater threat than Assad, international cooperation to fight the ISIS menace will remain incomplete. The Turks place a higher priority on attacking the Kurds, and have lucratively supported ISIS by allowing Turkey to be the main transit route for foreign recruits of the ISIS through illegal cross-border oil deals with black marketeers.[20] ISIS and its brutality seem to draw, with vengeance and visceral anger, on a bottomless reservoir of humiliation, or perceived humiliation, at the hands of the West. To the extent that ISIS is an ideology, does the situation not also warrant a comprehensive strategy to counter violent extremism?

What these cases, and this book, seek to draw attention to is how interventions in the past have gone disastrously wrong— and the fascinating syndrome of turning away from the scene of intervention once the vested interests of the intervening nations have been achieved.

We live in a dangerous world. The dangers, as alarming as it may sound, are not confined to the war-torn countries or failed states that have been the targets of interventions. Rather, the repercussions are felt in the region and beyond. The effects of destabilization and the unravelling of the countries which were subjected to interventions are being felt across the globe, including South Asia and Europe, which is witnessing desperate migration and an expansion in the influence of the ISIS.

The role of some of the 'neighbouring' states in fuelling the conflict has invited global attention. Can Dündar, editor-in-chief of *Cumhuriyet*, one of Turkey's biggest newspapers, and his Ankara bureau chief, Erdem Gül, were arrested on terrorism and espionage charges in November 2015. The two journalists were jailed after publishing a story in May that year that included photos and videos alleging that Turkish intelligence officials had smuggled weapons to Syrian rebel fighters in January 2014. In January 2016, they were sentenced to life imprisonment. They had upset the Turkish establishment because their report shed light on how Turkey had supported—or at least turned a blind eye to—the growth of extremist groups, including the ISIS.

Will global powers and the international community recognize the grave policy mistakes they have made in undertaking these perilous interventions? Will they learn the lesson that fomenting instability, militancy and regime change in countries while disregarding their sovereignty has serious negative consequences for all? This includes unleashing uncontrollable political and militarized forces and chaos while rarely achieving the intended objectives. There is, at the very least, a need for the international community to reassess the way it deals with such countries and situations in the future, taking into account objective factors and sound advice based on deep state and society issues and legacies ignored in the past.

It is equally essential to seriously revisit and agree on how the UN and its supreme organ, the UNSC, entrusted with ensuring peace and security and 'saving mankind from the scourge of war', are not used to give legitimacy to parochial interests and unilateral military actions. Violent extremism and terrorism are the real enemies and to deal with them and counter them in a holistic way—militarily, yes, but also politically, socially, culturally and psychologically—using all means at our disposal, including technology and media, and to build international solidarity around the fight against them are what is immediately needed.

It is time to eschew xenophobia, including Islamophobia, which would otherwise feed the ISIS narrative of hate and oppression of the Muslim ummah globally and give sustenance to terrorism and the perennial clash of civilizations. We must look at international cooperation from the perspective of addressing the root causes of disaffection among the youth in the countries of the Arab Spring and elsewhere, and the long-term issues of governance and sustainable development.

Finally, the Implications for India

What does this book mean for India and the policymakers out there?

Since I spent four decades in the Indian Foreign Service, the writing will reflect an Indian perspective: what lessons India has learnt from its own perilous intervention in Sri Lanka and from these other ones, and what has been India's position on them. What are the implications for India—a polyglot, secular country, the world's largest democracy, and a nation with the third largest Muslim population in the world—of the vicious cycle of perilous intervention, radicalization, terrorism and chaos set in motion in the Iraq–Libya–Syria–Yemen imbroglio?

There are profound implications for India because of its strategic, energy, trade and investment interests, as well as the presence of a large Indian diaspora in the Middle East. These developments in India's near neighbourhood will need to be carefully monitored for their potential impact on India amidst the widening arc of uncontrollable conflict in the Middle East; of the Shia–Sunni divide; and of the Wahabi Islamic jihadi ideology and forces. ISIS's violent extremism and terrorism, and the spreading of its influence and tentacles in our neighbourhood—in coordination with forces in Afghanistan and Pakistan—especially hold out threats to India, as they do to countries further afield in South-East Asia, Africa and Europe.

As a non-permanent member, India played a key role in trying to warn against the consequences of the perilous interventions and attempts at regime change in Syria and Libya in the UNSC. Even outside the UNSC, for years India has been asking that the international community unequivocally recognize the threat to international peace of violent extremism and terrorism that masquerade as freedom movements and struggles for self-determination for communities, peoples and territories.

It has also been warning against sponsoring militancy and terrorism directed at other countries, the results of which are evident in the creation of the Afghan Taliban and now the Pakistani Taliban. Nearly ten years ago, the UNGA adopted a global counter-terrorism strategy. Unfortunately, over the years only lip service was paid in two parts: the need for 'addressing the underlying conditions conducive to the spread of terrorism' and 'ensuring respect for human rights for all and the rule of law as the fundamental basis of the fight against terrorism'. Overwhelming political capital and resources were instead devoted to advocating military, security and law enforcement measures as attested by the number of Security Council resolutions and the various Security Council subsidiary organs devoted to terrorism and related matters. These measures may have killed many terrorists. But I don't believe they eradicated the 'isms' that fuel terrorism, which is largely the result of a constellation of fault lines stemming from poor and exclusive governance, short-sighted geopolitical aspirations and the unhindered spread of poisonous ideologies, among other factors.

Hardeep Singh Puri
June 2016

1

CHAOS, DESTRUCTION AND DESTABILIZATION

All in all it was just a brick in the wall.
All in all it was all just bricks in the wall.

—Pink Floyd, *The Wall*, 30 November 1979

There is nothing new or remarkable in saying that the world we live in is becoming an increasingly dangerous place. Be that as it may, some pertinent questions need to be kept in mind. First, are the forces that seek destabilization and chaos slowly inching ahead and winning the battle against the forces that seek to promote order and stability? Second, to what extent were the developments in post-2003 Iraq—also covering, inter alia, Libya, Syria, Yemen and Ukraine—foreseeable? Most importantly, were policy instruments available to stakeholders for other possible, more benign, outcomes?

The answers, like the questions themselves, are interconnected. They merit focused attention if we are to find solutions for the way ahead. There is a pressing urgency for this. The ISIS, a terror entity, now holds territory larger in size than the UK. If at all it represents an ideology,[1] as some seem to believe, a purely militaristic response may not suffice.

Well before military action was contemplated in Iraq in 2003, there were powerful political voices already advocating regime change, not only in Iraq but also in Iran and Libya. Exactly a year and a day after 9/11, Benjamin Netanyahu, then former and again to be elected prime minister of Israel, had the following to say in congressional hearings on 12 September 2002:[2]

> I think of 'the three'. Saddam is probably in many ways the linchpin, because it is possible to take out this regime with military action, and the reverberations of what happens with the collapse of Saddam's regime could very well create an implosion in a neighbouring regime like Iran.
>
> So I think that the choice of going after Iraq is like removing a brick that holds a lot of other bricks and might cause this structure to crumble. It is not guaranteed. With the assumption of regime removal in Iraq, implosion in Iran and implosion in Libya is [also] an assumption. It is not guaranteed. But if I had to choose, should there be military action first against Iraq or first against Iran, I would choose exactly what the President has chosen: to go after Iraq.
>
> I think that should be the step against Iraq, and I think it would actually stabilize Iraq. It might send a message. I think it will, to neighbouring Iran, to neighbouring Syria, and the people will wake up and they will say, 'We can have a real life. We can have choice. Our children can have a future. That is not a bad idea.'
>
> If you take out Saddam's regime, I guarantee you that it will have enormous positive reverberations in the region. And I think that people sitting right next door in Iran, young people, and many others will say the time of such regimes, of such despots, is gone. There is a new age.

This testimony was provided by Netanyahu a good seven months before military action against Iraq commenced on 19 March 2003 and continued till 1 May 2003.

It reveals quite a lot. One, Netanyahu had an obsessive dislike for all three regimes: in Baghdad, Tehran and Tripoli. Two, he was attracted to the idea of regime change in all three countries. Three, the testimony constituted a flawed narrative on WMDs. Four, the analysis of the likely consequences that would flow from the removal of at least two of the three bricks in the wall, Saddam Hussein and Muammar Gaddafi, as subsequent events have shown, was way off the mark. Netanyahu believed that removing Saddam would actually 'stabilize Iraq'. In fact, he said removal of Saddam's regime—he was willing to guarantee this—would have enormous positive reverberations in the region. Even though Netanyahu was speaking in his personal capacity, the fact that he was a former prime minister when he participated in the hearings and went on to become prime minister again, is, in itself, of considerable significance. It is entirely possible that the earlier 2002 congressional testimony would have continued to be buried in the archives of the United States Congress but for the fact that during his 2015 visit to Washington, Netanyahu revisited the same theme, and alert analysts saw through the scaremongering.

Military action in 2003 to topple Saddam Hussein occurred without United Nations Security Council authorization. A sceptical Council refused to be persuaded about the existence of WMDs then. Military action in 2011 to overthrow Gaddafi, ostensibly in the interest of protecting civilians, was with Security Council authorization for the use of force contained in Resolution 1973.[3] As per the original September 2002 prescription from Netanyahu, one more brick, Iran, still remains to be removed.

The chaos, destruction and destabilization between 2003 and 2011 have been widespread. Witness the rise, in the last decade, of the al-Qaeda, Boko Haram and the ISIS, the last being an unwanted but fast-growing child of failed interventions. As with most unwanted children, the paternity of this child too is known. Saner voices are now prevailing. There is an attempt to curb the urge to intervene. The nuclear 'deal' with Iran, which sought to significantly curb the military component of Iran's nuclear programme, provides that concrete proof. Addressing the UNGA on 28 September 2015, this is what US president Barack Obama had to say:

> The result is a lasting, comprehensive deal that prevents Iran from obtaining a nuclear weapon, while allowing it to access peaceful energy. And if this deal is fully implemented, the prohibition on nuclear weapons is strengthened, a potential war is averted, [and] our world is safer. That is the strength of the international system when it works the way it should.[4]

The route of unilateral, coercive military action, it would now seem, appears much less attractive and has far less to offer in comparison.

As history so often teaches us, good and evil are relative concepts. In case of the military action in Iraq in 2003,[5] three justifications were popularly cited: the WMDs, al-Qaeda links and the need for human rights and democracy. The WMD and al-Qaeda arguments, in retrospect, were based on manipulated falsehoods. Whilst the democracy argument merits a separate and more detailed analysis, what stands out is that against the 70,000 people who cumulatively lost their lives under Saddam, the weekly death toll in 2013 was between seventy and 100, with more than 100,000 Iraqis and 4,500 Americans killed.[6] Not surprisingly, there was a conspiracy of silence in Washington on the tenth anniversary of the military action. There was a bipartisan consensus, at least so it appeared, that the US was happy to wash its hands of Iraq. The US president confined himself to a well-crafted statement and saluted the courage and resolve of those who served in Iraq, honouring the memory of the 4,500 Americans 'who made the ultimate sacrifice'.[7]

The verdict of history, when finally delivered, is always laced with a strong dose of irony. The full folly of the 2003 Iraq misadventure unfolded over a decade with a series of other costly mistakes. The Security Council authorized military action in Libya following Resolution 1973 of March 2011, while its inaction in Syria in 2012 and 2013 will continue to haunt the international community. The sectarian fault lines opened up in Syria have already come to haunt the present global order. A discussion on the use of force or, for that matter, any discussion on the events in Iraq, Libya and Syria, would be incomplete without an understanding of political extremism and issues related to terrorism, including ideology, identity politics and their umbilical link to organized crime and the arms bazaar.

The ISIS, as explained subsequently, traces its genesis to costly policy mistakes and reflects deep-rooted alienation in the affected societies. To the extent that it represents a military challenge, it constitutes perhaps the greatest and most daunting strategic challenge and threat to international peace and security that the world faces today. The physical elimination of the ISIS will not by itself eliminate the deep-rooted underlying causes which gave rise to it.

Policymakers who ignore the lessons of history and do not acknowledge their own past mistakes are liable to repeat those very mistakes. This is how ISIS started, as the unwanted child of failed interventions and the neglected occupation of Iraq in 2003. It is the same prisons, drawing sustenance from the near-total absence of civil liberty in the countries of the region, which incubated the al-Qaeda that are now incubating the ISIS. To quote Michael

Weiss and Hassan Hassan from *ISIS: Inside the Army of Terror*, 'Whether by accident or design, jail houses in the Middle East have served, for years, as virtual terror academies, where brown extremist groups can congregate, plot, organize and hone their leadership skills inside the wire,'[8] and, most ominously, recruit a new generation of fighters.

The ISIS is arguably the most formidable extremist organization in history. Effectively in control of the Middle East's heart in Iraq and Syria, it has transformed from being a Sunni insurgent underground movement to a militarist quasi-state entity in a short period of time since mid-2014. Its degree of influence is evident in its geopolitical features. Having unfurled akin to an empire geographically, the ISIS physically operates across vast swathes between Iraq's eastern and Syria's western limits, exercising control over them as a transnational whole. Alongside, it also lays claims on lands as far as Libya, Algeria and Pakistan.[9] Politically, it is run by a close-knit cabinet of the ideologically committed, who 'manage the structures that keep the organization running, overseeing hundreds of towns, thousands of fighters and millions of dollars in finances'.[10] Its orderly modus operandi allows it to implement, with an iron fist, a ruthless and reactionary rendition of the sharia law in its lands. Consequently, anything in contravention of the ISIS's notion of society is crushed. Beheading smokers, butchering homosexuals, enslaving women, amputating thieves, contorting education and razing relics, it has embarked on an aggressive revisionism that has pushed the Iraqi and Syrian people back to the medieval age.

An open letter by 126 Muslim scholars to the ISIS in September 2014 meticulously condemned its gross misuse of Islamic tenets.[11] Yet, support for its cause continues to flow in from all corners. Despite vilifying most things Western as sacrilegious, it cleverly exploits the fruits of Western technology. Its outreach and propaganda campaign on the Internet has led to thousands of volunteers flocking in from dozens of countries to embolden the Islamic State's structures. Likewise, liberal donations from wealthy private sympathizers form a large chunk of its revenues. Economically, the ISIS has inflated into arguably the richest jihadist organization known, raking in over $3 million daily through sources that range from human trafficking and blatant looting to formalized levies and the smuggling of oil.[12] Militarily, its forces have managed to amass a daunting arsenal. Besides conventional AK-47s, rocket and grenade launchers, Stinger MANPADs, T-55 and T-72 tanks, Humvees, anti-aircraft and field artillery, it flaunts state-of-the-art weaponry, such as M 198 Howitzers with GPS (Global Positioning System) guidance.[13] According to Paul Jackson of the University of Birmingham, in zones lacking stable authority, warlords often step in to fill the vacuum as 'alternative sources of governance'.[14] However, the ISIS is now more than a motley crew of bandits. Its sheer size and strength today is reason enough to understand its evolution.

The ISIS traces its roots to the Salafi jihadist tenets of the al-Qaeda, selectively inherited by the Jama'at al-Tawhid wal-Jihad—or al-Qaeda in Iraq—after Saddam Hussein's fall in 2003. Harbouring ambitions of establishing an Islamic caliphate, in 2006, the Jama'at became part of the Mujahideen Shura Council, the umbrella Sunni conglomerate which led the armed resistance against American presence on Iraqi soil. As membership increased, the council soon matured into the ISIS.[15] In 2010, Ibrahim Awwad Ibrahim al-Samarrai—once an introvert orthodox Iraqi student with an inclination for soccer—was rechristened Abu Bakr al-Baghdadi, a fiery self-styled caliph-designate, who zealously commanded its ranks. Within a year, the ISIS made an international mark by teaming with the al-Nusra Front to reinforce the Sunni rebellion amidst the Syrian civil war. Meanwhile, in Iraq, the US left Nouri al-Maliki, once a Shia opponent of Saddam, in charge of Baghdad. However, the new Iraqi prime minister quickly proved sectarian for the nation's Sunni populace, which propelled Iraq towards a civil war.[16] Confident of its blitzing prowess, the ISIS, in 2014, vowed to wrest power, launched the 'northern Iraq offensive', crushed al-Maliki's troops, and planted their flags at Mosul, Iraq's largest city. By June, al-Baghdadi wielded enough authority to declare his coveted caliphate and call upon allegiance from the world over.

The mutation of the ISIS from a perceived 'terror outfit' into a self-proclaimed Salafi caliphate for Islam has marked a return of the old 'Mad Mullah syndrome' for Washington and its allies. The Islamic State's method and intent are not entirely new to the West, which also suffered major headaches over a similar situation in Afghanistan, where non-state religious extremists usurped power and bred global terror. The Afghan zealots, of course, started out as mujahids—fighters for the jihadist cause—against the Soviet occupants of their country in the early 1980s, then generously nurtured by the US. However, soon after the Russians evacuated Kabul, the al-Qaeda and the Taliban took over, biting the hand that fed them. Likewise, is the Islamic State too an unwanted consequence of the West's escapades in the Middle East? Surely, the US-led alliance cannot absolve itself of this mess entirely. The ancestral factions of the ISIS—from the al-Qaeda to the Mujahideen Shura Council—were all products of bungled Western policies. Making matters worse for the West, more direct links have been surfacing in the public domain for some time. In 2007, veteran political journalist Seymour M. Hersh noted a disquieting shift in the US's Middle East strategy under George W. Bush, which banked on the region's ancient sectarian gaps.

In West Asia, Shiite Iran and Hezbollah, along with Alawite-ruled Syria, were identified as the chief adversaries of American interests. Thus, in order to weaken these actors, Sunni detractors were sought to be empowered in collaboration with Sunni states such as Saudi Arabia. Moreover, it was reckoned that 'closer ties between the United States and moderate or even radical Sunnis' was a clever tool to keep a check on Iraq's al-Maliki government.[17] The shortcomings of such a perilous policy, however, were underlined during a controversial address to the Kennedy School at Harvard University in 2014 by US vice-president Joe Biden:

> The Turks ... the Saudis, the Emirates, etc., what were they doing? They were so determined to take down [Syrian president Bashar al] Assad, and essentially have a proxy Sunni-Shia war. What did they do? They poured hundreds of millions of dollars and tens, thousands of tonnes of weapons into anyone who would fight against Assad.[18]

As per Biden's outspoken verdict—for which he had to apologize later—the West's miscalculated largesse towards Sunni extremists in the Middle East through its regional partners ended up paving the way for the ISIS. Meanwhile, Republican senator Randal H. Paul of Kentucky candidly spoke to the Cable News Network (CNN) on the issue: 'I think we have to understand first how we got here ... One of the reasons why ISIS has been emboldened is because we have been arming their allies. We have been allied with ISIS in Syria.'[19]

Even more notoriously, in August 2014, during a talk with Iran's Press TV, a former contractor of the US Central Intelligence Agency (CIA), Steven Kelly, unabashedly admitted:

> [The ISIS] is a completely fabricated enemy. The funding is completely from the United States and its allies, and for people to think that this enemy is something that needs to be attacked in Syria or Iraq is a farce, because obviously, this is something

that we created, [and] we controlled. [Now], it has become inconvenient for us to attack this group as a legitimate enemy.[20]

By May 2015, the picture became clearer. Judicial Watch, an international watchdog, dug up a declassified release of the US Defense Intelligence Agency (DIA), which analysed American policy for the raging Syrian civil war. The state-sponsored report, from 2012, explicitly stated that 'the West, the Gulf countries and Turkey support the opposition [Sunni rebels], while Russia, China and Iran support the [al-Assad] regime'. The paper, stirring up a hornet's nest, went on to foresee the 'development of the … situation into a proxy war', and observed:

If the situation unravels, there is the possibility of establishing a declared or undeclared Salafist principality in eastern Syria … This is exactly what the supporting powers [the West] of the opposition [the Sunni rebels] want, in order to isolate the Syrian regime, which is considered the strategic depth of the Shia expansion.

However, the DIA's report also cautioned, with ominous accuracy:

The deteriorating situation … creates the ideal atmosphere for … unifying the jihad amongst Sunni Iraq and Syria. [The ISIS] could also declare an Islamic State through its union with other terrorist organizations in Iraq and Syria, which will create grave danger in regards to … the protection of [Iraq's] territory.[21]

Some warnings were, of course, voiced against reading between the lines of the memo.[22] However, such scepticism soon waned when Lieutenant General Michael T. Flynn was interviewed by Al Jazeera in August 2015. The former director of the DIA unequivocally upheld the prescriptive worth of the eyebrow-raising report on the crisis in Syria, recalling that he 'paid very close attention' to it while in office. Additionally, General Flynn affirmed Washington's tactic of abetting Salafist extremism against the Assad regime as being 'a wilful decision'.[23]

Many ISIS sympathizers are, in fact, home-grown. The experiences of prisoners—many of whom were incarcerated merely for expressing opinions that clashed with those of the state—kept in jails in Sunni-majority Arab states are of humiliation and torture. These experiences encouraged them to fight back with the sole aim of ridding these Islamic regimes of corrupt leaderships. This began as early as the 1980s, when Arab jails became incubators of al-Qaeda recruits and leaders. Some examples include Ayman al-Zawahiri in Egypt, who was Osama bin Laden's deputy and has replaced him as head of the organization, and Abu Musab al-Zarqawi in Jordan, who went to Iraq after the US-led overthrow of the Iraqi regime of Saddam Hussein and established al-Qaeda in Mesopotamia, which later spawned ISIS.[24] Even jails run by the US, such as Camp Bucca in southern Iraq, became breeding grounds for Islamic radicalization and terrorism. Camp Bucca provided an extraordinary opportunity, as it not only ensured safety but was also geographically close to the entire al-Qaeda leadership, in addition to giving these prisoners the chance to be together at one place.[25] In fact, this is where a senior ISIS official, Abu Ahmed, first met Abu Bakr al-Baghdadi.

The solution to the consequent mess does not lie in Western intervention, which has already proven to have dire repercussions. The West, with its limited understanding of what the general population in the conflict-stricken Arab countries wants from its leaders, and by imposing Western ideas of democracy and justice, has meddled in the politics of the region with drastic consequences. What is worse is the failure of Western political theorists to acknowledge the blunders that the West's association with autocratic rulers such as Gaddafi, Ali Abdullah Saleh of Yemen and Assad has resulted in—apparent in military interventions that involved arming rebels and the use of force. Thus, the partnership between Western nations and Arab regimes is detrimental insofar as it is believed to have originally led to the 'birth of Al-Qaeda in the 1980s and later spawned its derivative—the Islamic State—today';[26] these formed some of the 'push factors' (discussed later) for people to join militancy. However, the incredible pull of the ISIS that is drawing foreign fighters in large numbers cannot be ignored either.

A striking feature of the ISIS, claimed to be the most dangerous jihadist group operating in the world today, is the intensity with which the organization, using social media, is luring individuals from across the world to join them, and its alarming rate of success in this endeavour. The actual number of fighters remains shrouded in mystery. The CIA believes that around 40,000 fighters are part of the ISIS, while Russia puts the number at 70,000, and the Kurdish president believes the number can be as high as 200,000. This has, not surprisingly, resulted in extensive debates about the reasons for people, mainly the youth, to feel drawn towards the Islamic State, despite the international notoriety surrounding its violent ways. While one argument blames ideologies related to religion and culture that glorify radical Islam and persuade individuals to turn jihadists, another argument asserts that socio-economic factors of poverty, unemployment and economic stagnation lead to increased frustration because of the widening gap between expectations or aspirations and opportunities. These may be categorized as 'pull factors'.

In retrospect, perhaps the most significant mistake the US made in Iraq in 2003 was to overlook the disbanding of Saddam's army and the melting away of the Ba'ath Party cadres. The two factors have now fused to provide cutting-edge military leadership to the ISIS. *Time*, in fact, openly claimed that 'a big reason for [the ISIS's] success is the George W. Bush administration's decision to disband the Iraqi army shortly after the 2003 invasion'.[27] By August 2015, a report of the *Guardian* confirmed that up to 160 former Iraqi military officers had enrolled in ISIS ranks.[28] These were the 'push factors'.

The push factors could also be explained through the concept of 'frustrated achievers'.[29] Owing to the increased presence and impact of social media in this globalized world, deprivation becomes relative, and one may grow impatient with slow or absent upward mobility. In Western societies, which are home to various religious, racial and ethnic communities, invariably, there are instances of minorities having trouble with assimilation, integration and, in general, developing a sense of identity associated with the nation. Another reason for the youth joining the organization could simply be the extraordinary opportunity to be part of something special, new and, more importantly, meaningful; and associating with something as powerful as the ISIS may also make an individual feel rather empowered.[30] In some cases, it is also seen as a chance to seek redemption.

It is important to understand the push and pull factors not in isolation but as interconnected. When the youth belonging to a certain community remain unemployed and impoverished, they tend to be more vulnerable to radicalization of the kind propagated by the ISIS. In the countries of origin, particularly those in West Asia ruled by despots, the political scene was dominated by the lack of civil liberties and high rates of unemployment. The situation was made worse by Western intervention. For youth joining from the relatively affluent parts of the world, there was perhaps a quest for identity stemming from the pressures of assimilation. And the ISIS not only claims to practise true Islam as professed by Prophet Muhammad—in giving 'specific Koranic justification for their most gruesome acts'[31] and attracting those seeking some sort of religious redemption—but also addresses the desires and aspirations of those grappling with socio-economic issues, as it presents itself as an 'equal opportunity organization', which has everything 'from the sadistic psychopath to the humanitarian to the idealistically driven'.[32]

What has caused even more consternation in the international community is the phenomenon of women joining the ISIS. Social media is rife with reports and stories of young women from the UK, Norway, Sweden, France and many more Western countries travelling to Syria to marry ISIS militants. Yet, the assumption that the motivation for women to join the organization is solely to become 'jihadi brides' is much too simplistic. A significant part of the Islamic community in the Western world is angered by the persecution of Muslims, especially by Western opinion of how women should practise Islam, with the West often criticizing Muslim women's position. This has made women feel culturally and socially isolated in the visibly liberal Western societies. And ISIS, to them, seems to provide the solution. By joining the ISIS, they can fully embrace Islam—without having to conform to Western standards of gender roles—and be part of a 'sisterhood' of something meaningful. The role of women within the ISIS is, however, not restricted to the domestic domain. The organization has at least two all-female battalions in Syria's northern city of Raqqah, complete with women in burqas carrying rifles. Though these were reportedly formed to 'expose male activists who disguise in women's clothing to avoid detention when stopping at ISIS checkpoints',[33] they now help attract more women to the ranks of ISIS and generate support among them.

Some personal accounts of those who have been to Syria and joined the organization almost succeed in debunking the ISIS's utopian idea of a caliphate with idyllic notions of Islam and a good standard of living for all by highlighting the conditions of living under it, owing to sporadic access to electricity and water, terrible health care systems and the travails of life in a war zone. Considering these ground realities, the pull of the ISIS felt by thousands of young men and women in their teens to late twenties is, indeed, remarkable. From portraying itself as a caliphate, a utopian political state with centralized Islamic rule that promises a good lifestyle comprising free housing, electricity, water and other basic amenities, to appealing to prospective recruits through social media (Twitter, Facebook, WhatsApp, etc.), the ISIS has spectacularly demonstrated its global appeal. It has attracted youth from different parts of the world, most notably from some of the most developed Western nations emblematic of equality and modernity. And the youth are excited about the prospect of belonging to a group of like-minded people, of developing a personal identity validated by others,[34] and of overcoming socio-economic hurdles to be part of something new and thrilling.

In comparison to the al-Qaeda, which is recognized as a terror group, ISIS comes across more as an ideology that thousands around the world feel drawn towards. So, one needs to ask a key question at this point: can one bomb an ideology?

If not in self-defence, no country has the right to wage war. It is only the UN Security Council that has the authority to determine whether or not there exists a threat to international peace and security. Having made the determination, it is the Security Council alone that can authorize an appropriate response to deal with the threat. The laws of war do not, however, appear to be respected today in the real world. There is little hesitation or inhibition in undertaking military action when perceived national or other interests appear threatened. Equally, the arming of rebels without thinking through the consequences and the wilful encouragement of destabilization appear to take place frequently.

The Latin term '*jus ad bellum*'[35] can be broadly translated as the 'right to wage war'. In essence, it deals with the criteria for waging war and is concerned with whether the waging of war is just or not. The Westphalian order[36] based on state sovereignty placed strong emphasis on non-intervention. That, in practice, meant that the political or ruling dispensation could do pretty much anything or everything inside the country's borders as long as an internal situation or other actions did not develop in a manner that the Security Council deemed it constituted a threat to international peace and security. The post-war era, in a sense, can thus be looked at as one of absolute sovereignty. The establishment of the United Nations in 1945, the Universal Declaration of Human Rights in 1948, the enlarging membership of the UN, and various multilateral processes and negotiations have resulted in the gradual chipping away of the 'absolute' part of sovereignty.

An area where it is becoming increasingly difficult to cite sovereignty as a defence is that of mass atrocities, genocide, ethnic cleansing, crimes against humanity and war crimes. Another area that has escaped focused attention and intense scrutiny is the arming of rebels, the 'zero tolerance' norm for international terrorism notwithstanding.[37] By definition, terrorism breeds in countries that repress civil liberties and pursue policies that are not socially inclusive and do not encourage popular participation. At the same time, the financing and arming of rebel groups by the intelligence agencies of well-established democracies, ostensibly for laudable ends, have resulted not only in destabilization but also in widespread chaos. The decision to use force and wage war, including through the arming of rebels, should, by definition, be taken by whosoever is empowered to do so only after the most serious consideration.

How has the Security Council discharged this responsibility? Did it rise to the occasion in recent times and act in the interest of maintaining peace and security? On the occasions when it 'authorized' the use of force, did it do so based on a careful assessment that the military action would be anchored in and carefully circumscribed by 'proportionality'? Most important, was it really necessary to use force to achieve the objectives for which authorization was sought and provided?

There would appear to be considerable merit in examining some of the decisions that authorized the use of force and others in which authorization from the Security Council was not forthcoming. Was the Security Council made aware of the dangers inherent in the course of action being proposed? Were those dangers properly discussed and evaluated? If yes, why did the Council nevertheless decide to go down that road? The subsequent chapters deal with such situations and questions. One particular situation, when the Security Council authorized the use of force through Resolution 1973 in Libya, will continue to be cited as a game changer. In retrospect, was it a wise decision? Are the destabilization and chaos that prevail in Libya policy-induced?

There have, of course, been many instances when the Council, or rather its members, have refused to be persuaded by the evidence submitted to justify 'all means necessary', a euphemism for the 'use of force'. I recall an afternoon, on 24 April 2003, when along with other colleagues—the permanent representatives to the UN—I was in Chamber XIX of the Palais des Nations in Geneva, listening to the then secretary-general, Kofi Annan. The room overflowed with assorted representatives of member states, NGOs, the press and civil society.

The secretary-general's carefully crafted speech stressed the universality and indivisibility of human rights, regardless of gender, country or continent, or whether they concerned civil, political or economic rights. He stopped speaking around noon. What stood out and was immediately picked up by the world's wire services were his comments on the military action in Iraq. His carefully chosen words did not resonate well in some Western capitals. My American counterpart and friend Kevin Moley, in particular, was livid. Let us take a careful look at what the secretary-general actually said:[38]

> The decision to go to war without specific authorization by the Security Council has created deep division that will need to be bridged if we are to deal effectively, not just with the aftermath of Iraq, but with other major challenges on the international agenda.

Noting that threats to international peace and security may require a searching review of the adequacy of existing instruments, with a view to coming up with a collective response, he added:

> I say 'collective response' because I remain as convinced as ever that we are all safer—the large and powerful as well as the small and weak—in a system where all are governed by the international rule of law and principles set out in the United Nations Charter.

Emphasizing the obligations of the occupying powers, he continued:

> In the first instance, I hope the coalition will set an example by making clear that they intend to act strictly within the rules set down by the Geneva conventions and the Hague Regulations regarding the treatment of prisoners of war and by demonstrating through their actions that they accept the responsibility of the occupying power for public order and safety and the well-being of the civilized population.

That was in April 2003. In retrospect, it is clear that back then, parts of the West justified military action in Iraq by building on the perception that Saddam Hussein represented evil, possessed WMDs, and was in bed with the al-Qaeda, and that military intervention would serve to boost democratic forces. It is instructive to compare this with the situation in Iraq ten years later, in April 2013, some six to eight months before the emergence of the ISIS.

2

UNDERSTANDING THE
ARAB SPRING

Of the many stories doing the rounds about the Arab Spring, my favourite is the one told so eloquently by my friend and colleague at the International Peace Institute (IPI) in New York, Warren Hoge, former UN correspondent of the *New York Times*.

Moderating a discussion in the IPI's Distinguished Author Series, he said:

> We all have our recollections of the high hopes that the beginning of the Arab Spring in 2011 provoked. For many of us here at IPI, we remember in particular the visit to this stage in November of 2011 of Ahmed Maher, the charismatic 31-year-old founder of the April 6 Youth Movement that advocated democracy in Egypt.
>
> So giddy and high-spirited with the possibilities of the spreading uprisings was he that day that he showed up a little late, explaining with delight that on the way here he had been drawn into the Occupy Wall Street protests downtown. We asked him to compare what he saw with what he was experiencing in Egypt, and he said, 'I think the similarity is the youth, the spirit, the hope of change.'
>
> That was then.

Two years later, Ahmed Maher was arrested and charged with violating a law banning protests, and today he is serving a three-year jail sentence in Cairo, much of it in solitary confinement. In a letter he smuggled out of prison last year, you can hear the disillusionment he felt at the outcome that sounds almost quaint now.

'I met with some of the most famous and important figures of Europe, America, India, Korea and Turkey,' he wrote, 'and here I am now looking for a loaf of a stale bread to eat.'

What had begun as stirring popular mobilization was to descend into civil war, state failure, authoritarian renewal and, much too often, the deaths of participants.[1]

Ahmed Maher's story sadly is one of many. The hope, the optimism are gone. The recurring references now are to civil war, state failure and authoritarian renewal.

To say that the Arab Spring generated great excitement both in the region and the West would be an understatement. The self-immolation by a twenty-something fruit vendor in the Tunisian city of Sidi Bouzid in December 2010, gathering crowds in Cairo's Tahrir Square in February 2011, and the fall of Hosni Mubarak, the president of Egypt, on 11 February 2011 after a three-decade rule, tainted by unchecked corruption and concentration of power, sent expectations soaring and contributed to the development of a new narrative. There was great hope and anticipation, both within the region and outside, of good times ahead and of a new order emerging. That these momentous developments were taking place whilst the UN Security Council was considering Resolution 1970 on Libya appeared to lend credence to the view that the international community was seized of these events and had a sensible game plan to deal with particularly egregious violators of basic freedoms. This, in turn, raised two interrelated expectations. First, these unfolding events would resonate on a Western liberal democratic template. Second, the ferment on Arab streets and the strong and entrenched alienation of the people, particularly the youth, from the repressive regimes would lead to spontaneous uprisings against them. The early signs witnessed in Tunisia and Egypt fuelled the hype that a genuine democratic revolution, along the lines of what was witnessed in Eastern Europe in 1989,[2] was under way.

Articulation of dissent, even in its mildest form, was relatively new to the countries affected by the Arab Spring. Since the uprisings that swept across North Africa in the spring of 2011 were rooted in mass demands—among them political freedoms, social justice and human dignity—it is not surprising that the dominant view, at least in the West, was that they represented, at the very least, a yearning for the Western liberal type of democracy.

An act of self-immolation by an individual represents both extreme frustration and a sense of utter helplessness against a repressive environment. When Mohamed Bouazizi set himself on fire on 17 December 2010 in the Tunisian city of Sidi Bouzid, the action had overtones not limited to the local oppression and municipal context in which the fruit vendor's frustration was anchored. There was a remarkable similarity between the reactions that the act evoked in various Western capitals. Sample, by way of illustration, the carefully drafted statements that emerged from Paris, London and Washington. The French foreign minister Alain Juppe said on 16 April 2011:

> And then all of a sudden, in the town of Sidi Bouzid, without being influenced by any political or religious group, a young man sets fire to himself.
>
> Then, all of a sudden, step by step, the flame of freedom is spreading throughout the region. Egypt's youth rise up, Libya revolts, the Arab peoples rise up against the oppression. Citizens demand their dignity and forcefully voice their aspiration for

personal freedom, respect for human dignity and to be able to express their opinions freely—all these universal values dear to France, and not just to France since they transcend civilizations, cultures and borders and are all part of the United Nations common good.

This 'Arab spring' is the fruit of a sense of responsibility. I need only point to the attitude of the young Egyptians in Tahrir Square. I met them last month during my visit to Cairo. I listened to them talk to me about their projects, hopes and fears. I was impressed by their calm, but also by their refusal to let a victory—that of their people, not a party or religion—be taken away from them. I was won over by their enthusiasm and their dream of a reconciled, democratic Egypt, capable of giving work to her young people.[3]

At a G8 meeting in Deauville, France, in May 2011, French president Nicolas Sarkozy said 'it is critical that the popular revolutions in Tunisia and Egypt succeed'. He said mobilizing 'considerable aid' was among the central goals of the G8 meeting.[4]

British prime minister David Cameron echoed similar sentiments at the summit when he said:

I want a very simple and clear message to come out of this summit, and that is that the most powerful nations on earth have come together and are saying to those in the Middle East and North Africa who want greater democracy, greater freedom, greater civil rights: we are on your side.[5]

Obama joined his French and British counterparts when, in speaking about the self-immolation incident, he went on to say:

In too many countries, a citizen like that young vendor had nowhere to turn—no honest judiciary to hear his case; no independent media to give him voice; no credible political party to represent his views; no free and fair election where he could choose his leader.

He congratulated the people of the region for having 'achieved more change in six months than terrorists have accomplished in decades', by having their 'shouts of human dignity heard across the region, through the moral force of nonviolence'. He added:

> The United States supports a set of universal rights. And these rights include free speech, the freedom of peaceful assembly, the freedom of religion, equality for men and women under the rule of law, and the right to choose your own leaders—whether you live in Baghdad or Damascus, Sana'a or Tehran. And we support political and economic reform in the Middle East and North Africa that can meet the legitimate aspirations of ordinary people throughout the region.[6]

The mainstream narrative emanating from Western capitals was full of hope, expectation of imminent revolt and, with the benefit of hindsight, some wishful thinking. In retrospect, the narrative appears to have been predicated on a flawed assumption. Is it that flawed assumption which led to a completely wrong strategic diagnosis? More serious is the likelier scenario that the mainstream narrative was somewhat contrived.

The yearning for freedom and democracy, viewed in terms of an act that represents extreme frustration and helplessness, whatever the immediate cause and motivation, is and can be regarded as a significant pointer. A clamour for civil liberties—political, economic and social rights—is a given in any society, more so in those that have institutionally succeeded in denying basic rights to their citizens through a despotic hold on power. To that extent, the situation in the countries of the Arab Spring was qualitatively different from that prevailing in Eastern Europe in 1989. In the latter, the protesting citizenry wanted to have the lifestyle of their western European counterparts—both the democratic freedoms and the standard of living. The governments in West European capitals were not viewed as the 'enemy'. Rather, they were seen as providing the governance model which protesters in 1989 sought for their own countries. In the countries of the Arab Spring, on the other hand, Western governments were largely viewed as collaborators of the repressive regimes that had subjugated those who were now struggling to find their voice.

There is no doubt that the ferment, frustration and anger on Arab streets produced toxicity fuelled by repressive regimes. These regimes perpetuated their power by curtailing civil liberties in varying degrees. The lack of basic human rights and freedoms was problematic enough. The sense of economic denial and deprivation manifesting in high rates of unemployment in Tunisia and Egypt, the first two countries on the calendar of the Arab Spring, exacerbated by a new-found access to social media, facilitated rapid mobilization of large crowds, as, for instance, in Tahrir Square. The self-immolation in Tunisia's Sidi Bouzid was not, however, an isolated incident. The following well-documented cases provide insights into the prevailing mood in countries experiencing what came to be described as the Arab Spring.

Egypt

- Abdou Abdel-Moneim Jaafar, a forty-nine-year-old baker from a town outside Cairo, set himself on fire outside the Egyptian parliament in the capital on 17 January 2011. His act instigated weeks of protest and, later, the resignation of the Egyptian president, Hosni Mubarak, on 11 February 2011.[7]
- Twenty-five-year-old Ahmed Hashem Sayed, unemployed, set himself on fire in Alexandria and died from his burns in the second week of January 2011.[8]

Algeria

- A thirty-seven-year-old father of two, Mohsen Bouterfif, set himself on fire on 13 January 2011 during protests against rising food prices and unemployment. The trigger was apparently the refusal of the mayor of Boukhadra to meet with him and others regarding employment and housing issues.[9]

- Maamir Lotfi, a thirty-six-year-old unemployed father of six, set himself on fire in front of the El Oued town hall on 17 January 2011, again merely because he was denied a meeting with the governor.[10]

- A twenty-seven-year-old man burned himself in front of a police station in Jijel, just outside of Algiers; the reasons for his actions were unknown.[11]

- Abdelhafid Boudechicha, twenty-nine, was a day labourer who lived with his parents and five siblings. He set himself ablaze on 28 January 2011 in Medjana over employment and housing issues.

- Three people set themselves on fire in protest on 16 January 2011, expressing their frustration against the economy, escalating food prices and an unresponsive government.[12]

Mauritania

- Yacoub Dahoud set himself on fire in front of the presidential palace on 7 January 2011, declaring the right of Mauritanian people to choose their freedom.[13]

Tunisia

- About 107 Tunisians tried to kill themselves by self-immolation in the first six months after Mohamed Bouazizi's death.[14]

- Although it was Bouazizi's suicide that focused international attention on self-immolation, the practice had already become common in Tunisia prior to his death. According to Werner Ruf, a North Africa expert at the University of Kassel in Germany, 'Up to 15 per cent of the patients in the special clinic for burn victims in Tunis are victims of self-immolation.'[15]

Dissent, opposition and protest are legitimate expressions of differences in democratic societies. In 2010, when the so-called Arab Spring started, the countries of the Middle East, however, lacked the essential institutions, traditions and processes of social inclusion in which dissent and opposition could be assimilated. The absence of institutions that could assimilate the anger led to public demonstrations and protests, disproportionate use of force by the established regimes and the rapid toppling of 'presidents-for-life' in Tunisia, Egypt and later Yemen, as well as the grisly demise of Gaddafi, Libya's dictator for forty-two years.

In their recent work, *The Arab Spring: Pathways of Repression and Reform*, Tarek Masoud et al. observe:

> The Arab world's autocracies are protected by an array of political and economic factors that suppress dissent in ordinary life and crush opposition when it emerges. If such fortified systems could be overturned by hastily formed social movements in a matter of months, the region would have witnessed far more successful uprisings in earlier periods.[16]

Libya, the third country after Tunisia and Egypt to experience the so-called Arab Spring, became, perhaps by virtue of the universal dislike for its ruler Gaddafi, a target for regime change. Drawing inspiration from the winds of change discernible in the region, the Libyan opposition commenced as a movement for democratic rights, initially peacefully. Gaddafi, who had ruled Libya with an iron fist for more than forty years, however, decided to respond with the use of brutal force.

This prompted military action by the NATO, with due authorization from the UN Security Council. Conceived as the first manifestation of the Security Council's operationalization of R2P, the military action appeared initially to succeed and then went hopelessly wrong. Five years later, Libya as a state and as a country stands unravelled. Gaddafi's overthrow, initially welcomed, threw not only Libya but also several neighbouring countries—Chad, Mali, Niger and parts of Nigeria—into chaos.

Four years after the misadventure in Libya, Obama had this to say while addressing the high-level segment of the UNGA on 26 September 2015:

> In such efforts, the United States will always do our part. We will do so mindful of the lessons of the past ... not just the lessons of Iraq but also the example of Libya, where we joined an international coalition under a UN mandate to prevent a slaughter. Even as we helped people bring an end to the reign of a tyrant, our coalition could have and should have done more to fill a vacuum left behind.

The original narrative of the Arab Spring, predicated on flawed assumptions and objectionable approaches, is no longer mentioned or cross-referenced in positive terms by the so-called civilized world that sets the mainstream narrative.

How is it that so many got the strategic narrative of the Arab Spring so hopelessly wrong? And yet, not everyone did. India chose to be circumspect.

In a statement from New York, India's external affairs minister at the time, S.M. Krishna, commenting on developments in Egypt, welcomed the commitment of Egypt's Supreme Council of the Armed Forces to ensure a peaceful transition of power in a time-bound manner to establish an open, democratic framework of governance. 'We are proud of our traditionally close relations with the people of Egypt and wish them peace, stability and prosperity.'[17] India began backing the mass protests on 2 February 2011, terming them an 'articulation of the aspirations of the Egyptian people for reform'. Its ministry of external affairs had then said in a statement:

It is hoped that the current situation will be resolved in a peaceful manner, in the best interests of the people of Egypt. India wishes that Egypt, a fellow developing country with which it enjoys close and traditional ties, will continue to be a strong and stable nation, contributing to peace and prosperity in the region.[18]

India said it would be 'very positive' to requests by Arab countries to usher in democracy and help build institutions that sustain it. However, the offer made by Krishna was laced with caution. While interacting with newspersons on his way to Kuwait, he observed:

India does not believe in interfering in the affairs of another country. We will take the cue at an appropriate time depending on how they want India to help. India will be willing to be of some assistance to them. But let the situation arise.

India's position is that it is closely monitoring the events, and depending on how the situation develops, India will certainly try to position itself to be of advantage to forces of democracy so dear to India's heart.[19]

Addressing the high-level segment of the UNGA on 24 September 2011, Dr Manmohan Singh, the then prime minister of India, said:

We will succeed only if we adopt cooperative rather than a confrontational approach. We will succeed if we embrace again the principles on which the United Nations was founded—internationalism and multilateralism. More importantly, we will succeed if our efforts have legitimacy and are pursued not just within the framework of law but also the spirit of the law.

The observance of the rule of law is as important in international affairs as it is within countries. Societies cannot be reordered from outside using military force. People in all countries have the right to choose their own destiny and decide their future.

Such objective, clinical and contrarian assessments were not confined to countries like India. See what Henry Kissinger, the veteran American diplomat who served as secretary of state in the administrations of President Richard Nixon and President Gerald Ford, had to say:

The Arab Spring started as a new generation's uprising for liberal democracy [but soon] turned into paralysis. The existing political forces, embedded in the military and in religion in the countryside, proved stronger and better organized than the middle-class element demonstrating for democratic principles in Tahrir Square. In practice, the Arab Spring has exhibited rather than overcome the internal contradictions of the Arab-Islamic world and of the policies designed to resolve them … The original Arab Spring demonstrators' calls for an open political and economic life have been overwhelmed by a violent contest between military-backed authoritarianism and Islamist ideology.[20]

Delivering a speech to an international conference of Muslim clerics in the spring of 2013, the supreme leader of the Islamic Republic of Iran, Ayatollah Ali Khamenei, saw the so-called Arab Spring very differently. He viewed the developments in Tunis and Cairo as an 'Islamic Awakening'.

Today what lies in front of our eyes and cannot be denied by any informed and intelligent individual is that the world of Islam has now emerged out of the sidelines of social and political equations of the world, that it has found a prominent and outstanding position at the centre of decisive global events, and that it offers a fresh outlook on life, politics, government and social developments.

Islamic Awakening, which speakers in the arrogant and reactionary camp do not even dare to mention in words, is a truth whose signs can be witnessed in almost all parts of the world of Islam. The most obvious sign of it is the enthusiasm of public opinion, especially among young people, to revive the glory and greatness of Islam, to become aware of the nature of the international order of domination and to remove the mask from the shameless, oppressive and arrogant face of the governments and centres that have been pressuring the Islamic and non-Islamic East.[21]

Wishful thinking and unsuccessful manipulation partially explain the momentous developments that took place. The job of intelligence agencies is to monitor terror outfits like the al-Qaeda. Western intelligence agencies, which had considerable ground presence in the region, read the signals of unrest for change and fed them to their political capitals without much filtering. These agencies saw in the spontaneous outpouring of democratic aspiration a repudiation of terror outfits. This initial mistake was serious enough. It was soon compounded by another: the very costly mistake of arming select rebel groups when entrenched repressive regimes decided to use disproportionate force against unarmed civilians, as in Libya.

Soon, however, the unarmed civilian became only a talking point, a cover for the arming of rebels. There are no good, as against bad, rebels. Arming of rebels invariably has unintended consequences, mostly negative. The Arab Spring witnessed the perpetuation of another absurdity, the arming of what was described as a 'moderate opposition'. In Syria, in fact, the US embarked upon a $500 million programme to train the moderate opposition. This was a disaster, and the programme was discontinued, but only as late as October 2015, when it was found that just a handful of trainees could be accounted for on the battlefield, the others having either melted away or passed their equipment on to the enemy.

The consequences for Libya and its people of the authorized

use of force with the prior approval and sanction of the UN Security Council were devastating, leading to the unravelling of a country. The most serious miscalculation by the West was the misreading of the popular mood. In popular perception in these areas, the West was seen as part of the problem. Decades of support to repressive regimes—which deprived their populations of civil liberties, followed policies that were not socially inclusive and did not allow participatory governance—constituted the core of the problem. The jails filled with unemployed youth acted as incubators for the al-Qaeda. In Libya, ranked high in terms of human development index during the Gaddafi period, tribal affinities effectively prevented the post-Gaddafi scenario from following a Western liberal democratic template. Military action and the implementation of Resolution 1973 did not result in the 'protection of civilians', but a Somalia on the Mediterranean coast.

In terms of global political leadership there was a hidden cost to pay. The traditional allies of the US in this part of the world—Egypt, Saudi Arabia and other Gulf states—whose political classes had sustained themselves through political and military relationships with the superpower, suddenly found themselves facing new questions about the reliability of this alliance. As part of a complex relationship with Saudi Arabia, the US had been accommodative of the Wahabi extremism that emanated from that country. In a sense, this involved taking sides in the Sunni–Shia sectarian divide. The rationale for this was anchored in the expectation that on the issue of terrorism, countries that were part of the problem could be encouraged to become part of the solution. Could they? The jury is still out.

This also raises other deeper issues. The days of 'absolute' sovereignty are clearly gone. Failure to manage domestic political developments by a country will either invite interference and intervention or, in some cases where the consequences are particularly negative, also retribution. If sectarian fault lines are opened up, as between Sunni and Shia states, and sectarian considerations become the determinant for action, the prospects for maintenance of peace and security stand further eroded. This provides the tragic backdrop to what has happened in Iraq, Syria and Yemen and could, in all likelihood, happen elsewhere.

Equally, the Arab Spring forced the West to choose between idealism, embodied in democratic aspirations, and realism, through political and military alliances. In retrospect, the vote for democracy and idealism resulted in America abandoning its long-term political allies in the region, such as Mubarak, but the consequences, as in Iraq earlier and Libya and Syria now, proved disastrous.

Delivering the Third Gareth Evans Lecture[22] on 12 September 2013 in New York, Michael Ignatieff, Canadian author, academic and Liberal politician, said:

> We cannot fail to have noticed how reluctant our fellow citizens have become to support protection missions overseas. Let's be clear where the problem is: It is not compassion fatigue, isolationism or disengagement from the world. It's deep and justified distrust of all moralizing arguments, whether cast in the language of R2P or the language of humanitarian necessity, in favour of the use of force in international affairs. The evidence from opinion polls, from the recent House of Commons vote and from the evident failure of the president to secure support in Congress make it clear the public mood is, to quote a song from long ago: 'we won't be fooled again'.
>
> There is more to this than war weariness or sorrow at the human and financial cost of intervention. It goes beyond disillusion at the failures to build stability in Iraq, Afghanistan or Libya. The core problem is public anger at the manipulation of consent: disillusion with the moral and humanitarian

arguments used to extract popular consent for the use of force in Afghanistan, Iraq and Libya.

R2P was not used to justify two of these three cases, but its legitimacy as a vocabulary for international engagement cannot escape the general opprobrium that is falling upon all arguments to protect strangers in conflict-ridden countries far away.[23]

The choice of vocabulary used invariably points to the preferences and biases of the speaker or writer. Not every government joined in the support for a new democratic order in the Gulf and the Middle East. Those that were sceptical were simplistically categorized as being on the wrong side of the human rights divide in their own countries. Western think tanks and human rights organizations were unapologetic and shameless even when there were signs that the narrative was deeply flawed on several counts. It is one thing to encourage democratic protests through encouraging statements and moral support, and quite another to arm rebel groups and finance the destabilization of countries. The use of force and military action, whether authorized by the Security Council or otherwise, along with the arming of rebels, is an extreme step and, as experience the world over has shown, a sure recipe for disaster.

The supreme irony—and tragedy—is that the injection of this violence undermines the credibility and legitimacy of non-violent democratic protest. In turn, it becomes a catalyst for the brutalization of conflict. The inevitable outcome is a full-blown civil war in which a repressive regime uses brutal force without compunction against civilians—who may eventually no longer be unarmed, but in fact armed to the teeth. This is a scenario witnessed first in Libya and then in Syria. The original justification for intervention in such cases, couched in the language of morality—the 'protection of civilians'—becomes, in retrospect, an embarrassment.

Governments facing protest, the uninitiated might argue, have a right to insulate the state and its institutions from reckless violence. This could possibly have been argued if a post-Westphalian form of absolute sovereignty had currency. Increasing global integration, the free flow of information and the advent of social media now succeed in generating pressure that rebounds on domestic politics. If, as experience has shown, the protests are financed and armed from the outside, the established order feels no inhibition in seeking to suppress such armed protest through the brutal use of force. Two results inevitably follow. First, the ruling dispensation loses even the limited legitimacy it hitherto enjoyed. This is precisely what happened first in Libya and then in Syria. Second, a full-blown civil war and dismembering of the country follows. With the exception of Tunisia, the only country which appears to be succeeding in making a democratic transition, the Arab Spring has resulted in a militarized containment of the Islamic Brotherhood which emerged victorious in elections, in the unravelling of the state in Libya, Syria and possibly in Yemen, which is a work in progress in that direction.

The British prime minister's message of 26 May 2011 at the G8 summit spoke of 'the most powerful nations on earth' supporting 'greater democracy, greater freedom, greater civil rights' for 'the Middle East and North Africa'. But what have the results of this 'support' been?

When the world's leading industrial democracies individually and jointly decide to invest in a project for social and political change of the kind that the Arab Spring envisaged, it is reasonable to presume that some due diligence was done. It is politically incorrect now, and perhaps will be so for years to come, to say that Iraq under Saddam was infinitely better off than the emerging Islamic state under ISIS.

The US president asserted during his speech on the Middle East and North Africa at the White House on 19 May 2011:

> Those shouts of human dignity are being heard across the region. And through the moral force of non-violence, the people of the region have achieved more change in six months than terrorists have accomplished in decades.[24]

President Obama's statement needs careful evaluation. Democratic aspiration: full marks. But moral force of non-violence: when, where?

How will the Arab Spring be remembered? Perhaps it is too early to tell. Those who were lyrical about it, mostly in the West, supported by their think tanks and lobbyists, sought to manipulate the developments for regime change, and are perhaps now hoping for a scenario where the insurgencies in the region fade away. There is, however, an underlying reality that will not atrophy: the hope and positive effect that the popular protests represented. Repressive regimes governed these Arab nations for decades by successfully curbing dissent and employing brutal repression. Such methods of rule cannot endure forever. The political and economic projects of these regimes failed to deliver the basic goods and services that governance is required to. All said and done, the interventions into the crises were not arbitrary. They were triggered by the ruling regimes of the region, which supported non-state terrorist actors like the al-Qaeda and used brutal violence against their own people to open up sectarian fault lines. With the waters now muddied by the international interventions, the underlying toxicity in the Arab world is likely to remain for a considerable period of time. The region's democratic aspirations will have to find another opportunity to assert themselves.

The use of force, authorized or otherwise, combined with the arming of multiple rebel factions and the exposing of sectarian fault lines, forms a deadly cocktail for the Middle East. For some much-needed change in the current equation, the narrative on it must first change. The interveners and the regimes clinging to power must be able to converge towards the de-escalation of hostilities on a priority basis, without which the necessary solution to the region's politically burning climate shall continue to remain distant.

3

LIBYA: THE UNRAVELLING OF A COUNTRY

A total of 270 people (259 on board and eleven on the ground) were killed when the *Clipper Maid of the Seas*, operating as Pan American flight 103, exploded over Lockerbie, Scotland, after takeoff from Heathrow en route to New York's John F. Kennedy airport on the cold wintry evening of 28 December 1988.

Gaddafi's Libya in general and powerful individuals around him—like his intelligence chief, Abdullah al Senussi, and his brother-in-law—in particular were widely believed to have had a hand in the criminal act. The letter from the Libyan ambassador to the UN (chargé d'affaires ad interim) to the president of the Security Council on 15 August 2003 was part of a package settlement and thus carefully, even craftily, worded. Its operative provisions merely stated that Libya '... sought to cooperate in good faith throughout the past years to bring about a solution to this matter'. It said:

> Out of respect for international law and pursuant to the Security Council restrictions, Libya as a sovereign State ... has facilitated the bringing to justice of the two suspects charged with the

bombing of Pan Am 103 and accepts responsibility for the actions of the officials.[1]

Accepting responsibility for the actions of its officials was only one of the three demands made by the UN for lifting sanctions against Libya. The other two included a formal denunciation of terrorism, which Libya claimed it had already done, and compensation for the families of the victims. Libya offered up to $2.7 billion to settle the claims from the families of the 270 killed. This meant $10 million per family. The families of the victims, however, subsequently received $2 million less each because the US State Department did not remove Libya from the list of states sponsoring terrorism by the deadline stipulated by Libya. Libya's willingness to pay appropriate compensation was cited as evidence of its complicity. The spin in the Western media was that Libya, as a state, had accepted responsibility for the bombing.

Of the two Libyans indicted, only one was convicted. He too was released several years later on compassionate grounds. Abdelbaset al Megrahi was convicted by a special court in the Netherlands in 2001 and freed from a Scottish jail in 2009 because he was suffering from prostate cancer, stirring up a controversy later when he outlived doctors' expectations. A Libyan intelligence officer, Megrahi consistently denied any responsibility for the bombing. Many believed that the investigation itself had ignored crucial evidence and that Megrahi and the other Libyan, Al Amin Khalifa Fhimah, were 'sacrificed' by the Gaddafi regime in order to work out an acceptable 'settlement'.

Magnus Linklater, a leading Scottish political commentator, told Al Jazeera on 21 December 2013:

> Lockerbie is a huge cloud hanging over the Scottish justice system. It is almost as if the allegation that Megrahi is innocent is the default position. But that in its turn has not been tested

and it's been allowed to go unchallenged, and it is high time that it was properly challenged.[2]

The US announced resumption of full diplomatic relations with Libya only on 15 May 2006, after removing it from the list of countries that support terrorism. The two countries signed a further compensation agreement which resulted in Libya paying $1.5 billion into a fund to be used to compensate:

- Lockerbie victims with the remaining 20 per cent of the sum agreed in 2003;
- American victims of the 1986 Berlin discotheque bombing;
- American victims of the 1989 UTA flight 772 bombing; and
- Libyan victims of the 1986 United States' bombing of Tripoli and Benghazi.

During a televised discussion on 14 October 2015, former Secretary of State Hillary Clinton had this to say of the situation then:

> We had a murderous dictator, Gaddafi, who had American blood on his hands. He was threatening to massacre large numbers of Libyan people … and we had the Arabs standing by our side saying, 'We want you to help us deal with Gaddafi.'

What Clinton did not say is that in July 2009, as secretary of state, she had sent her assistant secretary for Near Eastern affairs, Jeffrey Feltman, to Tripoli, where he met Musa Kusa, Gaddafi's foreign minister, and expressed the US's 'desire to press the relationship forward' with new dialogues on trade, investment and political–military affairs. Feltman even floated the possibility of a meeting between Obama and Gaddafi at the UN. Obama and Gaddafi met at the G8 summit in July 2009.

At his last appearance at the UN, in September 2009, with a Libyan presiding over the General Assembly,[3] Gaddafi delivered a ninety-minute-long incomprehensible diatribe. The disgust of his audience climaxed when he tore up some paper which many thought to be the UN Charter. He then proceeded to dramatically fling the pieces over his shoulder at the Libyan chairing the high-level segment of the General Assembly.

Public attitudes and perceptions are not necessarily based on facts. Gaddafi's visit to New York in September 2009 was conditioned by some of these widely prevailing perceptions. As a result, the Libyan permanent mission to the United Nations in New York could not secure hotel accommodation for him and his large entourage. The Taj Group—owned Pierre on 61st Street opposite Central Park was initially chosen for the purpose but it backed out when the hotel management was informed about the identity of the visiting dignitary. The experience was to be repeated with several other hotels, with bookings refused as soon as Gaddafi's identity was revealed. A proposal to pitch a large luxury tent on a vacant site in New Jersey was also nixed when the local authorities realized that this was intended to accommodate Gaddafi and his entourage. He finally stayed in the Libyan permanent mission on 48th Street.

When protests started gathering momentum in Libya at the start of 2011 as part of the Arab Spring, Gaddafi's personal popularity was at an all-time low. There was virtually no support within the UN Security Council for Gaddafi in February 2011. Not one of the fifteen members of the Council wanted to be heard or seen saying or doing anything that would give the appearance of defending Gaddafi. He had burnt his boats with all Security Council members. It was against this background that the Human Rights Council in Geneva and the Security Council in New York considered action against Libya.

There is something about evil, especially when it manifests itself in those exercising political power in an authoritarian, almost tyrannical, way that the widespread havoc and destruction they cause invariably results in retributive justice. Those who live by the sword, as the saying goes, shall also die by it. And yet, evil, or perception of the perpetuation of evil by an individual, carries on. Shakespeare's Mark Antony's famous words, 'The evil that men do lives after them; the good is oft interred with their bones,' aptly capture the continuing consequences of this perpetration of evil.

Examples of evil incarnate in history are many. Attila the Hun, leader of the Hun Empire in Central and Eastern Europe 1,560 years ago, had a reputation for ferocity unparalleled in the records of barbarian invasions. Attila reportedly drowned in his own blood on his wedding night. Maximilien Robespierre, leader of the French Revolution and the force behind the Reign of Terror, ironically was guillotined without trial in 1794.

Adolf Hitler's strategies of territorial conquest and racial subjugation brought death and destruction to tens of millions of people. Nazi policies of genocide under his leadership reportedly killed some six million Jews. On 31 July 1941, Nazi vice chancellor Hermann Goering issued orders to Reinhard Heydrich, chief of the Nazi secret police, to prepare a comprehensive plan for the 'Final Solution'. The Wannsee Conference—held six months later on 20 January 1942 in the Berlin suburb of Wannsee and attended by fifteen senior Nazi bureaucrats—marked a turning point in the Nazi policy towards Jews. The gathered men understood that 'the evacuation to the east' was a euphemism for concentration camps and that the 'Final Solution' was to be the systematic murder of Europe's Jews, which came to be known as the Holocaust. Hitler's own end in a bunker on 30 April 1945, when Soviet troops were within a block or two from the Reich's chancellery, was true to the pattern of retributive justice that evil incarnate invariably attracts.

Pol Pot, the leader of the Khmer Rouge and the prime minister of Cambodia from 1976 to 1979, imposed an extreme version of agrarian communism. The combined effect of slave labour, malnutrition, poor medical care and executions is estimated to have killed around two million Cambodians (approximately one-third of the population). His regime gained special notoriety for singling out all intellectuals and other 'bourgeois enemies' for murder. In order to save ammunition, executions were often carried out using hammers, axe handles, spades or sharpened bamboo sticks. On 15 April 1998, Pol Pot was found dead in mysterious circumstances hours after the Voice of America publicized the Khmer Rouge's willingness to surrender him to an international tribunal.

The image of Saddam Hussein hiding in a small underground bunker near a farmhouse at ad-Dawr near his hometown of Tikrit, and the pictures of him being tested for DNA determination flashed by the world media, fit into the same pattern. He was found guilty of crimes against humanity—primarily, the vengeful 1982 Dujail massacre of Shiites—and sentenced to death in November 2006. This did not, however, contain the forces he had unleashed. His hanging on 30 December 2006, in some respects, created more serious problems for those over whom he had exercised excessive power.

If an attempt was to be made to characterize and grade the three most evil political rulers of contemporary times, Hitler, Saddam Hussein and Gaddafi would figure in most listings.

When the permanent representative of the Libyan Arab Jamahiriya to the UN, Abdel Rahman Shalgham, took the floor to address the Security Council meeting in an open session a little after 3.30 p.m. on Friday, 25 February 2011, he invoked some of these historical figures:

> Pol Pot, head of the Khmer Rouge in Cambodia, was asked why he executed one-third of his people. He said he did it because

of the people. Before invading the Soviet Union, Hitler recalled Rommel from Libya and told him, 'General, I intend to invade the Soviet Union.' Rommel told him, 'Operation Barbarossa will cost us 2 million lives.' Hitler responded, 'What does it matter if 2 million Germans die in service to the glory of the Fuehrer.'

Shalgham went on to say:

Libyans are asking for democracy, they are asking for progress, they are asking for their freedom, and they are asking for their rights. They demonstrated peacefully. They did not throw a single stone. They were killed. What did Brother Muammar al Gaddafi say? He said that people were using hallucinogens. These tens of thousands of people would need mountains of such pills to lose their minds in such a way. A pile of pills the size of the Akhdar Mountains would not be enough for that many people. Gaddafi and his sons are telling Libyans: 'Either I rule you or I kill you … I will burn Libya. I will distribute arms to the tribes. Libya will turn red with blood.'

On the same day, 25 February 2011, the Human Rights Council in Geneva passed a resolution expressing 'deep concern at the deaths of hundreds of civilians, and rejecting unequivocally the incitement to hostility and violence against the civilian population made from the highest levels of the Libyan government'. The resolution went on to call on the Government of Libya to meet its responsibility to protect its population, to immediately put an end to all human rights violations and to stop any attack against civilians. It also called on Libya to immediately release all arbitrarily detained people, to ensure the safety of all civilians (including those of third countries), to refrain from reprisals against people who had taken part in demonstrations and to immediately cease the blocking of public access to Internet and mobile networks. The operative part of the resolution was the decision to urgently dispatch an independent international commission of inquiry to investigate all alleged violations of international human rights law in Libya, to establish the facts and circumstances of such violations and, where possible, identify those responsible.

Even as the resolution was being considered and passed in Geneva, serious confabulations were already under way in New York. The permanent representatives of the UK and France, Mark Lyall Grant and Gerard Araud, under instructions from their respective capitals, started consulting Council members to seek a Council resolution embodying sanctions, an arms embargo and a referral of Gaddafi and his close collaborators to the International Criminal Court (ICC). It was clear that the PRs of the UK and France were coming under increasing pressure from their respective capitals. They felt they needed to be seen doing something in the light of growing criticism. The buzz was that the international community was a helpless bystander as Gaddafi and the coterie around him unleashed violence against unarmed civilians.

The pressures were a direct result of the narrative unfolding in the mainstream Western press, where a comprehensive and systematic demonization of Gaddafi was being carried out. This acquired the overtones of a campaign in the fifteen-day period between 11 February 2011, when Hosni Mubarak fell, and 26 February 2011, when Resolution 1970 was passed by the Security Council.

With illustrative flavour, a *Financial Times* article in February 2011 reminded readers how Gaddafi, prior to his rehabilitation as an 'allegedly responsible member of the world community', was known as the 'mad dog of the Middle East' during the days of former US president Ronald Reagan, and that his 'vicious killing spree against the people rising against him' only restored his disrepute, making the heralded 'great leader' seem 'like a disastrous Western bet' who was 'less welcoming to foreign investment than hoped'.[4] Another piece by the same newspaper found the 'lethal repression of demonstrators in Libya ... shocking, but not surprising', coming from a 'desperate regime' with a 'long history of quashing ... opposition'. It went on to underscore how Libya's 'oil riches ... failed to buy peace', leaving the country 'closed and dysfunctional', while assuring that the 'savage despot's' fall was worth welcoming, even if chaos replaced him.[5]

Meanwhile, the *Guardian* described the events as 'the bloodiest crackdown yet on pro-democracy protesters in the Arab world', viewing the 'Libyan leader [as] beleaguered at home and unwelcome anywhere abroad' with his 'diplomats resigning ... and ... fighter pilots defecting' due to the targeting of civilians.[6] Another article in the *Guardian* reminisced how everyone— including former British prime minister Tony Blair—'flocked to shake Muammar Gaddafi's hand' after Libya agreed to 'abandon its WMD programme in 2003'. However, while observing that his repressiveness made the Gaddafi of 2011 look 'very much like the old one', the article suspected that he may 'still be considered too valuable to lose, as US influence in the region decreases'.[7]

In contrast to the *Financial Times*, a piece in the *Times* refused to paint Gaddafi as a 'mad dog', instead seeing his moves as 'cleverly calculated'. Nonetheless, his rule was labelled a 'textbook dictatorship' that was 'consistent, effective and entirely ruthless', and he was termed 'brutal, touchy, exhibitionist ... capricious, overdressed, long-winded, [and] weirdly coiffured'.[8] The *Financial Times*, however, continued to see Gaddafi as fighting a cause that was 'surely ... lost' in lashing 'out viciously against the Libyan people'. It hoped that his 'misrule [was] coming to an end thanks to the bravery of the Libyans' and urged 'the wider world to do what it can to stem the dictator's capacity for mayhem'.[9]

As mentioned earlier, the Security Council met in an open session on 25 February 2011. Secretary-General Ban Ki-moon urged the Council to take urgent action and send a strong message to save innocent lives in Libya. Among the measures he suggested were trade sanctions, assets freeze, travel bans and accountability. This open session will, however, be remembered for the presentation of the Libyan PR, Shalgham, which proved to be a game changer in the fast unfolding events.

Sleepwalking into Chaos and Disaster

The Libyan ambassador's statement on 25 February 2011 was followed by the entire Libyan delegation 'defecting' and turning its back on Gaddafi. The permanent representatives of the Gulf states and several other representatives proceeded to congratulate the members of the Libyan delegation, who had officially declared their support for the 'opposition'.

The Council then proceeded to meet in a private session. A British draft, submitted by Mark Lyall Grant, had been tabled for discussion. Against the backdrop of the alarmist press reports and the defection of the Libyan delegation, the Council was inclined, as part of a desire to be seen to be doing something, to endorse a travel ban and impose an assets freeze and an arms embargo.

Many members, including India, however, wanted to be careful about the references relating to the ICC. India's doubts about the ICC referral had little to do with the fact that it was not a signatory to the Rome Statute.[10] India's main concern was that the Council needed to carefully determine the effect of an immediate ICC referral. Such a step might have had an effect completely opposite to what was intended. Germany and France felt that an ICC referral was the very minimum required, because this was the one measure, in their view, which would have a decisive restraining impact on Gaddafi. Other delegations, particularly Brazil, India, China, Portugal and Lebanon, felt that an ICC referral would have two unintended effects. One, it could queer the pitch and result in reprisals by Gaddafi. Two, while the 'threat' of an ICC referral could serve as a deterrent, an outright and immediate referral would leave him with no incentive for good behaviour.

The Russians were still hedging their bets. Russian PR Vitaly Churkin felt that this essentially required a judgement by the Council. He had some sympathy for the view that an ICC referral could be decisive in making Gaddafi see reason. He was, however, equally conscious of the real possibility that such a referral could jeopardize the lives of foreign nationals. Russia still had several hundred of its citizens on the ground awaiting evacuation. The Chinese and Indians had even more of their citizens in a similarly placed situation, 33,000 and 18,000 respectively. The fact that some Council members—including three of the five permanent members—were not part of the ICC was not without significance, but of no direct relevance to the decision. There had been several cases of ICC referrals which non-signatories to the Rome Statute had gone along with.

Resolution 1970 was passed by the Security Council on 26 February 2011 after a marathon twelve-hour session. The draft that had been submitted by the UK the previous day was sought to be substantively altered by an American amendment. It tried to shift the focus of the resolution from action under Article 41[11] of Chapter VII of the UN Charter by bringing in elements of Article 42,[12] which had the potential of being read as 'authorizing use of force'. The precise language suggested by the US sought authorization for member states to use 'all necessary means to protect civilians and make available humanitarian assistance'. As a student of trade policy, I was reminded of the Uruguay Round of Multilateral Trade Negotiations launched in September 1986, where issues related to services, intellectual property and investment were introduced into the General Agreement on Tariffs and Trade (GATT)—a legal framework of rights and obligations essentially governing the cross-border movement of goods—through cleverly conceived nomenclature, by merely adding an existing or non-existing trade relationship to it. In case of Resolution 1970, the US's ploy was to incorporate 'all necessary means' for the protection of civilians and humanitarian assistance as carte blanche for the use of force.

The atmosphere was tense as the Security Council met at the level of PRs around the horse-shoe table inside the UN building in New York. The exchanges became acrimonious. On the US amendment, Churkin observed that the suggested language was akin to a former US administration's attempt to describe intercontinental ballistic missiles (ICBMs) as 'peacemakers'. Strong words by Churkin and others caused Susan Rice, the influential American PR known to have direct access to the president, to backtrack. Delegation after delegation took the floor to point out that the intent all along had been to pass a resolution confined to targeted sanctions. Carte blanche for the authorization of use of force under Article 42 of Chapter VII would be incompatible with the objective of the resolution. Council members were not willing to authorize measures that had not even been discussed.

An attempt by Rice to introduce the issue of chemical weapons also did not gain traction. Churkin raised a strong objection to the reference to chemical weapons and said that a totally different element, unconnected with the matter at hand, was being injected to allow for language which could result in the 'use of force' under the garb of humanitarian intervention. Rice, however, persisted and said that language similar to what the US had proposed had been incorporated in Council resolutions on fighting piracy off the coast of Somalia. The Brazilian PR, Maria Luiza Viotti, presiding over the Council in February, pointed to a crucial difference: the Somali government had given its consent in the course of the anti-piracy resolution. Seeing that the Council was not willing to go down the Chapter VII route, the US finally backtracked, and, realizing its isolation, agreed to compromise on the language, which resulted in the withdrawal of the amended paragraph. New language was adopted in the resolution along the lines suggested by the Russians. In order to remove any unintended ambiguity, the resolution clearly stipulated, in the preambular section, that it was under Article 41.

On the ICC referral, the Council continued to be divided, with France, Britain and Germany on the one side asking for an immediate referral to the ICC, and China, India, Brazil, South Africa, Gabon, Portugal and Nigeria on the other favouring a calibrated approach. The latter group of countries was not against an ICC referral per se but suggested that, at that stage, the Council confine itself to a calibrated approach by merely threatening ICC referral and proceed towards referral only if compliance and good behaviour were not forthcoming.

In my intervention, I again drew attention to the fact that India and three of the five permanent Security Council members not being part of the ICC was only one aspect of the issue. India's primary concern was to put an urgent end to the killings. The safety of Indian nationals in Libya was critical to us and we needed to insulate them from possible reprisals. Rice agreed that a calibrated approach with the threat of referral in the first instance and a six-week compliance period for good behaviour might be a preferable course. It became clear, however, that the French and Germans were under different instructions. Nevertheless, the tough line India took on the ICC referral did have some positive impact. The resolution finally adopted made a reference to Article 16 of the Rome Statute, which provides that no investigation or prosecution may be commenced or proceeded with by the ICC for a period of twelve months if the Security Council makes such a request. This, with the additional language in paragraph 6, which stated that nationals of countries not party to the Rome Statute would be covered under their national jurisdiction, provided the cover we were seeking.

For a fuller understanding of how the final outcome of Resolution 1970 was shaped, one needs to comprehend the evolving situation in Libya, the actions of the Libyan delegation which had defected, the role of the Arab League and the part played by the global media. India's point that the Council might need to revisit the situation in Libya in the following weeks and that it was not prudent, therefore, to exhaust all the ammunition at an early stage was not lost on the members. The positions taken by Western delegations had to be seen against the backdrop of the pressure exerted by the media on governments in Washington, Berlin, London and Paris. The Council showed remarkable unity in not wanting to go down the route of Article 42 under Chapter VII. In the final analysis, Resolution 1970 was adopted unanimously with eleven co-sponsors. The only four countries which supported the Resolution but did not co-sponsor it were Brazil, India, Russia and China.

The tearing hurry to be seen to be doing something was in a sense understandable, given the spate of killings the Gaddafi machine had unleashed and especially since his mental make-up had been described as being akin to that of Pol Pot and Hitler. Looking back, it is also clear that the ICC referral was designed as a strong dose of medicine in the hope that more decisive action, in the form of use of force stipulated in Article 42, would not have to be invoked. The international community had no appetite for military action at that point of time. The ICC referral was, in retrospect, the first of many mistakes made by the Security Council.

Roble Olhaye,[13] a former PR of Djibouti, presented his credentials to the UN secretary-general on 18 January 1988. This made him the longest-serving PR and, hence, the dean of the diplomatic corps. He was also concurrently accredited to the US and as non-resident ambassador to Canada—an impressive diplomat by any yardstick. During his long tenure, he served on the Security Council, including as its president in February 1994. A professional accountant by training, he was a fellow of the Association of International Accountants and a member of the British Institute of Management. On 7 March 2011, Olhaye hosted a lunch in honour of Ban Ki-moon. The lunch at Felidia— the flagship restaurant of 'Italian cuisine queen' Lidia Bastianich at 243 E, 58th Street, New York, where she occasionally shows up—is described in Zagat[14] as providing 'superb meals' in a 'lovely' town house, ever an 'exceptional experience ... if your bank account permits'.

The ambassador's guest list for lunch contained all the important members of Ban Ki-moon's senior management team. Apart from the secretary-general himself, his chef de cabinet, Vijay Nambiar; the assistant secretary-general, Kim Won-soo; the head of the United Nations Development Programme (UNDP), Helen Clark; the head of the United Nations Children's Fund (UNICEF), Anthony Lake; the United Nations Fund for Population Activities (UNFPA) chief, Babatunde Osotimehin; the head of the UN Department of Political Affairs, B. Lynn Pascoe; and the head of the UN Department of Peacekeeping Affairs, Alain Le Roy, were present. Among the PRs, three of the permanent members of the Security Council—Lyall Grant of the UK, Susan Rice of the US and Gerard Araud of France—were there too. The other invitees included the PRs from countries serving on the Council: Maria Luiza of Brazil, Nawaf Salam of Lebanon, Joy Ogwu of Nigeria, and me. Also invited were the PRs of Qatar, Yemen, Ethiopia, Egypt and Denmark. In hindsight, it is quite clear that the host and the senior management of the UN had intended Libya to be the main item on the menu, the chef's $80 per head degustation menu notwithstanding.

The discussion at that lunch needs to be recalled for two reasons. One, there were the inexplicably hawkish positions of some participants. More importantly, the discussion clearly brought out that as late as 7 March 2011, there was ostensibly no agreement even amongst the five permanent members of the Security Council, the P5, as to what the next steps should be in Libya after Security Council Resolution 1970 had been adopted on 26 February 2011.

Helen Clark, who had served as prime minister of New Zealand, advocated 'strong military action' in order to prevent Gaddafi from inflicting untold misery on his population. Her advocacy for such action was designed to prevent the violence and killings which the Gaddafi machine was viewed as capable of unleashing. Anthony Lake, the UNICEF head, was much more circumspect. Having served as national security adviser in the administration of former US president Bill Clinton, he knew that the use of military means could not be without consequences, both for the country on which the military action was unleashed and for those waging war. The secretary-general, a good listener most of the time, was at his listening best. Nambiar and Kim Won-soo were also remarkably quiet. The most vocal discussants were, as on most such occasions, the gathered PRs, who quickly divided themselves into two groups, with the pro-interventionist group led by Araud of France, ably supported by Nassir of Qatar, and to a lesser extent by Abdullah al-Saidi of Yemen. Lyall Grant had very little difficulty in aligning himself with the charge led by Araud.

Half an hour into this discussion, Susan Rice, sitting on my left, suggested in a whisper that I ask Araud who would carry out the military operations in Libya if the Council were to authorize the use of 'all means necessary', a euphemism for military action.

Pat came his reply: 'Of course, NATO, led by the United States of America.' Rice's immediate response was that the US had so far made no such determination. Also that it was unlikely that the country would participate in a NATO mission unless nations of the region were equal participants in such an undertaking. Interestingly, the hesitation to use force, visible till March 2011, soon evaporated. The how and why of this need to be understood.

Bernard-Henri Levy, a French public intellectual, media personality and author, played an important role in influencing the French position on Libya. On 27 February 2011, before flying to North Africa, he called up French president Nicolas Sarkozy, whom he had personally known since 1983, and asked if he was interested in meeting with the Libyan rebels. Sarkozy answered in the affirmative. Levy soon made contact with the head of the interim National Transitional Council, Mustafa Mohammed Abdul Jalil, and met him on 3 March in a colonial villa by the sea in Benghazi, Libya's second largest city. After a short speech about liberty and justice, Jalil was posed with the same question: did they wish to meet the French president? On the condition that France would 'make a gesture',[15] Jalil agreed. This gesture was a press release by France, mostly noticed only in Benghazi, which greeted the formation of the NTC and was followed by the city being decorated with French flags.

A week later, and a week before Resolution 1973 was passed, on 10 March, Levy brought senior members of the so-called Libyan opposition to Paris to meet Sarkozy. They agreed to keep the initiative a secret, even from the French foreign ministry, only keeping British prime minister David Cameron in the loop. Even the French minister of foreign affairs, Alain Juppe, was not fully in the know. 'France's foreign minister was getting off a train in Brussels when he first heard that a rebel delegation had not only met with Sarkozy but gotten recognition as Libya's sole legitimate representatives.'[16]

In this meeting, Sarkozy 'agreed to recognize the opposition as the legitimate government of Libya, which shocked other European capitals and the French foreign ministry alike. He agreed to exchange ambassadors and to bomb three airports when he could.'[17] In addition, he promised to try and gather international support and work towards a Security Council resolution, failing which he and Cameron would anyway go ahead with 'the mandate of the European Union, the Arab League and the African Union'.[18] However, this plan was meant to be kept a 'secret'. The seeds had just been sown for mistake number two committed in Libya.

The US, meanwhile, welcomed an Arab League endorsement of a no-fly zone on 12 March.[19] It said that the US would advance its efforts to pressure Gaddafi to quit. Ideally, it would prefer a Security Council mandate before getting directly involved in Libya. However, the legitimization provided by a strong show of Arab support for a no-fly zone was, in all likelihood, expected to push the US's position in Libya beyond the construct of a 'humanitarian intervention'. While still emphasizing action under NATO, the US appeared to be showing signs of getting itself more directly involved. Fissures within the US administration, however, continued to surface. Defence Secretary Robert Gates remained sceptical. Dismissing what he called 'too much of loose talk' about imposing a no-fly zone over Libya and warning about huge costs, he nevertheless displayed some amount of flexibility. After the Arab League resolution, he said that the US would have no difficulty enforcing a no-fly zone if ordered to do so. On 11 March, Obama said in a press conference that the US was considering 'a wide range of actions to bring about that outcome', referring to Gaddafi's ouster.

These latest pronouncements pointed in the direction of an evolving American position. Obama had, for the most part of the Libyan crisis, been non-committal, and only reacted to the debates within his administration over the costs and benefits of intervention. The lack of appetite for another military entanglement with US troops still in Afghanistan and Iraq, sensitivities over American military intervention in yet another Muslim country, the absence of 'vital interests' for the US in Libya, risks of intervening in what appeared even then likely to evolve into a protracted civil war, and the lack of understanding of the Libyan opposition groups appeared to be some of the factors figuring in the US's calculation.

Meanwhile, influential leaders from both parties, including Senators John Kerry, Joseph Lieberman and John McCain, urged the administration to show greater assertiveness in dealing with Gaddafi, by supporting the rebel groups and imposing a no-fly zone. They also said that since Obama had said 'Gaddafi must go now', he had bound himself to act in ways that could lead to that outcome sooner rather than later. Failure to achieve that result, they felt, would not only send a wrong signal at a critical juncture in the region but also hurt the international standing of the US, besides exposing the country to threats from a wounded, abandoned despot.

The alternative scenario, the protagonists of intervention felt, would be a prolonged civil war and domination of jihadist and al-Qaeda elements. Meanwhile, the US was viewing the Arab Spring with increasing concern due to the growing tensions between pro-reform groups and governments in Yemen and Bahrain, and some signs of protests in Saudi Arabia. Robert Gates told Bahrain's king Hamad bin Isa bin Salman Al Khalifa during a visit to Manama that 'baby steps' towards reform would not help in addressing the political and economic grievances in the region. With the US sending a signal in favour of 'regime alteration' through serious and responsive reforms, rather than regime change, Gates said it was better if the change 'could be led' rather than 'imposed'.

When Secretary of State Hillary Clinton visited Paris for a G8 summit during 14–15 March, she spent nearly an hour speaking with Mahmoud Jibril, who chaired the executive board of the NTC and later served as Libya's interim prime minister during the civil war, alone. She 'stuck to her approved talking points, refusing to make any promises of support'.[20] Jibril, certain that he had 'failed to sway' Clinton, emerged 'drunk with rage', according to a witness.[21] The next afternoon, Sarkozy called Jibril to inform that the 'American position is shifting'.

On 14 and 15 March, Clinton met with Sarkozy. The French president was gung-ho about attacking Gaddafi, who by then was reversing rebel advances and regaining the offensive. After getting the measure of Jibril, Clinton agreed to American intervention if the UN backed it. Referring to her, *Vanity Fair News* reported:

> Viewing television images of Gaddafi's brutality from her quarters at the US ambassador's residence apparently strengthened her resolve. She took to seconding her husband's much-repeated line that the biggest mistake of his presidency was doing nothing to prevent genocide in Rwanda.[22]

On 15 March, Lebanon introduced a draft resolution in the Security Council in the afternoon session. A maximalist text, it sought the imposition of a no-fly zone banning all flights across Libya. It also sought to authorize 'all necessary measures', which implied military action. The US, at least insofar as the position articulated by Rice was concerned, wanted, in the first instance, a confirmation of serious and active participation by the Arab League in the imposition of a no-fly zone and other military operations. She clarified that, one, a naked no-fly zone by itself would not find favour in Washington; two, it would have to be accompanied by other measures, for which serious participation of countries in the region was a prerequisite; and three, a no-fly zone was an asset-intensive and extremely expensive proposition, which the US would be willing to consider only as part of a package.

Lebanon, on behalf of the Arab League, pleaded for the Council's authorization for a no-fly zone and other measures so that Gaddafi was prevented from committing massacres and reclaiming the entire country. It was during the course of this forceful advocacy that the Lebanese PR, Nawaf Salam, reminded Council members how Gaddafi's son, Saif al Islam, had warned that 'rivers of blood will run through Libya' in defence of the government, and thereby urged the Council to act and restrain Gaddafi. I recalled that the expression had first been used by Enoch Powell, a Conservative British MP, on 20 April 1968 in the highly popular 'Rivers of Blood' speech referring to immigration from the coloured Commonwealth. There had neither been a surge in immigration nor any blood, let alone rivers of it, down the Thames. Nawaf's reminder of Saif al Islam's scaremongering was, however, beginning to have some effect.

The Russians and Chinese continued to be sceptical but did not provide any indication of wanting to exercise the veto. China's preference was to abstain, and its PR, Li Baodong, used his margin of persuasion to convince Russia, Brazil and India as well. Russia appeared supportive, with some conditions. Nigeria, Gabon and South Africa were expected to support the resolution. In spite of the hype created by the UK and France, most Council members were agreed that the resolution being proposed would not have a positive impact on the ground. My recommendations to New Delhi were: one, we whittle down the resolution to enhance economic sanctions against individuals close to, and collaborators of, the regime; and two, express our reservations on the no-fly zone because it would amount to sanctioning military intervention, on which we had serious reservations. In my assessment, the resolution was being tabled entirely due to media pressure. We were able to buy time because of attention shifting to the nuclear meltdown in Japan.[23]

In order to fully understand the behaviour of Council members, it is instructive to go back to what the media, particularly in Western capitals, was saying between 26 February, when Resolution 1970 was passed by the Security Council, and 17 March 2011, when Resolution 1973 was passed. The *Independent* described Gaddafi's speech as a 'self-parody', in which he presented himself to Libyans more as a 'fellow resister' than a dictator by invoking 'Omar Mukhtar—hanged by Mussolini's colonial army—rather than [taking] the patronising tone of a Mubarak or a Ben Ali'.[24] In another report, it quoted selective parts of Gaddafi's two-and-a-half-hour-long televised 'fiery' speech, wherein he 'vowed to wage a bloody war if foreign powers dared to intervene', saying it would only 'plunge Libya into another Vietnam'.[25]

Reports in the *Guardian* and other leading dailies illustrated Gaddafi's 'ruthlessness, desperation and weakness',[26] insofar as he allegedly hired thousands of mercenaries or 'dogs of war',[27] and, in Cameron's words, was 'brutally repressing a popular uprising led by his own people and flagrantly ignoring the will of the international community'.[28] Another article in the *Guardian* quoted a rebel fighter who claimed that they did not 'have the capabilities to fight Gaddafi and his forces' as the latter had 'tanks and heavy weapons', but had their 'belief and trust in God'.[29] The *Financial Times* reported that the 'blood-stained dictator warned that his forces, steadily advancing on the rebel stronghold of Benghazi in eastern Libya, would 'show no mercy and no pity' to the 'rats and dogs' opposing him.[30]

The French media, *Le Figaro* in particular, extensively quoted world leaders and their condemnation of Gaddafi. While German chancellor Angela Merkel termed Gaddafi's speech 'very scary' and urged 'Libyan authorities to put an end to the violence against their own people',[31] Italian foreign minister Franco Frattini predicted, rightly so, a 'biblical exodus of migrants from Libya post the fall of Kadhafi [another spelling of Gaddafi] [as] a problem that no Italian must underestimate', and further considered it 'impossible to imagine what might happen in Libya after the fall of Kadhafi'.[32] Sarkozy, meanwhile, proposed the adoption of concrete sanctions against those involved in the ongoing violence who would eventually 'bear the consequences of their actions', as the international community could not 'remain a spectator in the face of these massive violations of human rights'.[33] A *Le Figaro* report also quoted Gaddafi as having warned against any attack or use of force by the international community in Libya, saying that 'he would turn the lives of whoever attacked Libya into hell'. According to the article, he further added that the 'Security Council has no mandate for such Resolutions, and its Charter [does] not interfere in internal affairs (since this was not a war between two countries)'.[34]

The Decision to Go to War, Resolution 1973

Without specifying the source of his information or providing any evidence in support, UN Undersecretary-General Lynn Pascoe told the Security Council on 14 March 2011 that the situation in Libya had been deteriorating rapidly, with Gaddafi's forces using heavy artillery and air and naval assets against civilians and rebels. Around the same time, the secretary-general's special envoy, Al Khatib, after one of his visits in March to Tripoli, reported back to the Council with a confidential briefing on his mission, which had the Council divided. While Russia, China, India, Brazil, South Africa, Portugal and Nigeria stated that Al Khatib's overall objective was to prevent further bloodshed and produce an outcome that resulted in a diffusion of the political crisis, France and the UK asked him to inform Gaddafi that the ICC referral had already been made and that he should get out. On 15 March, Al Khatib met India's feisty ambassador in Tripoli,

M. Manimekalai, who stayed on even as other missions vacated, and asked if any oil contract had been offered by Gaddafi to India. The ambassador responded that India is far too big a country for its policy to be influenced or formulated by any such suggestions or inducements. Meanwhile, Rashid Khalikov of the UN's Office for the Coordination of Humanitarian Affairs (OCHA) visited Tripoli and saw little opposition to the Gaddafi government there. It is also essential to recall that members of British special forces had been arrested and expelled by the Libyans in the first week of March, establishing beyond doubt that there was meddling in Libya well before there was any Security Council authorization.

The Lebanese PR, Nawaf Salam, speaking on behalf of the Arab League, said on 14 March that the Gaddafi regime had failed to implement Resolution 1970 and fulfil the legitimate aspirations of his people. He saw no contradiction in the Arab League's statement rejecting all forms of foreign intervention in Libya, and calling on the Security Council to impose a no-fly zone and establish safe areas. The demand for a no-fly zone had come from the Libyans, and the Arab League had merely endorsed it; once the Security Council authorized additional measures, their implementation, he argued, would not be regarded as foreign intervention.

The ensuing discussion showed the Security Council clearly divided, with the UK and France on one side demanding quick action by the Council to ostensibly prevent large-scale massacres. They argued that these would follow if Gaddafi's forces reached Benghazi within the next few days. Most of the remaining members asked questions about who would implement a no-fly zone and how and what its effects would be on the larger region. While Russia and China were most explicit in their opposition to the proposal, the Council's meeting on 14 March revealed, once again, the US's ambivalence on the issue.

In discussions in the Council on 16 March, Susan Rice termed the situation as 'exceedingly urgent and dire', and expressed serious concern at the reports of mass killings and large-scale disappearances of opposition figures. She said effective intervention would require not just prevention but protection of populations, for which a no-fly zone may not be sufficient. It was evident that Rice, along with others in the US administration, like Hillary Clinton, did not want another Rwanda-like situation on their hands. In that particular case, in spite of credible information and explicit written warnings provided by the force commander of the UN Assistance Mission for Rwanda (UNAMIR), Lieutenant General Romeo Dallaire, the impending genocide was not allowed to be brought before the Security Council.[35] Welcoming the Arab League's statement, Rice was of the view that implementation of such measures had to be part of a broader effort to protect civilians, and, towards that end, the US would consider additional measures, including—but not limited to—new sanctions. The US was also prepared to seriously consider the Arab League's proposal if there was 'active and serious participation of Arab countries', and therefore wished to ascertain the willingness of Arab countries to contribute to the implementation of their proposals. The interpretation of Rice's statement by the Council was that the US was not prepared to carry the can for the Arab League.

Churkin recalled the ineffectiveness of the no-fly zone in Bosnia[36] even when UN forces were present on the ground. Without clarity about rules of engagement, requirement of stationing troops on the ground and so on, the Council could not endorse the proposals, he felt. The Chinese PR, Li Baodong, added that while the Arab League had asked for a no-fly zone, the African Union had opposed any foreign military intervention, and that the latter's views also had to be considered. Moreover, the R2P principle could not be applied in a civil war situation because a no-fly zone, by itself, would be ineffective on the ground.

In my intervention, I said that it was clear that the Council unanimously wanted to prevent further bloodshed and was keen

on effecting cessation of hostilities. While empathizing with
the Arab League's concerns about the humanitarian situation in
Libya, I went on to say that we should act only after carefully
considering the proposals. While we were all subject to domestic
media pressures, these could not be the only lodestar for our
action. Having heard the US's position that Arab countries had to
actively participate in the enforcement of the proposed measures,
I stated it was necessary to know which countries from the region
would provide resources, how they would implement them, and
what their impact would be on the civil-war-like situation in
Libya. I also inquired how the proposals of a no-fly zone and no
foreign military intervention could be reconciled, considering
that assets for the imposition and sustenance of a no-fly zone were
available only with very few countries. These views were echoed
by Brazil, Portugal, Germany, Nigeria and Gabon. Interestingly,
the German PR, Peter Wittig, said that at that point of time the
Council should consider additional sanctions rather than the
imposition of a no-fly zone.

The South African PR Baso Sangqu said that the Council
should wait for the mission report by the African Union panel,
which would be in Tripoli on 17 March. Further, any Council
action should only be within the framework of the UN Charter.
Colombian PR Nestor Ostorio termed the situation grave and
felt there would be no contradiction in the rejection of foreign
military intervention and establishment of a no-fly zone once the
Council endorsed its imposition under a Charter-based mandate.
The Bosnian PR, Ivan Barbalic, said that based on his nation's
experience, a no-fly zone—though unable to stop massacres—
could at least reduce killings.

Our political coordinator in the Security Council, the highly
competent and effective Vinay Kumar, who had been monitoring

the proposed establishment of a no-fly zone, told me on 3 March 2011 that his discussions with his counterparts from the US, France, Portugal and the UK had indicated that there was limited, if at all any, support within their respective military establishments for the move. The dominant view even amongst the advocates of this step was that a final decision would depend on the extent of violence of the pro-Gaddafi forces. The anticipation was that the use of force would incite public opinion, which in turn might force political leaders to consider robust action. Hence the need for a no-fly zone. It was also evident that the proposal was not likely to gain traction till it was clearly established that Gaddafi was, in effect, using air assets against civilians and that the proposed strategy would ameliorate the condition of civilians. The assessment was that if the conflict dragged on, as was only to be expected, and civilian casualties mounted, further military measures, including a no-fly zone, would become a viable option on the table.

I had requested Vinay's assessment because we had received a circular message from our foreign secretary, addressed to India's ambassadors in Washington, Paris, Beijing, Moscow, Berlin, Geneva and New York. The operative thrust of the message was that having seen reports regarding NATO's contingency plans to impose a no-fly zone, modelled on the experience in Bosnia in 1993, we had serious concerns about the well-being of the 18,000-plus Indian nationals in Libya, only a third of whom had been evacuated by 2 March.

It was an emergency session of the Council that met on 14 March at the request of Lebanon to discuss the imposition of a no-fly zone and the establishment of safe areas in Libya, in pursuance of the resolution passed by the Arab League on Saturday, 12 March. By 15 March, it was clear that both the rebels and the government were violating the arms embargo in effect since February as per Resolution 1970, and that the Council continued to be deeply divided on military action against Gaddafi. Many members felt that open-ended military engagement would have serious implications not only within Libya but for the larger region.

The information available in New York indicated that the Arab League's resolution on 12 March was made possible only when Egypt joined the call for the imposition of a no-fly zone and the establishment of safe areas. The change in Egypt's position helped overcome opposition from Algeria, Syria, Sudan and Yemen. A meeting of UN ambassadors from the Arab countries took place on 14 March after the Security Council's closed session. The Egyptian ambassador, Maged A. Abdelaziz, informed the meeting that the Egyptian armed forces chief, who had visited Washington the previous week, had indicated that Egypt, with the largest army in the region, would not be in a position to participate in the imposition of a no-fly zone, let alone in any other military adventurism. As late as 14 March, there was no clarity on the source of the requisite military assets, the participants in military operations, and the likely implications of such additional measures. It was also not clear how the implementation of Resolution 1970—passed on 26 February—was faring. The Sanctions Committee, established in pursuance of Resolution 1970, was also scheduled to have its first meeting only on 17 March.

By 16 March, all delegations made up their minds. Russia said that the 'text is beyond repair'. Lebanon, the UK and France did not agree to the US amendments asking for unrestricted use of 'all necessary means' to protect civilians in Libya. The French, taking over the draft from the Lebanese, amended the authorization for the use of force to exclude 'an occupation force', in order to assuage the Lebanese and address the concerns of Portugal and South Africa. The Lebanese, under pressure and criticism from several Arab countries for going beyond the position of the Arab League, said that the exclusion of an occupation force was not enough, and asked for assurance that no foreign military intervention would take place 'on the ground'. The French, keen on an outcome, obliged by qualifying the language to 'exclud[e] an occupation force in any form in any part of Libyan territory'. Both the US and Lebanon agreed to this, leading to their co-sponsoring the resolution along with France and the UK.

In the evening session on 17 March, just before the voting, French foreign minister Alain Juppe remarked that the world was witnessing a Jasmine Revolution in Tunisia and democratic transitions in Egypt and Morocco, adding that the 'new Arab spring-time' was good news and that the international community should not be a mere spectator. He termed the situation in Libya alarming, with Gaddafi's forces marching towards Benghazi, and called on the Council to adopt the resolution. He stressed that 'we have very few days, perhaps hours, to respond to the situation and protect civilians'.

Meanwhile, as was noted later by the German Council of Foreign Relations:

> ... the German government did not learn of the shift in the Americans' position until the afternoon of March 16—and then, only because the US Ambassador to the UN, Susan Rice, informed her German colleague, Peter Wittig. There had been no phone call from Obama or Clinton to Merkel or Westerwelle [Foreign Minister Guido Westerwelle], no attempt to explain the astonishing turnaround in Washington. Members of the German government were taken by surprise. After all, they had received signals, even from the National Security Council itself, indicating that military operations would be possible only under Arab commands.[37]

I would not, normally, accept a press report to this effect. But in the best tradition of detailed reporting by young members of the Indian Foreign Service, we had received a comprehensive report from an officer at our embassy in Berlin, Amit Telang, following a revealing discussion with Knut Abraham, deputy head of the United Nations division in the German federal chancellery. It highlighted the background to Germany's abstention on Resolution 1973 on Libya. This decision, it was explained, followed due deliberation between Berlin and the German mission in New York. Telang was informed by his interlocutor that the US was also initially considering an abstention. The split within the American administration was obvious: while Gates was against military intervention, Clinton was in favour. If Gates had had his way, the US would have voted against the resolution. The German thinking was also that military intervention was not a justified course of action. Germany had explained its position to its European partners. The US informed Germany of the change in its position at the last minute. There was some displeasure in Berlin about France's unilateral decision to recognize the Benghazi group as a rebel government. The decision to abstain did not, however, affect Germany's commitment to NATO or to the Common Foreign and Security Policy (CFSP). The German chancellor's office felt that the abstention had been a strategic miscalculation, for which it now blamed Westerwelle. Merkel had some explaining to do, with 'diplomatic finesse'.

Sarkozy, meanwhile, had been quick to hit the phones, rallying the international community to support military intervention in Libya, as Juppe flew to New York. And by the time of the Security Council vote on 17 March, 'Washington voted along with France and Britain for a resolution authorizing the use of force in Libya to protect the civilian population, while Russia and China abstained. That night, Sarkozy called [Bernard-Henri] Levy to tell him, "We've won".'[38] Two days later, as Gaddafi's forces reached Benghazi, France began bombing Libya. Levy's position remained that he had 'no role, except having had, one evening, in Benghazi, the crazy idea to pick up the phone and call [his] country's president and recommend that he receive a delegation from Free Libya'.[39]

Except Gabon, all delegations submitted their Explanation of Vote (EOV) after the adoption of Resolution 1973. Delegations voting in favour stated that new measures were essential as Gaddafi, apart from violating Resolution 1970 adopted unanimously by the Council, continued to attack civilians. If not stopped now, the further march of pro-Gaddafi forces would lead to a bloodbath. Nawaf Salam of Lebanon said action under the resolution may not guarantee peace in Libya but would provide some hope for the people of Libya. Mark Lyall Grant termed the Gaddafi regime illegal and said the UK would work closely with France, the US, NATO and the Arab states in enforcing the no-fly zone. Susan Rice termed the resolution a powerful response to the call of the Arab League and added that the future of Libya was to be decided by the Libyan people themselves, and that the US would support them for their universal rights. Baso Sangqu of South Africa found comfort in the amended language of Operative Para 4 (OP4), which reflected the French 'googly'—a cricketing term—'… while excluding a foreign occupation force of any form on any part of Libyan territory'.

Abstaining delegations, other than Germany, noted that the resolution did not clarify their concerns about the use of military force, including details of who would participate and the other aspects of specific measures. Brazil showed its apprehension on the effectiveness of OP4, about protection of civilians, and noted that it may affect the very people it intended to protect. Its PR, Maria Luiza Viotti, stressed the need for the use of diplomacy and dialogue. Churkin of Russia attributed the abstention to their principled stand against use of military force, and regretted that the passion of interventionists had prevailed and that Resolution 1973 transcended the Arab League's resolution. The Russians also did not allow Shalgham, the Libyan PR, to sit at the Council table because he had by then defected to an opposition government not recognized by the UN. Li Baodong of China said it was against the use of force in international relations, and that China's many specific questions on the resolution did not receive answers.

Germany itself, which had earlier moved several amendments on financial aspects but always expressed apprehensions about military measures, said that the Gaddafi regime had become illegal and must go. Peter Witting said that military actions would result in protracted military conflict affecting the entire region and added that Germany would not contribute any forces.

Resolution 1973 on Libya was adopted by the Security Council on 17 March 2011, with five members—Brazil, Russia, China, India and Germany—abstaining. The other ten voted in favour. A resolution in the Council can see the light of day, in terms of Article 27(2), '… by an affirmative vote of nine members'. There was high drama in the run-up to the vote. By convention, Council proceedings can commence only when all fifteen members are present. Baso Sangqu, my highly spirited and competent colleague, who, despite his young age, is a veteran of many multilateral battles, initially chose to stay away, ostensibly because he was awaiting instructions. The Nigerian PR, Joy Ogwu, an academic who had served as her country's foreign minister previously, had made it clear that she was under instructions to vote with South Africa, no matter which way South Africa decided. In other words, if South Africa had chosen to abstain, along with India and Brazil—its partners in the IBSA (India, Brazil, South Africa) Dialogue Forum—and Nigeria joined the members abstaining, the resolution would not have received the nine affirmative votes required. The French PR later told me that Baso's temporary absence had given the movers of Resolution 1973 the jitters. His explanation was that South Africa's eventual affirmative vote was the result of Obama and Sarkozy working the telephone to President Jacob Zuma. My own assessment was that the South Africans faced a genuine dilemma. How could they be seen voting against a resolution which specifically called for mediation by the African Union?

Resolution 1973, passed on 17 March 2011, '… stresses the need to intensify efforts to find a solution to the crisis which responds to the legitimate aspirations of the Libyan people and notes the decision of the Secretary-General to send his Special Envoy to Libya and of the Peace and Security Council of the African Union to send its ad hoc High-level Committee to Libya with the aim of facilitating dialogue to lead to the political reforms necessary to find a peaceful and sustainable solution'.

The ink on Resolution 1973, authorizing 'all necessary means', a euphemism for the use of force, had barely dried when NATO warplanes were in the Libyan skies dropping lethal arsenal. The war, which started in March 2011, continued well into August–September 2011. But the decision to go to war and effect 'regime change' had been taken even before Resolution 1973 was passed. The decision for a regime change constituted mistake number three—which followed the premature ICC referral and the refusal to undertake a limited management of the conflict in Benghazi, instead authorizing a carte blanche for the use of force in Libya. These were, in fact, not the only mistakes. Even after authorizing the use of force, the Council could have reviewed the evolving situation and asked those undertaking the military operations to halt action once the Gaddafi regime had been degraded. This decision was not, however, taken by the Security Council. In fact, this passage of Resolution 1973 would have been jeopardized if regime change had been specifically mentioned in the text. This was a tacit understanding amongst two of the permanent members, with the third, the more important one, exercising neither judgement nor leadership. Resolution 1973 was a carefully negotiated package which contained provisions for a ceasefire and mediation by the African Union. But as soon as the military machine was unleashed, the proponents of war had no use for the provisions of ceasefire and mediation.

Consider this. Resolution 1973 had five points: ceasefire with the mediation of the African Union, use of all necessary means to protect civilians, a no-fly zone, an arms embargo and targeted sanctions. How was the resolution implemented? As soon as it was adopted, the overenthusiastic members of the international community stopped talking of the African Union. Its efforts to bring about a ceasefire were completely ignored. The only aspect of the resolution which was of interest to them was the 'use of all necessary means'—to bomb the hell out of Libya. In clear violation of the resolution, arms were supplied to civilians without any consideration for the consequences. The no-fly zone was selectively implemented only for flights in and out of Tripoli. And the targeted measures were implemented insofar as they suited the objective of regime change. All kinds of mechanisms were created to support one party to the conflict and attempts were made to bypass the sanctions committee by proposing resolutions to the Council. It goes without saying that the pro-interventionist powers did not ever try to bring about a peaceful end to the crisis in Libya.

Samantha Power, special assistant to the president and senior director for multilateral affairs and human rights in the National Security Council, called India's ambassador in Washington, Meera Shankar, on the afternoon of 21 March 2011 to emphasize that the action in Libya was 'a humanitarian mission only', with the aim of protecting Libyans and other civilians. The American objectives, as indicated by her, were to enforce a no-fly zone and then hand over operations to countries like Turkey and Qatar as quickly as possible. She mentioned that Obama was keen to distance himself from the operations once a no-fly zone had been adopted. She explained that the US and others acted in haste because of messages from NGOs like Red Cross that time was running out. She repeatedly emphasized that the military operations were 'not about regime change but about implementing the will of the Security Council for a no-fly zone and protecting civilians'. Power was less than confident about possible outcomes. The best case scenario, according to her, would be for the international community and the UN to stand together, along with this enforcement action, leading to a situation in which people around Gaddafi would ask him to go into exile. India's ambassador, in turn, stressed our concern for the safety and security of our diplomatic personnel and the 2,000 or so Indians who remained in Libya at that point of time.

In another message, India's ambassador said that Gates as well as Admiral Michael Mullen, the chairman of the joint chiefs of staff, had reiterated that the US's role was limited to functioning as part of the coalition forces. While the country had led the coalition forces till then, it would not have a 'preeminent role' in future. The US had agreed to provide its 'unique capabilities' at the 'front end', and then hand over the primary responsibility to others in 'a matter of days'. Gates said that the coalition would, in future, not be led by NATO due to the sensitivities of Arab countries. He did not clarify as to who was to take over command from the US.

The denunciation of Gaddafi, fuelled by the Western press and supported by think tanks—with one notable exception, to which I will turn shortly—had built pressure on policymakers in the capitals of three permanent member nations of the Security

Council. The 'black swan' moment[40] came when Gaddafi used the threat of violence as part of his 22 February 2011 speech about fighting 'till the last drop of blood'.[41] Given his megalomania, his track record of being quick to use brutal violence against domestic dissent, and the fact that the Libyan state under him had been widely perceived to have been associated with criminal acts of international terrorism, it is not surprising that few disbelieved Gaddafi and even fewer wanted to take chances with him. Even more importantly, the assessment was that Gaddafi believed he was facing a threat from those who wanted to overthrow him and unravel the Libyan state.

In some respects, he was not wrong. He was the Libyan state. He had established it four decades earlier in 1969 after overthrowing King Idris, who had held together a weak conglomeration of tribes, in a military coup d'état. He was not mistaken in thinking that amongst those who wished to see him go were in fact people actively associated with the al-Qaeda. Libya, it will be recalled, was one of the largest providers of recruits to terror outfits like the al-Qaeda. Be that as it may, given the extent of destruction to which Libya had been subjected, it would be worthwhile to objectively examine what Gaddafi actually said in his February speech. This examination is best undertaken by listing the interpretation of those who did not buy into the mainstream Western narrative cited earlier in the chapter.

What exactly did Gaddafi say? As per a *Global Research* article:

> The White House claimed that Gaddafi had threatened to massacre the people of Benghazi with 'no mercy', but the *New York Times* reported that Gaddafi's threat was directed at rebel fighters, not civilians, and that [he] promised amnesty for those 'who throw their weapons away'. Gaddafi also offered to allow rebel fighters to escape to Egypt if they preferred not to fight to the death. Yet President Obama warned of imminent genocide.[42]

The *New York Times* had indeed reported that though on 17 March 2011 Gaddafi had warned the residents of Benghazi that 'an attack was imminent'—'"we are coming tonight," Colonel Gaddafi said'—'[s]peaking on a call-in radio show, he promised amnesty for those "who throw their weapons away" but "no mercy or compassion" for those who fight'.[43]

In a televised speech on 22 February 2011, Gaddafi had urged the people of Libya to save themselves before the 'march' began. He had said there would be a peaceful march from inside the cities and streets 'to save the children' and 'arrest those who harm them'. Only if that did not work would a national march, led by him, follow.[44] In fact, in most of his speeches, Gaddafi had condemned only the handful of people who were participating in the rebellion and had targeted his verbal attacks on the West and NATO, abusing them and daring them to switch to the Libyan channel. He continued to speak to the Libyan people as his proclaimed own, whom he intended to keep safe from the outside threat.[45]

Reviewing the episode, Alan J. Kuperman, an American expert of public affairs, noted that '... contrary to conventional wisdom, Gaddafi ... never threatened or perpetrated revenge killings against civilians in areas that [the Libyan government] recaptured from the rebels [even though] the government did attempt to intimidate the rebels by promising to be relentless in pursuing them'.[46] His argument cited the direct address by Gaddafi, of 17 March, to the 'rebels of Benghazi', whereby he urged them 'to throw away [their] weapons exactly like [their] brothers in Ajdabiya and other places [had]', reminding his listeners how they were never pursued by the regime after 'they laid down their weapons and [turned] safe'.[47] Kuperman assessed that 'there [was] no reason to believe ... that a bloodbath would have occurred in Benghazi [as] Gaddafi had not threatened to attack civilians there and had not perpetrated such violence in any of the other cities that his forces had recaptured from rebels'.[48]

An Al Jazeera report revealed in July 2011 that Gaddafi had once allegedly advised Europe to ground its planes and hold discussions with the Libyan people.[49] On those lines, in a televised speech on 29 April 2011, the Libyan leader had the following to say:

> The Security Council should hold a meeting when there is a war between two or more countries, like there is now between Libya and NATO. That would truly be a reflection of the UNSC doing justice to Libya, instead of interfering in its internal affairs. We are ready to negotiate with, talk to anyone—France, Britain, Italy, the United States—who stepped down recently—the European Union and NATO. We are ready to talk. We are not at the end of 1950 to say that Libya's independence must be like this, or like that. All these questions would arise had we been a colony; but Libya is an independent state, a member of the UN, with every right to determine what its state system should be like, and who will lead it.[50]

However, Gaddafi's reputation continued to precede and haunt him. Given his portrayal as a crusher of 'many revolts … by force', Hugh Roberts,[51] a historian of the Middle East, highlighted that the NTC rebels had 'good reason to fear that once Benghazi had fallen to government troops, they would be rounded up and made to pay the price'. Thus, the rebels saw a remedy in convincing 'the international community that it was not only their lives that were at stake, but those of thousands of ordinary civilians'. However, 'in retaking … towns' captured by them, Gaddafi's 'forces committed no massacres at all … nothing remotely resembling the slaughter at Srebrenica,[52] let alone in Rwanda'. In fact, asserted Roberts, 'the only known massacre carried out during [Gaddafi's] rule was the killing of some 1,200 Islamist prisoners at Abu Salim prison in 1996', which, despite being a 'dark affair', may not have been directly ordered by him.[53] Yet, the *Financial Times* reiterated how

Gaddafi was called the 'mad dog of the Middle East' by Ronald Reagan,[54] and how his Libya was 'regarded as the foremost State sponsor of terrorism ... rightly denounced for [a] dreadful human rights record',[55] including a 'long history of quashing the slightest sign of opposition',[56] just as the *Guardian* questioned Gaddafi's 'conceit' in abolishing 'the conventional state' to replace it 'with an organic system that empowered the masses'.[57]

In retrospect, several things become clearer. First and foremost, there was the role of the Clinton-era bleeding hearts: those who served in Bill Clinton's administration and carried the 'guilt of Rwanda' into the Obama administration. Susan Rice maintained an unusually low profile in Council consultations. It was only when the interventionist lobby succeeded in getting Obama's consent for the US's participation in military operations against Libya, a day before Resolution 1973 was adopted, that she sprang into action to propose an amendment seeking authorization for the use of 'all necessary means' for the protection of civilians, which would allow for military operations by land, air and sea. This was then ring-fenced by the French to exclude 'boots on the ground'.

Within a week of Resolution 1973 being passed by the Council, it was clear to most of us that the US had been dragged into the process somewhat reluctantly. Richard Haass, a highly respected member of the American strategic community who had served in various posts in the defence and state departments and had been the president of the Council on Foreign Relations since 2003, gave an interview to Tavis Smiley of PBS (Public Broadcasting Service) on 24 March 2011. During the talk, he explained that it was not a war in which one ethnic group intended to commit genocide on another, but that it was a purely political affair. He refused to believe that Gaddafi intended to eliminate a large segment of the Libyan population, nor that it was a humanitarian crisis comparable with Rwanda, Darfur or the Balkans.[58]

Haass went on to argue that oil was not the real reason the US was involved in Libya, claiming that it was involved because people misread the situation and saw it as a potential humanitarian crisis. He further stated that the US administration also misread the situation in believing that if they did not act in Libya, it could turn the tide against progressive or pro-democracy forces throughout the Middle East. According to him, there was a lack of clarity in that the US had implied the necessity of removing Gaddafi, while the UN Resolution 1973, for the rest of the world, only required Gaddafi pulling out of certain cities. Thus, Haass stated, there was a disconnect between the ambitious goals of the US and the more limited objectives of the international community, reflected in the lack of diplomacy on the part of the Americans in certain places.

Explaining further, Haass emphasized that even if there was a humanitarian crisis at hand, there were alternative solutions to establishing a no-fly zone. He noted that the military component of the episode was not at all thought through. Haass also argued that the US had made a mistake in calling for Gaddafi's ouster and initiating war crimes proceedings against him, because this removed any incentive for him to compromise. Asserting that the Americans took diplomacy off the board very quickly, he emphasized that they were unwise in escalating their goals, for they did not know what the opposition intended to do in the event that Gaddafi was ousted. He went on to express his wonder about how the US could jump in with both feet despite so much uncertainty about the consequences of its actions. Lastly, he emphasized that although Gaddafi was a tyrant, he was also willing to make some decisions the Americans liked. He noted that the US failed to appreciate that it was dealing in a world with shades of grey, in that there were evil people who nonetheless could do things that were in its interest. With that, Haass concluded that the US had exclusively been dealing with Gaddafi as if he were evil incarnate, but that there were other dimensions worth consideration as well.

Washington lacked the appetite for a long-drawn-out military operation. This became clear within two days of the commencement of operations. The US started talking of the need to hand over the lead role to NATO and other participants. Araud was worried and often expressed anxiety as to what would happen if the US pulled out.[59] The Chinese assessment, conveyed in a discussion with me on 23 March—when Li Baodong came to see me—was that with military expenditure already in the vicinity of approximately $400 million per week, with little economic interest in Libya, and the presidential elections in the US due the following year, the US was keen to end its involvement in military operations, since the situation in Libya could only slide into civil war. Notwithstanding the outward unity and commonality of purpose, tensions were already evident by the last week of March between Washington and London, and Washington and Paris, on the way forward in Libya. It was clear as daylight that Gaddafi was a wild card whose behaviour could not be predicted. If, by some chance, he survived the combined onslaught of NATO with the participation of the world's leading military machines, the power struggle in Libya would be long-drawn and bloody—something in which the US had no interest in participating. Without US support, France and the UK could not conceivably get the support of the 'coalition of the willing' and the international community for their preferred course of action all along: regime change.

Towards the end of March 2011, our assessment—that is, the assessment of the permanent representatives of countries serving on the Council, including two of the permanent members, Russia and China—was that the US would carefully gauge the unfolding situation and calibrate its position accordingly. If the situation in Libya unfolded in a satisfactory manner, the US would claim credit. That would be couched in moralistic terms of having acted decisively to protect civilians from the madness of a present-day

Pol Pot, and that too with specific authorization of the Security Council. If, on the other hand, the situation deteriorated into civil war, as was widely expected, it would withdraw. In retrospect, it got the worst of both ends.

On the eleventh anniversary of the 11 September 2001 terror attacks in the US, armed militants stormed the diplomatic premises of the US consulate in Benghazi, setting the building on fire. Ambassador Christopher Stevens, computer specialist Sean Smith and Central Intelligence Agency (CIA) contractors Tyrone Woods and Glen Doherty—both former Navy Seals—were killed in the battles of that night.

'A broken system overseen by senior leadership contributed to the vulnerability of American diplomats—in one of the most dangerous cities in the world,' said Republican committee member Susan Collins of Maine as part of the bipartisan Senate committee that was instituted to inquire into the circumstances of the tragedy. Republican vice chairman Saxby Chambliss said the committee's report showed that despite a deteriorating security situation in Benghazi, the US government did not do enough to prevent the attacks and protect the diplomatic facility. The report also said that subsequent investigations showed the participation of many militant groups in the attacks, including al-Qaeda in the Islamic Maghreb, the Libyan militia group Ansar al-Sharia and members of the Yemen-based al-Qaeda in the Arabian peninsula. Were these not the groups that Gaddafi had claimed were out to overthrow him and destabilize Libya? On whose side, then, did the US, France and the UK intervene in the full-blown civil war that was in progress when these tragic events unfolded?

There are several other aspects to the Benghazi events that are mind-boggling. Evidence, on record, shows that the embassy had repeatedly requested additional security. An embassy cable on 25 June had expressed the fear that Islamic extremism was on the rise in eastern Libya around Benghazi and noted that the black flag of al-Qaeda 'had been spotted several times flying over government buildings and training facilities'. On 2 August, Stevens himself had sent a cable requesting eleven additional bodyguards, noting 'host nation security support [to be] lacking and [unable to] be depended upon to provide a safe and secure environment for the diplomatic mission of outreach'.[60] Their requests for additional security were repeatedly denied as per the testimony of security officials before the House Oversight Committee in December 2012. The actions of those responsible for the security of overseas American diplomatic premises borders on the bizarre. A well-armed sixteen-member security detail from Libya was removed in August, a month before the attack, and replaced by Libyan security personnel that, Stevens had told them, could not be relied upon. Based on the documents released by the House Oversight Committee, on the day of the attack on the American consulate in Benghazi—11 September—the White House situation room started receiving emails at about 1 p.m. that the mission was under hostile surveillance. The Pentagon's only response was to send a drone equipped with a video camera so that everyone in Washington—at the White House, the state department, the Pentagon and the CIA headquarters—could see what transpired in real time.[61]

A discussion in the Council in early April 2011, barely three weeks after the passage of Resolution 1973, merits specific mention in this context. The discussion involved a somewhat sharp exchange between Mark Lyall Grant and me. Without referring to me by name, he said some in the Council were 'playing Aunt Sally'. In his view, there was no evidence of arming of rebels or the stationing of ground troops in Libya because there was no arming taking place. Without hesitation I asked for the floor and said that, without wishing to comment on who Aunt Sally was, there were clear indications that rebel groups were being armed in violation of Security Council resolutions. Also that the arming was taking place without due diligence, and that before long evidence of such misguided actions would not only surface but would do so along with all the unintended and negative consequences. I also made a passing reference to the special forces of some Council members who were guiding operations on the ground. I added that the fig leaf of a perfectly executed intervention—no civilian casualties and a barely armed opposition—would become increasingly problematic. It was also increasingly clear that the goal of regime change was getting the better of all other objectives. I stressed that the objective of regime change was neither mentioned in Resolution 1973 nor approved by the Council. It had become clear that Gaddafi had been demonized so much that coalition partners were not likely to back down without his removal from power, notwithstanding reported negotiations with Libyan emissaries in London and Athens.

Gaddafi was found hiding in a culvert west of Sirte, a city halfway between Tripoli and Benghazi, when he was captured by NTC forces. The brutal nature of this extrajudicial killing, with an aluminum rod piercing his posterior and a shot between the eyes, may have satisfied sections of Libya's tribal society that had been at the receiving end of Gaddafi's forty-year rule. However, the curse of Gaddafi not only visited Libya but is now being played out in many other countries. Since his rule depended largely on hired mercenaries and not entirely on an organized state army, Gaddafi's fall immediately led to an outburst of private armies, which contributed to the wider destabilization of the region. The assassination of Stevens in Benghazi, the fall of northern Mali to Tuareg rebels, the consequent French military action in Mali, and the capture by Islamic jihadists of an oil facility in Algeria were fallouts, and the transformation of Libya into a Somalia on the Mediterranean coast is still a work in progress.

Iraq had set the stage for Libya almost a decade prior to it, but there are, of course, crucial differences between the two. The military action in Iraq was undertaken by a 'coalition of the willing' when the UN Security Council refused to provide authorization. The NATO military action in Libya followed the passage of Resolution 1973 in March 2011. The establishment of a no-fly zone was part of a package of other provisions, such as freezing of assets, negotiation of a ceasefire and mediation by the African Union. In hindsight, it is entirely possible that the resolution would not have been approved if members of the Council had known the Security Council's authorization would be used in a selective manner only for military action, ignoring the other provisions. It is also abundantly clear that the 'protection of civilians' provision in the resolution ended up being subordinated to the larger objective of regime change. The jury is still out on whether regime change was the original objective. It was never mentioned and was, in fact, vehemently denied during discussions within the Security Council. Clearly, regime change became the objective soon after Resolution 1973 was adopted. The Libyan ghost resurfaced in discussions on Syria, where, like Libya, the original dissent and resentment to authoritarian rule on the part of unarmed civilians was slowly but surely transformed—through active moral, financial and military encouragement from Qatar, Saudi Arabia and the West—into an armed insurrection. It is as yet unclear whether Bashar al-Assad will meet the same fate as Saddam Hussein in Iraq and Gaddafi in Libya. Only time will tell.

4

SYRIA: THE MULTILAYERED AND STILL UNFOLDING TRAGEDIES

> Hegel remarks somewhere that all great world-historic facts and personages appear, so to speak, twice. He forgot to add: the first time as tragedy, the second time as farce. Men make their own history, but they do not make it as they please; they do not make it under self-selected circumstances, but under circumstances existing, already given and transmitted from the past. The tradition of all dead generations weighs like a nightmare on the brains of the living.
>
> —Karl Marx,
> 'The Eighteenth Brumaire of Louis Napoleon', 1852

Presenting her last report to the Security Council on 28 May 2015, the outgoing undersecretary-general for humanitarian affairs, Valerie Amos, painted a dire picture. She recalled that since her first briefing to Council members on 13 March 2012, a year after the civil war had started in Syria, she had repeatedly pleaded for the Security Council to take action and halt the killings, which stood at the horrific figure of 220,000. She also mentioned a figure of one million injured, almost four million refugees, 7.6 million internally displaced, 12.2 million in need of humanitarian assistance, and 422,000 people living under siege conditions. According to the Syrian Center for Policy Research, the death toll stood at 470,000 in February 2016, with 11.5 per cent of the country's population 'killed or injured' since 2011, and over ten million displaced internally and abroad.[1]

Even a fraction of these numbers should have been sufficient to stir the conscience of the international community and provide the impetus for the Security Council to act. And yet, it did not. Between 2011—when the civil war started—and 2016, the Security Council tried to address the conflict on several occasions. The stage was, however, set by the four double vetoes exercised by China and Russia on 4 October 2011, 4 February 2012, 19 July 2012 and 22 May 2014. The Council's inaction constituted a severe self-indictment and the most comprehensive statement not only of its ineffectiveness but also its complete irrelevance to today's emerging threats to international peace and security. How was this tragic impasse reached? A comprehensive understanding is important not only for its own sake but perhaps even more for finding a way forward towards a possible solution.

The Syrian civil war is in several respects sui generis. Characterized by extreme, even unprecedented, brutality, it is continuing to result in widespread destruction, both in human and material terms. It has unravelled the Syrian state and made its borders—drawn up by imperialist cartographers—irrelevant. Large parts of contemporary Iraq and Syria are claimed by the caliphate that the ISIS proposes to establish. A defining characteristic of what is happening in Syria, perhaps entirely unique, is that disputants on both sides appear to prefer chaos and disintegration to seeking a negotiated political settlement. An understanding of the multilayered tragedies that have unfolded and besieged the Syrian people will not be possible without a proper historical perspective.

Syria was another country that attracted attention from the West during the Arab Spring. As elsewhere in the region, the number of disaffected people willing to be co-opted to fight alongside the al-Qaeda and assorted terrorists of all hues made it an attractive candidate for regime change. Dissent, initially peaceful, soon began to draw inspiration from developments in Libya. The three easy steps witnessed in Libya—a Security Council resolution, arming of rebels and NATO military action—became the model for Syria. The rebels, openly armed by Qatar, covertly by Saudi Arabia, and clandestinely by others in the West and the Gulf states, expected the same outcome in Syria. 'Regime change' had, however, always been the unstated objective, as far as at least three of the permanent members of the Security Council were concerned, in the case of Syria as well. Journalist Charles Glass wrote in October 2015:

> A Syrian friend, now living in exile, told me that the American ambassador, Robert Ford, just before he withdrew from Damascus in October 2011, tried to recruit him to take part in a government that he promised would shortly replace Assad's. When the French ambassador to Syria, Eric Chevallier, left Damascus on March 6, 2012, he told friends he would be back when a post-Assad government was installed 'in two months'.[2]

Given the Libyan experience and the strategic interests of Russia in Syria,[3] the Security Council refused to oblige. Russia and China vetoed three draft resolutions in 2011–12 and one more in 2014. Unilateral military action by NATO or a coalition of the willing was not forthcoming either.

Syria's demographics made it susceptible to internal conflict: 12 per cent Alawites (Shias) and 10 per cent Christians formed a cosy compact, with the Sunni business class collaborating to lord over a predominantly (78 per cent) Sunni population. The opening up of sectarian fault lines was only a matter of time.

Saudi Arabia, Qatar and other Gulf countries started supporting predominantly Sunni armed groups. The US, the UK and France were never enamoured by Bashar al-Assad in the first instance. Influenced by the democratic elixir of the Arab Spring and fuelled by wishful thinking, they saw in the evolving situation in mid-2011 an opportunity to reorder the world on democratic lines. They underestimated the Syrian approach to dealing with dissent. In 1982, Bashar al-Assad's father Hafez had used brute force to quell dissent in Hama and, as subsequent events showed, the son had no qualms in doing so either. His subsequent decision to wage war against those opposed to his regime—whom he ab initio characterized as terrorists—removed whatever little inhibition might have existed in arming rebels opposed to the Assad regime. Since Iran and Russia were supporting the Assad regime in different ways, the opposing three permanent members of the Security Council—the US, the UK and France—felt even more reassured about the righteousness of their cause and the course of action they had adopted. The full implications of this did not become clear, as is invariably the case, till much later. It is only when it became evident that the Libyan experience was going hopelessly wrong that doubts about the approach to the crisis in Syria also began to rise.

It was both easy and convenient to see the evolving situation in Syria through the mere prism of security. The Assad family's own track record, particularly the 1982 Hama massacre (discussed later in the chapter), was always a convenient starting point in any conversation. Viewed against this background and the democratic aspirations unleashed by the Arab Spring, it is entirely understandable that the mainstream narrative in the West, at least till 2012, viewed developments in Syria in terms of a brutal and repressive regime targeting innocent and helpless civilians demanding their democratic rights during the Arab Spring.

Calls for direct military intervention by the West grew from early 2012. There was, however, very little appetite for it in Western capitals. It was election year in the US, and polls indicated a consistently clear majority against a military intervention in Syria. Also, the Libyan experience was already beginning to demonstrate that distinctions between 'good' and 'bad' rebels are at best illusory. The assassination of Ambassador Christopher Stevens in Benghazi had reinforced the view that:

> ... arming opposition forces, while improving their chances in the near term, can militarize and divide a society in ways detrimental to its recovery.[4]

It was clear that should Assad be overthrown militarily, Syria's unravelling would be even more problematic than that of Libya.

There was yet another complicating factor. There was no guarantee that a significantly upgraded military arsenal supplied to Syrian rebels would not be used against American allies, particularly Israel. Well before these factors contributed to the realization that military intervention in Syria would be a mistake, Obama had already set the tone for the American position. He declared on 7 March 2012: 'For us to take military action unilaterally, as some have suggested, or to think that somehow there is some simple solution, I think is a mistake.'[5]

This was in marked contrast to his position some seven months earlier: 'We have consistently said that President Assad must lead a democratic transition or get out of the way; he has not led. For the sake of the Syrian people, the time has come for President Assad to step aside.'[6]

With the US president having ruled out unilateral military action, the British and the French—the other two permanent members of the Security Council—naturally turned to the Council to get a Libya-like authorization for the use of force. This made it necessary to get Russia and China on board, apart from the non-permanent members of the Security Council.

It is useful to recall that in the Libyan case, it was possible to pass Resolutions 1970 and 1973 in the UN Security Council essentially because the distrust between Moscow and Washington could be bridged during Dmitry Medvedev's presidency. But a strong difference of opinion and approach between Medvedev and Putin was already evident in their views on the Libyan crisis. Visiting the Republic of Udmurtia, a Russian federal subject, in March 2011, days after the Security Council had authorized the use of 'all necessary means' under Resolution 1973, Putin criticized air strikes over Libya as 'defective and flawed' and 'as a medieval call for crusades'. He conceded that he was not troubled by the idea of military intervention per se but was concerned by the ease with which decisions on the use of force are taken in international affairs. He said:

> This is becoming a persistent tendency in US policy. During the Clinton period, they bombed Belgrade. Bush sent forces to Afghanistan and then, under an invented false pretext, into Iraq, eliminating the entire Iraqi leadership, even children in Saddam's family. Now it is Libya's turn, under the pretext of protecting the peaceful population. But in the bomb strikes, the civilian population gets killed. The Libyan regime did not meet any of the criteria of a democratic state, but that does not mean that someone is allowed to interfere in internal affairs to defend one or the other side.[7]

Medvedev's response was interesting:

> At the moment, various words are being used to describe the events taking place. I think we need to be very careful in our choice of wordings. It is inadmissible to say anything that could lead to a clash of civilizations, talk of 'crusades', and so on. This is

unacceptable. Otherwise we could see a situation far worse even than what is happening today. We must all keep this in mind.[8]

Change of power equations within the Kremlin in the second half of 2011 and Putin's re-election as president in March 2012 altered the dynamics in the Council altogether. Botched attempts by the West to raise questions on Putin's re-election queered the pitch still further. The Western media and think tanks had voiced allegations of 'election fraud' well before and also after Putin's election. David Kramer, the president of Freedom House, widely believed to be funded by the US state department, went on record for *Foreign Policy* on 1 March 2012 to predict:

> Even if the system delivers the required results, clear evidence of rigging may lead voters to reject the election as unfair and illegitimate. Moreover, the authorities' stifling of the Russian public's voice runs the risk of creating an even more combustible environment in the period after March 4. The balloting, whatever its outcome, is therefore unlikely to extinguish the rising desire for real change. Unless and until that change is permitted, Putin's continued pursuit of simulated democracy will fail to achieve even a simulation of stability.[9]

The line and approach of Freedom House and its parent organization, the National Endowment for Democracy (NED), soon found resonance elsewhere. The Wall Street–funded American Enterprise Institute (AEI) penned an editorial, titled 'Putin's Pyrrhic Victory', which was carried by the *Los Angeles Times*. It stated: 'Putin's win will be a Pyrrhic victory. Far from enhancing the Putin regime's legitimacy, the election will diminish it further in the eyes of a significant part of the Russian population.'

Let us now turn to China, another important player, in fact a crucial one, because it is also a veto-wielding permanent member of the Security Council. Thomas J. Christensen, former US deputy assistant secretary of state, makes the following observation in his latest book:

> The lessons of Libya would have strong consequences for how China and Russia addressed UN action during the Syrian civil war. After Libya, China more predictably opposed any UN condemnation of Assad's regime, much less any sanctions. China joined Russia in vetoing three draft Resolutions in 2012 to condemn and sanction Assad's regime, in August 2013 blocked consideration of a use-of-force resolution, and in May 2014 vetoed a draft resolution to refer the Syrian civil war to the International Criminal Court. While Putin's Russia took the lead in opposing the United States' and European efforts at the UN, China was steadfast in its support of the Russian position, despite the fact that countries like Saudi Arabia, with whom China has had close ties, strongly supported the rebels and wanted the UN to actively oppose Assad as well. China also found diplomatic comfort in the region because Iran was strongly supportive of Assad and strongly opposed to the UN draft resolution.[10]

The lack of appetite in Washington for military intervention and the complete reluctance of Moscow and Beijing to countenance a Libya-like authorization for the use of force in Syria are starting points in understanding the current mess in Syria. But the entrenched long-term historical factors also need to be listed in order to comprehend why the developments in Syria have unfolded in the manner they have, leading to the virtual dismemberment of the country.

Watching the Syrian tragedy unfold in 2011 and 2012 from a vantage point inside the Security Council, the student of history in me felt the urge to look for pointers from past experience. Imperial cartographers, by the very nature of the tasks assigned to them, were appointed to serve the interests of their masters. These interests, their own creativity, and, most often, their mindsets divorced from reality invariably produced arbitrary and artificial divisions which later proved problematic.

In the midst of the First World War, two Allied diplomats— Frenchman François Georges-Picot and Briton Mark Sykes— secretly agreed on the post-war division of the Ottoman Empire, which had entered the conflict on the side of Germany and the Austro-Hungarian Empire, into respective zones of influence in the Sykes–Picot Agreement of 1916. Britain was allocated control of areas roughly comprising the coastal strip between the Mediterranean Sea and River Jordan, Jordan, southern Iraq, and a small area including the ports of Haifa and Acre, to allow access to the Mediterranean. France was allocated control of south-eastern Turkey, northern Iraq, Syria and Lebanon. The agreement is considered to have shaped the region, defining the borders of Iraq and Syria.

In a fascinating account of what reportedly transpired, based on declassified documentation, Middle East historian James Barr remarks in *A Line in the Sand* (2011) that 'even by the standards of the time, it was a shamelessly self-interested pact'.[11]

As Barr recalls in his book, in December 1915, Sykes, a young member of the British parliament, was summoned by Lloyd George, the prime minister, to advise his cabinet on deciding 'the future of the Ottoman Empire' following its defeat in the First World War, without hampering 'Britain's fragile alliance with France'. The prescription, in Barr's words, 'was to shape the modern Middle East'. While Sykes was to 'mastermind' the division of the Ottoman Empire between the British and the French, he was, in fact, a 'lesser expert on the subject than he led the cabinet to believe'. For one, he spoke neither Arabic nor Turkish, contrary to the prevalent belief. The initiative, nonetheless, went ahead based on a map and a three-page precis carried to the meeting by him. In a discussion that ensued between Arthur Balfour, the foreign secretary, Herbert Kitchener, the secretary of state for war, and him, Sykes suggested, pointing to his map, that Britain retain 'such country south of Haifia'. As Kitchener understood it, this implied that the demarcation line for British possessions was to commence from the Haifa coast and extend eastwards. Sykes, clarifying his position to a still sceptical Balfour, sliced his finger across the map and connected the port city of Acre in the west to the Kurdish city of Kirkuk in the east. Lloyd George, keen on 'the destruction of the Ottoman Empire', liked the proposal. H.H. Asquith, the leader of the opposition, too, eventually, acquiesced despite warning earlier about the 'dangers of disturbing "a hornet's nest of Arab tribes"'. After the day's work was done, a content Sykes summed it up as 'practical politics'.[12]

Based on a general understanding of British and French spheres of influence, the pact was the manifestation of an approach that can only be described as 'to the victor belong the spoils'. The Sykes–Picot Agreement map—with its clean national borders cutting across ethnic, linguistic and religious lines— was formalized and made official in 1920 with the San Remo Agreement. The agreement has dominated conversations about European incursions in the Middle East and has been soundly condemned by pan-Arab and Arab nationalists as artificial, illegitimate and undeserving of recognition.

But London and Paris were by no means the only Western capitals where the division of spoils received attention. The Ottoman Empire, long coveted by various other empires, was also very much on Washington's radar. In 1919, President Woodrow Wilson appointed a commission headed by Henry Churchill King, president of Ohio's Oberlin College, and Charles R. Crane, a wealthy businessman and connoisseur of Arab culture. Officially called the 1919 Inter-Allied Commission on Mandates in Turkey, the King–Crane Commission was an official investigation by the US government concerning the disposition of non-Turkish areas within the former Ottoman Empire. Between June and August 1919, the members of the Commission travelled from Constantinople to Palestine, Lebanon, Syria and the southern reaches of Turkey. They journeyed as far south as Beersheba and as far east as Amman and Aleppo to determine the wishes of the region's inhabitants concerning a post-war settlement. Wilson instructed the Commission to 'acquaint itself as intimately as possible with the sentiments of the people of these regions with regards to the future administration of their affairs'.[13]

Meanwhile, the Balfour Declaration of 1917—a letter from British foreign secretary Balfour to Walter Rothschild, a leader of the British Jewish community, for transmission to the Zionist Federation of Great Britain and Ireland—had stated:

> His Majesty's government views with favour the establishment in Palestine of a national home for the Jewish people, and will use their best endeavours to facilitate the achievement of this object, it being clearly understood that nothing shall be done which may prejudice the civil and religious rights of existing non-Jewish communities in Palestine, or the rights and political status enjoyed by Jews in any other country.[14]

The tensions inherent in the Balfour Declaration presented yet another problem for the post-war settlement, and the fate of Palestine was a central part of the King–Crane Commission's work.

Western scholar David W. Lesch writes that for all intents and purposes, the Westphalian nation state system was crudely imposed on the Middle East. Centuries of pre-existing orientations were cast aside. Lesch goes on to say:

> The Ottomans had the good sense to administer most of the Levant as provinces that more or less aligned with their

natural ethnic, religious, geographic and economic trade route orientations. For instance, today's Iraq comprised the Ottoman provinces of mostly Sunni Kurdish Mosul in the north, mostly Sunni Arab Baghdad in the center, and mostly Shiite Arab Basra in the south. What comprised today's Syria, Lebanon, Israel, Jordan and Palestine was administered as smaller provincial units centered on major cities. These administrative units were by no means perfect, but, for the most part, the Ottomans, despite the stresses and strains that confronted them in the 1700s and 1800s leading up to the Great War, bargained and negotiated their way with local powers to produce relative stability.[15]

The defining characteristic of the governance systems in place in the countries of the region for decades prior to the Arab Spring was that strong men maintained an iron grip on power, with little or no civil society, even less civil liberty. In order to retain absolute power, they displayed no hesitation in using brute force to suppress dissent. Also, they did not hesitate to undertake killings on a large scale to stay in power.

Brutalization has a demonstrative effect and is designed to instil fear in citizens. Any discussion of this phenomenon, of strong men instilling fear through the use of brute force and violence in the Syrian context, has to commence with Hama, the worst massacre in Syria's modern history, carried out by Hafez al-Assad in February 1982. Ironically, it was the Arab Spring and inspiration from the Libyan uprising that made it possible for ordinary Syrians to focus for the first time on the 1982 massacre and express open defiance thirty years later on the anniversary of the massacre.

On 2 February 1982, Hafez al-Assad seized the western city of Hama and bombed its centre with fighter jets, enabling tanks to roll through its narrow streets, crushing an armed rebellion by an estimated 200 to 500 fighters from the military wing of the Muslim Brotherhood, a transnational Sunni Islamist organization founded in Egypt in 1928. The subsequent twenty-seven-day military campaign left somewhere between 10,000 and 40,000 people dead and almost two-thirds of the city destroyed. This violence has been documented by credible international human rights organizations like Amnesty. Hama's population in 1982 was 250,000, and almost every family there lost a member.

The strategy of instilling fear in Hama's residents succeeded. Accounts of the eyewitnesses and victims recorded at the time lend credence to the view that it was indeed the senior Assad's intention to instil fear. 'Through us, he wanted to teach all Syrians that challenging the regime would lead to this, and it worked. It worked for thirty years,' recalled a respondent.[16]

Writer and author Wendell Steavenson demonstrates that the senior Assad's Hama strategy was effective:

> The Muslim Brotherhood threat to Hafez al-Assad's regime was neutralized. I talked recently to Hafez's brother Rifaat al-Assad, once a right hand of the regime, who is widely blamed for overseeing the Hama massacre. Now in exile, he divides his time between a grand house in the Avenue Foch in Paris and a house in Mayfair in London. He has always denied being anywhere near Hama on February 3, 1982. I asked him, though, if he has now condemned the action … He demurred for a moment. 'We could not have succeeded without doing it,' he told me.[17]

The repression by Hafez al-Assad elicited critical comment across the board—not only from human rights organizations in the West but also from the right-wing and left-of-centre press and from Syrians both inside the country and outside. Upon his death in June 2000 after thirty years as the president of Syria, the *New York Times* argued that '[Hafez al-]Assad's longevity in office rested on a rigid intolerance of dissent, most starkly illustrated at Hama in … [1982]', going on to label his Syria 'a suspicious police state'.[18] Around the same time, the *Economist* said that 'his repressive habits' grew with the 'opposition to [his] autocratic rule', and saw the Hama rebellion as a culmination of the 'resentment that much of Syria's Sunni Muslim majority felt at being ruled by a member of a small Shia sect'.[19] The Fourth International's World Socialist Web Site saw the Hama massacre as 'summ[ing] up his ruthlessness in crushing internal dissent. The Hama massacre took place under conditions of deepening economic crisis, increasing social inequality and rising popular discontent.' It also cited that 'between 1982 and 1992 thousands were arrested for political dissent and [around] 10,000 were executed'.[20] In 2002, Syrian journalist Subhi Hadidi described the Hama incident as 'a genuine, premeditated cold-blooded massacre [whereby] "carte blanche" [was given] to the use of … all means of repression … [in] destroying entire neighbourhoods … including mosques and churches'.[21]

Fast-forward thirty years to 2012 and two questions need to be addressed. One, how has Bashar al-Assad been able to maintain his own iron grip on power, given the limited support he has enjoyed? Two, how has the international community reacted to these developments?

On the first, Steavenson has an explanation:

The Assads are Alawites from the mountain villages above the coastal town of Latakia. The regime has always relied on family and clan ties, on an Alawite-dominated intelligence and military establishment. In this crisis, Bashar has managed to convince the wider Alawite community that this is an existentialist fight for them, too, that if his regime falls, they will be cut to pieces by a vengeful Sunni majority. The band of regimist thugs known as the *Shabiha*—[named] after Alawite bandit smuggling gangs that operated in the seventies—have been mostly drawn from the Alawite population, and are at the forefront of the crackdown on protests and opposition neighbourhoods. It didn't have to be this way. Plenty of Alawites were fed up with Assad's corrupt and oppressive regime as any other Syrian; many Alawite villages are poor and ignored. But his strategy of playing the sectarian card has, by now, and so much horror later, proved effective. He has effectively taken the Alawite population hostage to protect his family and his regime.[22]

The Alawite region became a part of Syria as a by-product of the notorious Sykes–Picot Agreement. It was placed under the French mandate after the end of the First World War. After defeating and evicting the British-backed Syrian king Faysal in 1920, France, in a divide-and-rule strategy, partitioned Syrian territories into four parts, one of which was Latakia, where most of the population was Alawite. Alawite territory was geographically crucial because French forces could use it to control the whole Levant coast—the eastern portion of the Mediterranean Sea. Although Latakia lost its autonomous status in December 1936, the province continued to benefit from a special administrative and financial regime. In return, Alawites helped maintain French rule in the region. For instance, they provided a disproportionate number of soldiers to the French mandate government, forming about half of the troupes spéciales du Levant. Today, as mentioned at the outset, Alawites comprise 12 per cent of Syria's population, or about two million people. They mainly live in the mountainous areas of Latakia on the north-western coast, where they constitute almost two-thirds of the population.

Repression by Bashar al-Assad was being documented well before the advent of and during the Arab Spring. The following comments, drawn from a cross section of opinions, are illustrative. A 2010 Human Rights Watch (HRW) report stated that Syria remained under a state of emergency since 1963, allowing its 'security agencies … to detain people without arrest warrants … and regularly engage in torture. Special courts set up under

Syria's emergency laws ... sentence people following unfair trials.'[23] In March 2011, the *Times* argued that Assad, who was 'learning, with a jolt, that his tyranny is not immune to the Arab Spring', was 'an international menace who specializes in slyly orchestrating a tag team of terror with President Ahmedinejad of Iran'.[24] Meanwhile, the *Guardian* quoted a Syrian writer who talked about the 'historical oppression' of his people and called the Assad regime a form of 'internal colonialism' that has 'robbed ... bombed ... and impeded' Syrians for long, subjecting them to 'arbitrary arrest and imprisonment'.[25]

A month later, the *Times* reported how 'tanks were sent into the heart of a Syrian city [against the ongoing] anti-government rebellion [and protesters were] fired upon'.[26] By May, a leading Syrian human rights organization claimed that 'Syrian security [had begun] releasing detainees with unhealed wounds caused by torture in order to spread panic and fear among people' protesting.[27] In early 2012, with the rebellion descending into a civil-war-like crisis, Genocide Watch cited a report of the UN Office of the High Commissioner for Human Rights (OHCHR) to warn that the 'death toll in Syria [had exceeded] 5,400 [which was] over five times more than the estimated deaths in July 2011', flagging it as conclusive evidence that 'the al-Assad regime is committing intentional crimes against humanity'.[28]

It is useful to delve into the concept of the 'Shia crescent' at this point. It explains, to some extent, the background of the sectarian strife under way, with the realities of demographics playing into civil-war-like situations in many countries, including Yemen. The Shia crescent was not just a geographic designation but a warning that King Abdullah of Jordan had issued after the collapse of Saddam Hussein's regime. It spoke of the consequences of a string of countries where the Shias were either the majority and held power (Iraq and Iran), were of a sizable minority in close proximity (Saudi Arabia and the Gulf states, with the exception of Bahrain, where they constitute an overwhelming majority, but are nevertheless not in power), formed a plurality (Lebanon), or maintained close ties with Iran (Syria, although technically run by Alawites). Without a doubt, his comments belied the racism consistent with the Arab Shias' historical discrimination at the hands of both religious and secular Sunni Arab rulers.[29]

Indeed, King Abdullah is widely accepted to be the first person in a position of authority to have used the term. The *Washington Post*, in December 2004, quoted him as saying:

> If pro-Iranian parties or politicians dominate the new Iraqi government, a new 'crescent' of dominant Shia movements or governments stretching from Iran into Iraq, Syria and Lebanon could emerge to alter the traditional balance of power between the two main Islamic sects and pose new challenges to US interests and allies.[30]

In a 2006 interview with Al-Arabiya TV, Mubarak had deliberately conflated Arab Shias with Iranians and questioned their fidelity: 'There are Shias in all these countries [of the region], significant percentages [of them], and Shias are mostly always loyal to Iran and not the countries where they live.'[31]

Independent commentator Rannie Amiri cites three seminal events 'punctuating the apprehensions of King Abdullah II, Hosni Mubarak, and the royal families from the Gulf countries to Morocco' regarding Shias. First, the return of Ayatollah Ruhollah Khomeini to Iran and the 1979 Islamic Revolution; second, the 2004 fall of Saddam Hussein's regime in Iraq, along with the end of Ba'ath Party rule, both of which had persecuted and brutally suppressed the country's Shia population for decades.[32] The third was the integration of the Shia group Hezbollah into Lebanon's political structure and the widespread popularity of its leader, Sayyed Hassan Nasrallah. After nearly two decades of occupation, with Hezbollah forcing the Israelis to withdraw from Lebanon in 2000 and battling them to a draw in the July 2006 war, Nasrallah became one of the most admired leaders in the Middle East. The silence of the region's heads of state when Lebanon came under relentless Israeli bombardment in 2006 was in contrast to the support both he and his Hezbollah had found on Arab streets.

Ingrained in the fifth school of Islam[33] is the notion of resistance against despotic rule and rulers. This dates back to the epic battle fought on the plains of Karbala in present-day Iraq by the grandson of Prophet Muhammad, Hussain, against the tyrannical reign of Caliph Yazid ibn Muawiya in the year 680 CE. Outnumbered by tens of thousands, Hussain and his small band of followers fought bravely but were brutally massacred. The 'tragedy of Karbala' continues to serve as inspiration to the Shia, endowing them with the belief that standing up to oppression and injustice, no matter how great or at what odds, is an act of faith. The events of Karbala were recalled by Khomeini in the 1979 Revolution deposing the Shah and even by anti-government protesters after Iran's elections in June.

Although it would be incorrect to conclude that Shias are in a continuous state of revolt against the established order of the state, their 1991 uprising against Saddam in the aftermath of the first Gulf War, Hezbollah's battles against the militarily superior Israeli army in the 1990s and 2006, and the recent clashes between Zaidi Shia rebels and the governments of Yemen and Saudi Arabia are all viewed with a leery eye by the Sunni political class in the Middle East. The 'Shia crescent' is feared by the Sunnis precisely because if it became a reality, it would threaten their authority and power, and their influence might be swept aside by the people as quickly as was the Shah's.

Saudi Arabia and Bahrain have recently been harshly criticized by HRW for overtly discriminatory practices towards, and torture of, their Shia citizens. If Arab Shias are accorded fair and equal rights, given the full benefits of citizenship, not treated as fifth columnists, not conflated with 'Persians', and allowed the same dignity and religious liberties as all other citizens, domestic harmony would exist and render ineffective the use of sectarianism to further anti-Iranian sentiment.

The prevailing Shia–Sunni rift, coupled with the ongoing conflict, acutely impacted even the region's smallest minorities. The Druze, in particular, need to be mentioned. A discreet sect of Abrahamic unitarians, the Druze, estimated to be about a million in number, have settlements in Syria, Israel, Lebanon and Jordan. Since their relationship with mainstream Islam has been known to be uneasy, they are threatened existentially by the al-Qaeda as well as the ISIS. While the former seeks to forcibly assimilate them as Sunnis, the latter aims at their complete enslavement or extermination. Amidst the tensions, a majority of the Druze in Syria oppose Assad, while the few in the Israel-occupied Golan Heights support his regime. A sizable number of Druze also serve the Israeli state. Nonetheless, since unclaimed car bombings rocked Druze and Christian settlements near Damascus in November 2012, anti-Assad factions such as the Free Syrian Army saw an upsurge in the number of Druze joining their cause.

Insofar as the international community is concerned, it is important to recall three decisive influences that were at play in 2011 and 2012. The first was the expectations raised by the Arab Spring and the second was the Libyan experience, which involved the Security Council's authorization for the use of force and the arming of rebels. Finally, a larger number of other countries felt by this time that Assad should be held to account on domestic processes, including political reform, and that free and fair elections be held through a negotiated political settlement between different Syrian parties.

The previous chapters traced the heightened and misplaced expectations from the Arab Spring and the Libyan experience which, by February 2012, was beginning to go hopelessly wrong. These developments also coincided with the thirtieth anniversary of the Hama massacre. A civil-war-like situation with sectarian overtones was clearly evident in Syria by February 2012. Efforts for a negotiated political settlement in the intervening period were at best feeble and half-hearted.

When India presided over the UN Security Council in August 2011, we managed to obtain Council endorsement for a unanimous statement by the president of the Security Council. The following are the highlights of the Statement at the 6,598th meeting, held on 3 August 2011:

> The Security Council expresses its grave concern at the deteriorating situation in Syria and expresses profound regret at the death of many hundreds of people.
>
> The Security Council calls for an immediate end to all violence and urges all sides to act with utmost restraint, and to refrain from reprisals, including attacks against state institutions.
>
> The Security Council reaffirms its strong commitment to the sovereignty, independence and territorial integrity of Syria. It stresses that the only solution to the current crisis in Syria is through an inclusive and Syrian-led political process, with the aim of effectively addressing the legitimate aspirations and concerns of the population, which will allow the full exercise of fundamental freedoms for its entire population, including that of expression and peaceful assembly.
>
> The Security Council calls on the Syrian authorities to alleviate the humanitarian situation in crisis areas by ceasing the use of force against affected towns, to allow expeditious

and unhindered access for international humanitarian agencies and workers, and cooperate fully with the Office of the High Commissioner for Human Rights.

A unanimous presidential statement from the Security Council calling for a ceasefire and the commencement of an all-inclusive political process appeared to us to be quite an achievement in light of the double vetoes by China and Russia. An additional difficulty was that one of the members of the Council, Lebanon, had difficulty in going along with the contents of the presidential statement. Since I wanted to press ahead, the Security Council secretariat suggested a way forward, drawing on precedents from the 1970s during the Iran–Iraq War.

This extract from the authoritative Procedure(s) of the UN Security Council describes the events:

> A more recent case of dissociation from the Presidential Statement occurred in 2011. At a meeting held on 3 August, the President (India) read out a Presidential Statement on Syria, which he prefaced by stating, 'After consultation among Council members, I have been authorized to make the following statement on their behalf'. The Deputy Permanent Representative of Lebanon then took the floor. She first quoted the Permanent Representative of Lebanon as having affirmed at an earlier meeting that 'what takes place in Lebanon affects Syria, and what takes place in Syria affects Lebanon'. She then stated, 'As Lebanon believes that Presidential Statement S/PRST/2011/16 adopted today does not help to address the current situation in Syria, Lebanon dissociates itself from the statement.'[34]

Since the dissociation statement was made after the statement had been adopted by the Council, the Lebanese statement was entered into the record.

Eight days later, an IBSA delegation comprising senior representatives of India, Brazil and South Africa called on Bashar al-Assad and his foreign minister, Walid Muallem, on 10 August 2011 in Damascus to discuss the situation in Syria and to find a way forward. They were reassured of the president's commitment to the reform process, the introduction of multiparty democracy, including through revision of the constitution in consultation with the people of Syria, and that national dialogue would continue to give shape to the new laws to arrive at a suitable model for the economy. The process of revision of the constitution, the visiting delegation was told, would be completed by February–March 2012. Assad acknowledged that some mistakes had been made by his security forces in the initial stages of the unrest and that efforts were under way to prevent their recurrence. The Syrian foreign minister reiterated that Syria would be a free, pluralistic and multiparty democracy before the end of the year. Following the IBSA initiative, more essentially, there were reports—many credible—that Assad considered the idea of domestic reform and accommodation of the opposition. The granting of amnesty to several extremist prisoners in 2014 provided hints of this later. However, at the time, there were claims that Assad was willing to invite certain members of the opposition for informal discussions. The opposition, nonetheless, emboldened by the three seemingly conventional steps of intervention witnessed in the case of Libya—a Security Council resolution, the arming of rebels and military action—were not willing to meet Assad halfway. Syria has been, in a sense, a sui generis case of both sides wanting settlement only on their terms.

In some respects, the IBSA initiative was unique in that it was genuinely anchored in the belief that if both sides walked back from the violence and Assad was held accountable for corrective action domestically, it could provide the basis for a genuine Syrian peace process. The mainstream thinking and the dominant narrative was that as a result of this process, Assad would step down. In retrospect, the main and only difference between all parties boiled down to when Assad would have to step down, with the Saudis and the Gulf Cooperation Council (GCC)—backed by the British, the French, and, most of the time, by the Americans—insisting that his stepping down was a precondition for the process to start. The Russians, who in 2011 under Medvedev could still have exercised some leverage with the Syrians, were not willing to agree to the predetermined sequentiality sought to be imposed by the GCC.

There were two factors that the somewhat simplistic approach of the GCC had not taken into account. One was the widely held belief that if Assad were to step aside, or be physically removed, there would be a bloodbath, with the annihilation of the 12 per cent Alawite population. Given the deep sectarian divide, it was not clear which country could, or would, provide security guarantees. The other consideration, not always explicitly mentioned, was the other elephant in the room, Iran. With Russia, as a permanent member of the Security Council, required in any negotiated settlement between the parties, there was gross underestimation of the need to requisition the help of Iran, Russia's ally in the region. As with most other contentious issues that affect the region, the countries of the Middle East invariably failed to agree to include Iran and Israel on a possible list of invitees to a regional peace process.

It is entirely possible, as the Russians continued to argue from 2012 onwards, that whilst they had qualitatively higher interests in Syria than in Libya and the Council's decision on Syria came under Putin's leadership, their leverage with Assad was overestimated. In fairness to the Russian thinking and position, intervention on behalf of an armed opposition with barely distinguishable links to terrorist groups, as was being suggested by either side, did not merit serious consideration—more so in the context of the unfolding Libyan experience. But it also became increasingly clear that the US, which could have leaned on the Gulf states to allow a ceasefire and an all-Syrian peace process to commence, was itself flip-flopping.

On 14 April 2012, with renewed determination to make a tentatively agreed ceasefire work, the Security Council passed Resolution 2042, which authorized the dispatch of an advance team of up to thirty unarmed military observers to Syria to monitor compliance with the 'ceasefire agreement'. Annexed to the resolution was the six-point proposal of the joint special envoy of the United Nations and the Arab League, Kofi Annan. Given the scale of violence and brutalization on the ground, the six-point proposal was, at once, both visionary as also bordering on the reckless.

The proposal urged commitments towards: one, 'an inclusive Syrian-led political process', even if it required an interlocutor; two, 'an effective United Nations supervised cessation of armed violence' from all sides; three, the 'timely provision of humanitarian assistance to all areas affected by the fighting', ensured by a 'daily two-hour humanitarian pause' in hostilities; four, intensifying the 'pace and scale of release of arbitrarily detained persons'; five, freedom of movement for journalists; and six, freedom of association, especially for peaceful demonstrations. The unarmed observers were tasked with establishing and maintaining contact with both sides of the conflict. Neither the armed opposition groups, encouraged by their supporters, nor the security forces had any real incentive in making the ceasefire stick or work.

Annan, speaking at the Brookings Institution in Washington on 18 October 2012, said he was able to broker an agreement among the major powers on the six-step Syrian transition plan at a meeting in Geneva in June, attended by both Hillary Clinton and Russian foreign minister Sergei Lavrov. But immediately after the meeting, the US and European nations went to the Security Council to try to get a resolution under Chapter VII that Russia had made clear it opposed, because such a resolution had been used to authorize NATO military interventions in Libya. Russia and China vetoed the measure, Annan quit a month later, and the Syrian conflict has grown more militarized.

The Syrian conflict was 'not winner-take-all', Annan said. 'Neither side [is going to] give up, unless presented with a [political] alternative.'

Military intervention is not the answer in every situation, Annan observed further, adding that in the case of Syria, he believes it would make things worse. Syria would not implode, he said, but would explode, and spread instability and sectarian strife across the region, as increasingly witnessed.

The question that now stands is: is Syria irretrievable?

According to Reuters, Amos Gilad, the strategic adviser to Israeli defence minister Moshe Yaalon, expressed fears in June 2015 that Israel's neighbour Syria may be 'undergoing a de facto partition', noting that Assad 'controlled just a fifth of Syria, and may end up in charge of a rump state dominated by his minority Alawite sect'. 'Syria is gone. Syria is dying', he said, predicting that history will remember Assad as 'the one who lost Syria'. The report argued that given Assad's steady loss of territory, 'pro-government forces [were] focusing their efforts on shoring up control over a western area of Syria stretching north from Damascus through Homs and Hama to the Mediterranean coast, including the heartland of the Alawites'. Israel—despite being a long-time enemy of Syria—has meanwhile preferred 'largely ... to keep out of the insurgency next door', while worrying that 'Assad could be toppled by more hostile Sunni Islamist insurgents'.[35]

It was clear in 1982, when the senior Assad carried out the

Muammar Gaddafi, the leader of Libya from 1969 to 2011. In his last appearance at the United Nations in September 2009, he delivered an extended incomprehensible diatribe. Public perception of him was so unfavourable that the Libyan Permanent Mission to the UN in New York could not secure hotel accommodation for him and his entourage. He was brutally killed in October 2011, six months after the UN authorized military action in Libya.

family, circa 1994. While Hafez al-Assad (seated) ruled Syria with an iron grip ecades from 1971, his son Bashar (standing, second from left) took over after 2000 and has presided over the unending civil war in the country since 201

China and Russia exercising their vetoes on Syria in the Security Council for the first time on 4 October 2011, with Nigeria's permanent representative, Joy Ogwu, presiding.

Ambassador Puri presiding over the UN Security Council in August 2011. He was president of the Council once again in November 2012. To his right is Ban Ki-moon and t

Syrian refugees arrive at Skala Sykamias, Lesbos island, Greece, in October 2015. Since the start of the civil war in 2011, more than 7 million people have been internally displaced in Syria while over 4 million, out of a national population of 22 million, have fled the country.

The temple of Baal-Shamin in the ancient city of Palmyra, Syria. The Islamic State destroyed many of the city's nearly 2,000-year-old structures before the Syrian army

Ambassador Puri with then US secretary of state Hillary Clinton and Indian external affairs minister S.M. Krishna in September 2011.

Ambassador Puri with Susan Rice, his American counterpart on the Security Council at the time and later the US national security adviser, in August 2011.

Ali Abdullah Saleh, president of Yemen from 1990 to 2012. In 2011, over 16,000 Yemenis took to the streets in Sana'a, the capital city, in mass protests against unemployment and a worsening economy. The demand list soon escalated to calls for the resignation of Saleh, who eventually gave up power in favour of his vice-president, Abd Rabbuh Mansur Hadi.

Viktor Yanukovych, the then president of Ukraine, with Vladimir Putin, the then prime minister of Russia, in April 2011. In February-March 2014, with Putin now president, Russia annexed Ukraine's largely Russophone Crimean peninsula, days after the Ukrainian

Prime Minister Rajiv Gandhi signing the Indo-Sri Lanka Peace Accord with President J.R. Jayewardene of Sri Lanka on 27 July 1987 as Hardeep Puri, then posted at India's high commission in Colombo, turns the pages of the document. Others in the picture include: (L to R, front row) Panruti S. Ramachandran, P. Chidambaram, K. Natwar Singh, P.V. Narasimha Rao and A.C.S. Hameed; assisting President Jayewardene is his secretary, Menikdiwela; and (L to R, second row) High Commissioner J.N. Dixit, Deputy High Commissioner Nirupam Sen and Joint Secretary Kuldeep Sachdev.

Farewell call:
Ambassador
Puri gifting
a portrait
of Mahatma
Gandhi to
Secretary-
General Ban
Ki-moon on
the completion
of his term
at the UN in
February 2013.

murderous assault on Hama, and clear as daylight when his son used brutal force against his own citizens, that the ruling dispensation would go to any extent to stay in power. Given that Alawites constitute only 12 per cent of Syria's population, the government is not representative. Also, its legitimacy has to be anchored in its ability to co-opt the support of citizens other than the Alawite population. It could also be argued that given the death toll, the physical destruction, and the overall unravelling of the Syrian state, it is perhaps no longer even in the interest of the Alawite population that Assad continues.

The easy success in achieving regime change in Libya—even though it had costly repercussions—coloured judgement and led to unrealistic expectations in Syria. Syria, however, proved to be an entirely different ball game. It has taken four years for the major stakeholders to realize that a military solution in Syria may not work.

Addressing the UNGA on 28 September 2015, this is what Obama had to say:[36]

> But while military power is necessary, it is not sufficient to resolve the situation in Syria. Lasting stability can only take hold when the people of Syria forge an agreement to live together peacefully. The United States is prepared to work with any nation, including Russia and Iran, to resolve the conflict. But we must recognize that there cannot be, after so much bloodshed, so much carnage, a return to the pre-war status quo.

He then went on to make what was perhaps the most significant suggestion on Syria:

> Yes, realism dictates that compromise will be required to end the fighting and ultimately stamp out ISIL. But realism also requires a managed transition away from Assad and to a new leader, and an inclusive government that recognizes there must be an end to this chaos so that the Syrian people can begin to rebuild.

The willingness to work with Russia and Iran and to consider a 'managed transition' from Assad could provide the basis for a possible situation.

The US, Britain, France and some Gulf states have never tried to make a secret of their continued arming of the opposition to Assad. Characterizing those being armed as a 'moderate opposition' amounts to a definitional absurdity. Agence France-Presse (AFP) carried an interesting report on 26 September 2015, according to which the Pentagon had noted that 'a group of US-trained Syrian rebels had handed over ammunition and equipment to Al Qaeda's affiliate in the country, the Al Nusra Front … in exchange for safe passage', contradicting its earlier 'denials of reports that some fighters had either defected or handed over gear'. The article cited Pentagon spokesperson Captain Jeff Davis, who had said that the New Syrian Front 'did, in fact, provide six pick-up trucks and a portion of their ammunition to a suspected Al Nusra Front group'. Colonel Patrick Ryder of the Central Command unit 'overseeing [the] efforts against the Islamic State' observed that 'pick-up vehicles and ammunition represented about 25 percent of the equipment issued to the group by the US-led coalition'. The report concluded that 'the development was another embarrassing setback for the US effort to "train and equip" moderate Syrian rebels to fight IS jihadists in Syria', which was a 'US$ 500-million programme, originally aimed to ready around 5,400 vetted fighters a year for three years', and yet, was failing to find 'suitable candidates' to train.[37]

Meanwhile, the rationale for Russia's direct, as against the four-year-long indirect, involvement in Syria was set out forcefully by Prime Minister Medvedev when he addressed Russian state TV on 17 October 2015:[38]

Of course we are not fighting for specific leaders; we are defending our national interests, on the one hand. And secondly, we have a request from the lawful authorities (of Syria). That is the basis we are working on. The president said it is obvious that if we don't destroy these terrorists there, they will come to Russia. We do not want the IS to head Syria. It should be civilized, legitimate authorities. Who will lead Syria is for the Syrian people to decide. Russia is working on the basis that Assad is the legitimate president. US operations in Syria had 'practically zero' impact on IS. Only Russia's intervention changed the situation.

Earlier in the week, before Medvedev set out Russia's position, Moscow had expressed outrage that the US had declined to host a Russian delegation on Syria led by Medvedev. 'I think this is stupid behaviour. As a result of such decisions or a refusal to hold talks, the Americans just demonstrate their weakness,' Medvedev said.[39]

The last day of September 2015 had marked a major turning point in the Syrian conflict. Russia's move of launching its first air strikes inside Syria had brought an entirely new proxy dynamic to the crisis and upset the regional and global balance of power in the war-battered country. Obama's statement that Russia risked getting embroiled in a quagmire in undertaking military action in Syria was greeted by an angry response from Moscow. This wishful thinking represented an all-time low, claimed Moscow. Russia claimed its jets were targeting ISIS militants. Washington and its allies claimed, however, that Russian strikes seemed to target areas controlled by more moderate rebel groups fighting the regime of Bashar al-Assad. The debate surrounding the use of the term 'moderate' was understandable. The CIA did control or back opposition to the al-Nusra Front in Syria. The immediate aim of the Russian air strikes was to shore up the Assad regime, believed the West. The attack on Homs, in particular, was viewed as critical. The underlying motivation for Russia's bold action appeared designed to protect its geostrategic interests in the region. The country has long had a naval facility in Tartus, and established an airbase in Latakia to facilitate its 2015–16 military intervention in the crisis. If these were bombed, it would be a strategic blow to Russia.

The move also pre-empted a Western plan to threaten the current regime in Damascus. The large flow of refugees in the summer of 2015 stemming from the Syrian conflict had begun to focus European minds on how to resolve the underlying problem. Britain, France, Jordan, Turkey and Washington had commenced serious discussions on the need and feasibility of creating a no-fly zone over Syria. Those zones were intended to create areas of safety inside Syria for opposition forces and for thousands of displaced people, reducing the refugee flow. The tactic would theoretically prevent the Syrian air force from attacking rebels and their supporters. But the presence of Russia makes it almost impossible for the US and its allies to risk such a no-fly zone, lest it choose to enter into a serious global confrontation.

As the Damascus government was weakening and showing fatigue following nearly five years of civil war and sanctions, Putin 'moved to stop the rot', as one former Western intelligence official put it. Through use of his air force, navy, and, possibly, soldiers, he would be effectively propping up the Assad government to allow for a carving up of a 'useful Syria',[40] including Damascus and the home of Assad's Alawite sect in the west, around Latakia.

Will the direct Russian military engagement facilitate an eventual political deal or settlement? All the pointers are, however, in an opposite and more worrisome direction. The military intervention by Russia adds a new layer of uncertainty to the possibility of a political solution to the Syrian conflict. During the seventieth session of the General Assembly in September 2015, it became clear that both the US and Russia remained at odds on how to move forward on the Syrian quandary. Obama spoke of the 'dangerous currents' that risk 'pulling us back into a darker, more disordered world', a euphemistic rebuke of Russia's action in Ukraine (discussed in a later chapter), and questioned the actions of 'major powers that want to ignore international rules and impose order through force of military power'. 'In accordance with this logic, we should support tyrants like Bashar al-Assad, who drops barrel bombs to massacre innocent civilians because the alternative is surely worse,' he said in comments that seemed to be aimed directly at Putin.[41]

Meanwhile, Putin expressed the view that 'to refuse to cooperate with the Syrian government and its armed forces, who are valiantly fighting terrorism face to face, would be an enormous mistake'. But there was hope in Putin's address. In an attempt to get one up on his American counterpart, he called on the need for a 'genuinely broad international coalition' to fight the ISIS, including a Security Council resolution to 'coordinate' military action. This idea received indirect backing from several countries, including France.

In a piece carried by the Associated Press (AP) in October 2015, Henry Kissinger argued that Russia's unilateral military action in Syria was the latest symptom of the disintegration of the American role in the region's stability since the days of the Arab-Israeli war of 1973. The destruction of ISIS, Kissinger felt, was more urgent than the overthrow of Assad, who had already lost over half the area he once controlled. Insofar as the future of Syria was concerned, Kissinger recommended:

> As the terrorist region is being dismantled and brought under non-radical political control, the future of the Syrian State should be dealt with concurrently. A federal structure could then be built between the Alawite and Sunni positions. If the Alawite regions become part of a Syrian federal system, a context will exist for the role of Mr Assad, which reduces the risks of genocide or chaos leading to terrorist triumph.[42]

Echoing Kissinger's point, Irish journalist Patrick Cockburn noted that the 'drama of Russian military action, while provoking a wave of Cold War rhetoric from Western leaders and the media, has taken attention away from ... the failure over the last year of the US air campaign—which began in Iraq in August 2014 before being extended to Syria—to weaken Islamic State and other al-Qaeda-type groups'. He reminded readers how, despite the Western coalition's 7,323 air strikes by October 2015, the great majority of them by the US Air Force, 'the campaign has demonstrably failed to contain IS'. Thus, the Irish journalist saw Russia's participation in the actions against the Islamic State crisis as a mere bid to take advantage of this failure, typical of a 'great power rivalry'.[43] In a piece for the *Independent*, Cockburn also pointed out that Russia's involvement would significantly risk and inhibit the efforts of Turkey, which has been more concerned about the military–political assertions by the Syrian Kurds along its Syrian–Kurdish border, as part of the anti-ISIS coalition.[44]

At the time of finalizing this chapter in April 2016, the ground realities continued to paint a discouraging picture, in general, and posed adverse consequences for some nations, in particular. Since October 2015, multilateral talks on the Syrian crisis, which commenced at Vienna amongst eighteen countries, the UN and the European Union (EU), have aimed at a political solution to the mess in Iraq and Syria. Initially, Washington continued to show suspicion over Iran's participation in the discussions, despite Ban Ki-moon urging otherwise. The talks could only begin, in the first place, after Moscow's demand on Egypt's inclusion was yielded to. The deliberations, nonetheless, were quick to stagnate, as Russia and the US disagreed on Assad's post-conflict political role on the one hand, and Saudi Arabia continued to doubt Iran's part in the negotiations on the other. By November, despite the prevailing discord and the Russian scepticism over the working groups at Vienna, a joint peace plan was issued by all members of the process, which was endorsed by the UNSC's Resolution 2254 in December. No consensus on the political futures of Assad or his opposition in Syria could be reached, however.

Meanwhile, even as its rifts with Iran remained, Saudi Arabia, an important regional member of the West-led coalition against the ISIS, kept a majority of its military focus directed at its bombardment of the Houthi rebels in Yemen, levelling a Médecins Sans Frontières (MSF) medical facility in the process in January 2016. Speaking to the *New York Times*, UN Deputy Secretary-General Jan Eliasson observed that the 'deep distrust between Saudi Arabia and Iran' has always been 'one of the most important obstacles' during conflicts in the Middle East.[45] Likewise, Turkey too kept itself engrossed with the Syrian Kurds.

In January, another round of the talks began at Geneva, and was to include Syria's government and opposition. For the process, Staffan de Mistura, the freshly appointed UN special envoy for Syria, intended to rake in a wide array of local stakeholders. While Turkey, however, pressured the exclusion of the Syrian Kurds from the talks, the Saudi-supported High Negotiation Committee (HNC) of the Syrian opposition was reluctant to participate. By the month's end, when the HNC did send a delegation to Geneva, it included a noted member of the Salafist Jaysh al-Islam outfit, which was deemed a terrorist front by Russia and Iran for its fight against Assad. The deliberations, nevertheless, were under way by 1 February 2016, only to be suspended merely two days later in the aftermath of the northern Aleppo offensive by the government forces. On 22 February, Russia and the US jointly imposed a forceful cessation of hostilities amidst all parties committed to Resolution 2254. The ceasefire, although, did not apply to the ISIS, thus leaving enough scope for continued worsening of the situation in the Middle East.

While there is an ongoing attempt to make the ceasefire last in order to produce a lasting political process for all stakeholders, Russia's direct military involvement in the crisis, which commenced in September 2015 upon Assad's request and resulted in six months of aerial bombing against the opposing rebels, has only left the Syrian government's position relatively strengthened. Even though Putin ordered a withdrawal, by and large, from Syria in March 2016, Russia continues to maintain an active military role in the situation, especially since it now has an established airbase in Latakia, sharing space with the Bassel Al-Assad International Airport.

Though elusive, nonetheless, peace for Syria continues to be sought through sporadic international efforts. On 18 April 2016, as the *New York Times* reported:

> In a strongly worded statement, the White House said that Mr. Obama had urged Mr. Putin to use his influence with President Bashar al-Assad of Syria to press him to stop attacks against opposition forces and abide by his commitment to [the] ceasefire.[46]

5

YEMEN AND THE OTHER
ELEPHANT IN THE TENT

My earliest recollections of Yemen are clouded in memories of
brief stopovers in the leafy port city of Aden in the late 1950s
or early 1960s, accompanying my parents by ship from Bombay
(now Mumbai), to Karachi, Aden, Port Said in Egypt and then on
to Genoa in Italy. That brief stopover was repeated three years later
in the reverse direction when my father completed his assignment
and we were returning to India. That was the prescribed route
then, or, in Government of India parlance, the 'approved' route
for anyone assigned to an Indian diplomatic mission in Europe.
Air travel was still relatively rare. Two identical passenger ships
of Italian shipping company Lloyd Triestino (now called Italia
Marittima), MV *Asia* and MV *Victoria*, built in 1953, with a
displacement of 11,500 tons, operated as luxury liners between
Italy and the Far East. My memories are of a thriving port city,
bustling commerce, and the good looks of its population. I was
too young to understand the unfolding political developments
a year before the Yemen Arab Republic, also known as North
Yemen, was set up in 1962. This set the ground for the civil war
between the royalists, who had hitherto ruled the country, and
the republicans backed by Egypt.

Fast-forward from 1962 to 1978. Ali Abdullah Saleh came to power and held office—first as the president of North Yemen until 1990 and then as that of the current Republic of Yemen, formed after the North's unification with South Yemen that year—till he was forced to quit in 2011. His method of ruling, which he likened to 'dancing on the heads of snakes', would include 'destroying civic forms of association and any kind of institution that existed in Yemen, whether from the Zaidi monarchical period or from the few presidents who ruled before him in the republic'.[1]

Yemen featured regularly on the agenda of the Security Council during India's tenure in 2011–12. In early 2011, over 16,000 Yemenis, exasperated with the existing system, took to the streets in Sana'a, the capital city, in mass protests emulating the Arab Spring. While the protests initially echoed the reasons for dissent in Tunisia and Egypt—unemployment, worsening economic conditions, and so on—the demand list soon escalated to calls for Saleh to resign, even as attempts were made to make changes to the constitution that would allow Saleh to continue in office for another ten years.[2] The GCC drew up an agreement forcing Saleh to give up power in favour of his vice-president, Abd Rabbuh Mansur Hadi.

Fifty-two years after I last saw Yemen, I was all set to visit the country again. This time because India was serving its seventh term as a non-permanent member of the Security Council. That visit—which would have been my third—alas, could not take place. The physical security of the fifteen members of the UN Security Council could not be guaranteed for a short five-hour transit visit not even involving an overnight stay.

The Security Council undertakes visits to global hot spots, including those on the Council's radar and those where there are missions mandated by the Security Council. In 2012, the Council was strongly inclined to include a short stopover in

Yemen en route to Afghanistan. To cut a long story short, even this had to be called off in spite of the US offering to provide physical security, including armed personnel carriers (APCs) for the visiting members of the Council. The undersecretary-general for safety and security in the UN, Gregory Starr, decided that because Sana'a airport was not secure for landings and take-offs, security clearance for the visit could not be granted. The visit finally took place in early 2013, on 27 January, when India was no longer on the Council.

In April 2011, the deal for Saleh's exit prepared by the GCC saw him saying 'yes' twice, only to back down until he finally signed the power transfer agreement on 23 November 2011. As a central component of the negotiated agreement, a National Dialogue Conference was established (eventually commencing in March 2013) to bring together 'all forces and political actors, including youth, the Southern movement, the Houthis, other political parties, civil society representatives and women'[3] for the rebuilding of a future Yemen. Many, however, still felt excluded from this arrangement and this feeling only grew over time. In May 2012, the secretary-general issued a statement encouraging all sides to play a full and constructive role in implementing Yemen's political transition agreement in accordance with Security Council Resolution 2014. In June 2012, a Security Council resolution focused on the second phase of the transition and expressed the Council's readiness to consider further measures, including those part of the implementation mechanism under Article 41[4] of the Charter. The second phase of the transition process was to focus on:

- Convening an all-inclusive National Dialogue Conference;
- Restructuring the security and armed forces under a unified professional national leadership structure and ending all armed conflicts;

- Steps to address transitional justice and to support national reconciliation; and
- Constitutional and electoral reform and holding general elections by February 2014.

The resolution also mentions the threat of al-Qaeda in the Arabian peninsula (AQAP). In 2013, the presidential statement reiterated Council members' readiness to consider sanctions against individuals who interfered in the political transition process.

As we left the Security Council on the completion of India's two-year term in 2012, I recalled a conversation with Abdullah al-Saidi, the permanent representative of Yemen, well before he left his post and joined the New York–based IPI in March 2011. Al Saidi is a cerebral and erudite diplomat—a thinking person well liked by his peers. I had inquired about how Yemen would fare in the Arab Spring and how the dynamic of the Houthi revolt in the northern part of the country would play out. He appeared sanguine. I was less so.

Growing somewhat in tandem with other developments since 2004 was the Zaidi Houthi movement, led by descendants of the monarchs who had ruled Yemen for years before the establishment of a republican state. The Houthis belong to a Shia sect—Zaidism—which advocates rule by an imam, a sayyid, in a legitimate Islamic government. The movement started off as a revivalist response to the growing Salafist influence in the northern part of the country, with the latter seeming to enjoy the support of the Saleh government as part of a divide-and-rule strategy. State support for American operations against Islamic extremist groups, in this case the al-Qaeda, worsened tensions between the Houthis and the government; and many rounds of conflict led to the deaths of over a thousand people and the displacement of more than 100,000 from the northern territory.

In the context of Islamic extremism and the growth of terrorism, Yemen earned the dubious distinction of being the first country where a terrorist group demonstrated its ability to hold territory, with a division of the al-Qaeda—the AQAP—managing to set up its primary bases in certain remote areas of the country. The AQAP was able to achieve this primarily through marriage ties in the region and the state's inability to fight back.[5] This left the Houthis, as Bernard Haykel, director of the Institute for Trans-regional Study of the Contemporary Middle East, North Africa and Central Asia at Princeton University, asserts, as the group most capable of defeating the AQAP. But the possibility of the Houthis taking on the al-Qaeda has been obliterated by repeated attempts by the Saudis and their Western allies, primarily the US, to subdue the former.

Saudi Arabia has always been the other elephant in the tent, sometimes visible, at other times less so. Its uncharacteristic boldness in its move from discreet influence to brazen military intervention in the politics of Yemen can only partially be explained by the assumption that the Houthis are 'an Iranian proxy force similar to Hezbollah in Lebanon'.[6] For the Saudis, Yemen has always been a red line and Iran was not to meddle in it.[7] This has motivated Saudi involvement in Yemen for some time now, and has allowed Saudi leaders to defend their campaign 'as a strike against Iranian influence in the Middle East'.[8] If the Houthis emerged victorious, it would imply, according to this view, the Saudi kingdom sharing its borders with a Shia-ruled country, which may subsequently drive the oppressed Shias of the kingdom to rebel, thereby resulting in Saudi Arabia losing its 'own sphere of influence to the Iranians'.[9] Explaining the Saudi intervention, Mustafa Alani of the Gulf Research Centre blamed the US's 2015 nuclear deal with Iran that would increase Iranian influence in the region, and further said:

It started with Lebanon, then Syria, then Iraq and now Yemen. It's like a domino, and Yemen is the first attempt to stop the domino … Now there is an awakening in the region, a counter strategy, and Yemen is the testing ground. It is not just about Yemen, it is about changing the balance of power in the region.[10]

Hezbollah, in public perception, is associated with the Houthis.[11] Both a political party and a paramilitary organization, it is disciplined and has a professional fighting force. Even though the Iranian Revolutionary Guard—a branch of the country's armed forces—reportedly supports the Houthis financially and militarily, helping them develop along the lines of the Hezbollah, failure to acknowledge the deeper roots of the Houthis in Yemen, and ignoring that their relationship with the Yemeni state predates any apparent association with Iran or the Hezbollah group constitute a major error of analysis. Yet, the Saudis have made that very mistake, which has resulted in innumerable blunders in a country already fraught with violence and conflict. Ironically, if the Saudis were to succeed, it could possibly benefit Iran. For, the Houthis, even if removed from power, would not be annihilated and would be replaced with a weak government in need of permanent support—resulting in a 'long bleeding of Saudi resources at the expense of further internal instability'.[12]

The military operations carried out by the Saudis in Yemen, beginning in 2015, with the corporate help of the US and Britain,[13] included the bombing of several areas and have led to the death of countless civilians. In a bid to defeat the Houthis, the Saudis have been training some Yemenis, which has resulted in intense battles that have destroyed cities. They have justified their actions by claiming that Hadi specifically requested help in March,[14] citing Article 51[15] of the UN Charter, against the Houthi advances that threatened his rule. The justification for Saudi military intervention is, however, problematic on many grounds. To begin with, as a news report[16] by the Nairobi-based Integrated Regional Information Networks (IRIN) points out, Article 51 deals with threats from the outside, while the threats to Hadi's rule came from a domestic group—the Houthis—and did not directly pose a threat to the Saudis. In addition, having resigned (even though a large part of the international community continued to refer to him as the president of Yemen) and fled the country following Houthi military aggression in January 2015, Hadi had lost legitimacy to seek international help; and determining who really was in control in Yemen was challenging as most territories and most of the armed forces came under the control of the Houthis. In seeking help from Saudi Arabia, what Hadi was essentially doing has been described in the following words: '… a quasi-legitimate president living in Saudi Arabia asks that state to go bomb and strafe his own country and his own people, and invokes collective security as justification'.[17]

A Middle East analyst examines the legality of the intervention and explains why the Saudi military actions in Yemen are justifiable neither by domestic nor by international humanitarian laws.[18]

According to domestic Yemeni law, intervention by other countries to stabilize its domestic unrest requires parliamentary approval (Article 37) and 'a decision by the National Defence Council, in a meeting presided over by the elected president of Yemen' (Article 38). Neither of these conditions was met for the Saudi intervention.

As per international law, Saudi intervention would have been legitimate if Hadi still held office as the president of Yemen when he requested the Saudis, who in turn had sought and been granted permission from the Security Council for the use of force.

From the perspective of humanitarian law, the Saudis' 'use of illegal weapons has violated the laws of war and resulted in the killing of innocent civilians and children, as well as destruction of infrastructure in Yemen'. Besides, 'by preventing the delivery of humanitarian aid to the war victims and injured persons, Saudi Arabia has caused a devastating humanitarian catastrophe for the people of Yemen, specifically, and the region as a whole'.

In undertaking the actions they did, the Saudis have clearly overstepped the legal system of not just Yemen but also the international community, in addition to demonstrating complete disregard for the Security Council. The colossal damage done in Yemen—killing innocent civilians, weakening the infrastructure and worsening the 'extremist situation' by creating space for them to expand through frequent attacks on Yemen's southern border[19]—'has created bad blood between Yemenis and their rich Gulf neighbors that will poison relations for years'.[20]

What has also drawn the ire of sections of the international community is the Saudi leadership that has been described as 'impulsive and rash'.[21] The military offensive under the leadership of the newly ordained deputy Crown prince and defence minister has come in for particularly harsh criticism. Eighty-year-old King Salman bin Abdulaziz Al Saud delegated all power to the apple of his eye, twenty-nine-year-old Mohammad Bin Salman Al Saud, on 23 January 2015, proving that Saudi Arabia is an 'absolute monarchy with absolutist power'.[22] As events unfolding in 2015 demonstrated, the defence minister, new to the political dynamics of the region, appeared to be unaware of its many pitfalls, primarily because the Saudi bureaucracy does not appear to have passed on knowledge of experiences of dealing with Yemen to its next generation of policymakers. Further, the Saudis were used to dealing with their neighbour through tribal leaders and people with long-standing relationships with Saudi Arabia, and none of those people or relationships was alive or sustained.[23] The young Salman's character traits were demonstrated to the world when he staked his country's future, along with his own, on being victorious in the war. To achieve this, within two months of his appointment in January 2015 and with no prior military experience, he gave orders for Operation Decisive Storm, coercing the Houthis through air strikes to restore Hadi's government.[24] Instead of sticking to the traditional Saudi approaches that avoided any engagement in domestic or regional violence, the younger Salman convinced his father of the need for a quick and swift war to defeat the Houthis.

This placed Riyadh in a quandary. The Saudi request for ground troops from Pakistan and several other countries to take on the Houthis resulted in some loss of face. Apart from explicit help from some countries, with the United Arab Emirates sending in over 3,000 troops, and Qatar and Senegal deploying more than 1,000 and 2,100 troops in Yemen respectively, the responses from all others were cautious and carefully hedged. Pakistani prime minister Nawaz Sharif, regarded as close to the Saudi royal family because he himself had sought refuge there in difficult times, voiced his concern about how the Saudis had 'prematurely jumped into the war without a viable strategy for victory' and were now 'panicking' while trying to find allies for their campaign.[25] Yet, Saudi Arabia enjoyed internal support for the coalition-led intervention.

It was widely believed that Saudi Arabia had given an international dimension to what was primarily a domestic conflict,[26] possibly to demonstrate its strength and capacity to the Arab world as well as the US. Despite this, the Saudis managed to garner support from the UK and the US. Although the latter's primary interest in Yemen stems from the al-Qaeda's presence in the country, its unsolicited participation in the conflict has had an effect contrary to its aims. By supporting the Saudis in the attacks against the Houthis—the only group deemed capable of fighting the AQAP—American policy further strengthened the hold of the al-Qaeda in the region.

In its issue of 25 March 2015, *Foreign Affairs* asserted the need for the West to recognize the significance of Houthi leadership:

The United States may need to look beyond alarmist slogans and flag burning to open a direct line of communication with Houthi leadership. Hadi's government is powerless and has fled a political confrontation with the new Houthi government in acknowledgment that it lacks sufficient public and tribal support to wage a campaign against the Houthis. Those loyal to the Houthi family have emerged as one of the most effective military forces combating the expansion of al Qaeda and the Islamic State of Iraq and al-Sham in the Arabian Peninsula. If the West turns its back on the Houthi leadership because of slogans, opportunistic aid from Iran, or Hadi's protestations, it might end up forsaking a serious partner in the Middle East.[27]

The US built up the military capacity of some groups in Yemen to fight the al-Qaeda during the reign of Saleh as head of state. Most of these groups, trained and armed, ended up fighting Saleh's enemies. In one particular well-documented instance, one of the multiple drone attacks that the US carried out on the basis of coordinates provided by Saleh proved to be a major embarrassment. The coordinates provided had nothing to do with the al-Qaeda, and the convoy, in fact, belonged to Saleh's enemy.[28] Haykel goes so far as to describe the US's policy in Yemen as a 'catastrophe', suggesting that Yemen 'is a real mess' and that the 'United States has wasted a tremendous amount of goodwill, abused its power through the killing of lots of civilians, and has increased the presence of al-Qaeda in Yemen', despite having classified the AQAP in Yemen as the 'network's deadliest franchise'[29] earlier. The US has viewed Yemen through a single prism—of the al-Qaeda and terrorism. In first supporting Saleh for thirty years, then Hadi, followed by the Houthis against the al-Qaeda, and now the Saudis against Yemen and the Houthis, the Americans have been accused of changing allies in Yemen as if they were changing shirts.[30] Saudi Arabia's deep mistrust of the US was embedded in this oscillating attitude, which was apparent in the former attacking Yemen without informing the US, in a show of strength.[31] Another reason for the Saudis adopting an independent position could be the fear of abandonment by the US—which has in the past deserted common allies Mubarak and Saleh. In addition, the economics of shale oil has altered not just the position of the US as the biggest buyer of Saudi oil to that of a major competitor but has also jeopardized the profits of the Saudi ruling class and their role in world politics.[32]

Irrespective of the reasons for Saudi or Western intervention, Yemen's condition has continued to deteriorate. There have been repeated attempts to bring the warring parties to the negotiating table. Jamal Benomar, who was the UN mediator in the negotiations that led to the Transition Agreement in 2011 and was later, in 2012, appointed UN special representative of the secretary-general for Yemen,[33] urged them to bring the 'spiraling conflict to a halt' and 'shape the country's future without causing total social collapse'.[34] He played a key role in bringing the National Dialogue Conference—a ten-month series of peace talks—to a close in January 2014.

The latest phase of the Sana'a military intervention, including comprehensive aerial bombardment, commenced on 25 March 2015. In a visit to Saudi Arabia, Benomar presented the outline of an agreement that he nearly pulled off. This involved the warring Yemeni parties, including twelve political and tribal factions which were close to a power-sharing deal. The Houthis had apparently agreed to withdraw their militias from the cities they had occupied, and even approved of the inclusion of Hadi in the executive body that would temporarily run the government. The only problem was that Benomar was presenting this to his designated Saudi interlocutors at a time when internal power equations in the House of Saud were dramatically changing. As mentioned earlier, given that the deputy Crown prince had staked his future on being victorious in the war on Yemen, there was no scope for Benomar's plan to work.

Benomar himself faced a lot of unfair criticism for becoming an active political player, instead of being an unbiased mediator, and was driven to resign from his post later in 2015 following loss of support from the Gulf nations. His resignation was accepted by the secretary-general on 16 April 2015. Ismail Ould Cheikh Ahmed of Mauritania was announced as his successor.

After having sanctioned a political mission under Benomar, the UN's role in Yemen could be characterized as passive and inert at best. The UN's reluctance to assert itself could be on account of any number of reasons. In any recording of history, the kid-glove approach to Saudi Arabia and the perceptible political tilt against Iran by the US must be correctly mentioned.

Presidential statements released by the Security Council also failed to make any mention of Saudi Arabia, let alone condemn its actions.[35] While the UN did make attempts at brokering talks in Geneva about the deteriorating situation in Yemen as it slid deeper into turmoil—with more than 21.2 million people (more than 80 per cent of the population) in need of aid, around thirteen million facing food shortages, and 9.4 million experiencing difficulties in access to water—they failed to bridge differences.[36] One of the key reasons for the failure of these talks may have been the clash between their primary objective, which was to secure a 'ceasefire, agreeing on a withdrawal plan for the Houthis and stepping up humanitarian aid deliveries', and the demands made by Hadi and other representatives of the state that made it clear that there was no room for negotiation with the Houthis.[37]

What needs to be noted here is that while the Security

Council was taking steps, albeit small, towards initiating dialogue between the various actors involved in the conflict, Hadi and his government continued to impose conditions such as 'no negotiations', thereby using the Council to achieve narrow partisan political purposes, while Prime Minister Khalid Bahah called the Geneva meeting, which was to be held a week later on 15 June 2015, 'merely a consultative process'.[38] Hadi failed to acknowledge that the Houthis, marginalized for sixty years, accounted for nearly 40 per cent of the population and could not be asked to simply withdraw from large areas of the country they had successfully seized.

On 27 January 2013, a Security Council mission was sent to Yemen, the primary purpose of which was 'to reaffirm the continued support of the Security Council for the ongoing political transition process in Yemen, in accordance with the Gulf Cooperation Council Initiative and Implementation Mechanism leading towards elections in February 2014'.[39] This mission expressed its readiness to resort to 'further measures, including under Article 41 of the Charter of the United Nations' in the event of there being 'actions aimed at undermining the Government and the transition process'.[40] The Council was essentially opposed to the idea of using force in Yemen, even while identifying the precariousness of the humanitarian situation in the country. The report also makes a few references to the 'Friends of Yemen', which includes some members of the international community, who were to assist Yemen through the crisis and democratic transition by offering economic and political support, and helping form relevant policies and reform structures.

It is ironic that Riyadh, one of the 'Friends', itself bears major responsibility for causing further chaos and devastation in the country today. The UN's political stand has remained largely unaltered, a hands-off posture involving the expression of concern without wishing to even acknowledge the real problem. Even the EU recognized that the Saudi bombings had 'dramatically worsened the already fragile situation in the country and risked having serious regional consequences'.[41] In the midst of the domestic chaos and foreign military intervention, the UN has merely gone to the extent of declaring Yemen a level-3 humanitarian emergency, the highest on its scale,[42] and condemning Saudi air strikes on Sana'a airport that were hindering the travel of humanitarian aid workers.[43]

The latest Saudi military intervention in Yemen that began in early 2015 was overtly supported by the US. An official statement from the White House confirmed that Obama had ordered 'logistical and military' support to the Saudi-led operations. All the UN had to say was that it was aware of the military operation and was 'still checking details'.[44] UN deputy spokesman Farhan Haq announced to the media, a few hours prior to this military operation being undertaken by the Saudis, that the UN did not believe in military actions to resolve the conflict.[45] In addition to bombing parts of Houthi-held areas in Yemen that killed many civilians, Saudi Arabia also announced its intention of arming anti-Houthi forces,[46] and eventually did so—as the coalition 'dropped weapons to tribes allied to Hadi's government',[47] a move that had already proven to be disastrous in Libya and Syria. At the beginning of the Saudi-led coalition in 2015, Benomar warned: 'It would be an illusion to think that the Houthis could mount an offensive and succeed in taking control of the entire country and it would be equally false to think that President Hadi could assemble sufficient forces to liberate the country from the Houthis.' In this light, he observed that 'any side that would want to push the country in either direction would be inviting a protracted conflict in the vein of an Iraq-Libya-Syria combined scenario ...'[48]

There is increasing realization that what is ensuing in Yemen is not a crisis that can be solved militarily and that the Houthis, who represent almost half the country's population, cannot simply be criminalized and eliminated.[49] Despite this growing awareness, it is appalling that little was done about the Saudi military action. A couple of months into the intervention, the UNOHCHR acknowledged that hundreds of civilians had been killed and at least 300,000 displaced since the start of the Saudi-led air strikes, yet the UN continued to be a silent spectator. It continued to rely on talks, with Ban Ki-moon reiterating 'his urgent call on all Yemeni parties to engage in these consultations in good faith and without pre-conditions in the interest of all Yemeni people'.[50] Generally, the UN has appeared rather helpless and incapable of adopting a stricter stance vis-à-vis the visibly unlawful intervention in the form of use of force carried out by Saudi Arabia and its allies.

Following developments in Iraq in 2003, and in Libya and Syria since 2011, the UN appears to have relegated itself to such irrelevance that Saudi Arabia and its allies have not even attempted to approach the Security Council and seek authorization for the 'use of force' in a country grappling with a serious humanitarian crisis. In April 2015 the Council adopted Resolution 2216, through which it reiterated 'its support for the efforts of the Gulf Cooperation Council in assisting the political transition in Yemen' and commended 'its engagement in this regard'. In doing so, the Council surprisingly went ahead and sided with the aggressors, that is, the Saudis and their coalition members. In October 2015, the UN's humanitarian chief, Stephen O'Brien, appeared alongside Saudi government officials at a press conference, where he welcomed the humanitarian aid offered to Yemen by the King Salman Humanitarian Aid and Relief Centre, and said that the UN had been able 'to establish a strong sense of relationship and partnership' with the agency.[51] Thus the UN was essentially approving the procurement of aid for Yemen from a country that was actively involved with it in a military conflict. The UN, an organization that was set up with the intent of saving 'succeeding generations from the scourge of war', reaffirming 'faith in fundamental human rights, in the dignity and worth of a human person', and establishing 'conditions under which justice and respect for the obligations arising from treaties and other sources of international law can be maintained',[52] is today playing the role of a passive bystander as one country breaks international law and another falls prey to unimaginable man-made devastation.

After visiting Yemen in August 2015, Peter Maurer, the president of the International Committee of the Red Cross (ICRC), said that Yemen had witnessed more physical destruction in five months than Syria had in four years of the civil war. MSF, which offers medical care in extreme conflicts, stated that the situation in Yemen was worse than in any country in which they operated. Tragically enough, the coalition forces led by Saudi Arabia carried out the bombing and destruction of an MSF hospital in northern Yemen on 26 October 2015. The six consecutive air strikes, widely condemned by the international community, appeared to be a 'deliberate targeting of the medical facility',[53] since the MSF country director claimed that the coalition was being provided with the hospital's GPS coordinates regularly.[54] HRW has criticized both militias and the Saudi-led coalition for war crimes.

UNICEF, the World Health Organization (WHO), Oxfam and other organizations have stated that tens of thousands of Yemeni children suffer from severe malnutrition, and over a million are at severe risk. They have also warned of acute water insecurity. Twenty million people are facing shortages. The ICRC, MSF and others have pointed to the number of facilities that have been forced to close down. This is anything but a 'normal war'.

6

CRIMEA/UKRAINE: 'LEGITIMATE' RUSSIAN INTERESTS?

A political crisis erupted in Ukraine's eastern and southern parts in early 2014. Between 27 February and 19 March that year, the largely Russian-speaking Crimean peninsula, militarily cut off from the Ukrainian mainland by Russian troops, managed to secede unilaterally to the Russian Federation. The event stunned the West, particularly because it entertained the hope of Ukraine integrating with the EU at some point of time. Ironically, neither Russia nor Europe, given their own economic preoccupations, was in a position to offer much of a future to Ukraine's distraught citizens. Nonetheless, the Crimean issue became a tussle between the two sides, seen unequivocally by the US and Europe as a case of Russian bullying stretching to the extent of annexing another country's sovereign territory. Legally, the Russian overreach was indeed a breach of Ukraine's sovereignty. Politically, it was painted as a mere preservation of Russia's strategic interests. As a consequence, the Ukrainian crisis has become another case study of the relevance and effectiveness of the Security Council in tackling international crises which include great power interests.

On 6 March 2014, Shivshankar Menon, the former foreign

secretary who, as the national security adviser, was the most influential figure in the Indian foreign policy establishment then, said about the unfolding events in Ukraine: 'There are … legitimate Russian … interests involved, and we hope … there is a … resolution to them.'[1] India had been an ally of the erstwhile Soviet Union and subsequently, though to a lesser extent, of Russia—an ally for which the Russians have not hesitated in demonstrating their support in the past. Taken out of context, the Indian reaction, if it can be called that, would appear to suggest that if the powerful have interests, 'intervention' and 'takeover' are understandable. It was perhaps not what the diplomat had intended.

I don't wish to offer an interpretation of the remark. However, it can be argued that given the impunity with which international law and state sovereignty were being violated all around, the Russian step was merely one—which the West now protests against the most—in a long list, including Iraq, Kosovo, Libya, Syria and Yemen.

The Russian position was made clear in Putin's address to the State Duma on 18 March 2014, in which he appealed for 'admitting to the Russian Federation Crimea and Sevastopol' a day before the annexation. He set out the Russian position justifying Crimean separation from Ukraine. By citing a 96 per cent referendum vote in favour of 'reuniting with Russia', he emphasized how 'everything in Crimea speaks of [a] shared [Russian] history and pride', tracing the peninsula's past since the days of Vladimir the Great to its 'handing over like a sack of potatoes' to Ukraine in 1991. He protested that despite accepting Crimea as 'Ukrainian territory', Russia had seen Russian-speaking people being 'subjected … to forced assimilation' across the region. Critiquing the inefficacy of the Ukrainian state, he asserted that having 'had enough of the authorities', millions of 'Ukrainian citizens ... fled to' Russia for jobs worth over $20 billion annually. Putin termed the ouster of Ukraine's pro-Russia president, Viktor Yanukovych, in February 2014 a 'coup' and blamed it on the 'nationalists, neo-Nazis, Russophobes and anti-Semites [who] continue to set the tone in Ukraine'.[2]

'Those who opposed the coup,' he argued, 'were ... threatened with repression,' with the 'first in line' being 'the Russian-speaking Crimea'. Russia, thus, 'could not abandon Crimea and its residents' and had helped 'create conditions' for them to 'peacefully express their free will regarding their own future'. Then, Putin turned his attention to the internationalization of the issue:

What do we hear from our colleagues in Western Europe and North America? They say we are violating norms of international law. What exactly are we violating? Russia's armed forces never entered Crimea; they were already in line with an international agreement ... As it declared independence ... the Supreme Council of Crimea referred to the United Nations Charter which speaks of the right of nations to self-determination. [It] referred to the well-known Kosovo precedent: a precedent our Western colleagues created ... when they agreed that the unilateral separation of Kosovo from Serbia—exactly what Crimea is doing now—was legitimate. The [United Nations] International Court [of Justice] agreed with this approach ... in its ruling of 22nd July 2010. We keep hearing from the United States and Western Europe that Kosovo [was] some special case. One should not try so crudely to make everything suit their interests, calling the same thing white today and black tomorrow. Our Western partners, led by the United States of America ... believe in their exclusivity ... that they can decide the destinies of the world. To make their aggression look legitimate, they force the necessary resolutions, and if for some reason this does not work, they simply ignore the Security Council. They hit Afghanistan, Iraq, and frankly violated the ... Security Council resolution on Libya, when instead of imposing the so-called no-fly zone over it, they started bombing it too.[3]

By Putin's rationale, the kettle had no right to call the pot black. If the Crimean case was to be that of an annexation, the American-led interventions since Kosovo were as unjustifiable, leaving the West no reason to meddle in or complain about Crimea. Russia anticipated the support of its BRICS partners (Brazil, India, China and South Africa) and the negative reaction of the West as it went ahead in Crimea. Meanwhile, the Security Council was reduced to a bystander as the entire saga reeked of a face-off between the West and Russia. In a sense, the so-called strength of the Council also constitutes its major weakness. It is helpless in the face of an entrenched interest of one of its permanent members if that member has no hesitation in exercising its veto power. Both the US and Russia have repeatedly demonstrated this.

It is useful to recall the long history of Russia's interests in Ukraine. Having wriggled out of the Russian shadow following the collapse of the Soviet Union in 1991, Ukraine has since asserted its own identity as a nation state, with the capital Kiev being called Kyiv.[4] While this may also apply to several other post-Cold War nations, the socio-political and geopolitical complexity of Ukraine's eastern and southern skirts, which have historically housed majority populaces that are ethno-linguistically Russian and have felt closer to Mother Russia, is to be borne in mind. Thus, the belt has remained a hotbed of political unease. Eastern Ukraine has the Donetsk and Luhansk oblasts (an administrative division), colloquially referred to as Donbass, seeking secession to compose a confederation called Novorossiya—or 'New Russia'— reviving the imperial Russian name for the region. In the south, more notably, Crimea has always attracted Russia's attention for its national interests, owing to geostrategic, historical and demographic factors.

A peninsula dislocated from the Ukrainian mainland, Crimea separates the Sea of Azov from the Black Sea and is the only political entity between Russia and Ukraine other than the water bodies and an international border. Sevastopol, at the southwestern tip of Crimea, further enhances the peninsula's strategic value. Succeeding the ancient Greek port of Chersonesus, the city boasts a long pedigree of imperial patronage. Through its history, Sevastopol has remained a pivot for influence over the entire peninsula, making Crimea a maritime gateway to the Mediterranean for centuries, first as a Greco-Roman colony, then as a Mongol khanate (kingdom) and finally as an Ottoman protectorate. Such was its strength under Turkic-Mongol rule that, in 1571, Crimea invaded Muscovy (medieval Russia) and set Moscow ablaze.

The tide turned by 1774, when the Ottoman Empire, having lost the Russo-Turkish War, had to surrender the Crimean peninsula to Russia's imperial fold. However, the Crimeans revolted, then expressing loyalty towards the Turks. Tsarina Catherine the Great of Russia was swift to respond. She trampled the rebellion, installed a puppet ruler, and encouraged ethnic Russian settlements in the peninsula. Finally, the inevitable annexation of Crimea by Russia occurred in 1783, based on fragile assurances of mass consent by the Russian military leader, the tsarina's favourite, Grigory Potemkin. With that, the Ottoman port of Aktiar was fortified into the naval base of Sevastopol and has docked the Russian Black Sea Fleet since. That history repeats itself was shown by the 2014 annexation of Crimea by the Russian Federation.

Stalin's forced deportations of ethnic Crimeans after the Second World War or Khrushchev's gifting of Crimea to the Ukrainian Soviet Socialist Republic did not matter much legally, since such reshufflings were domestic concerns of the then Soviet whole.

However, as the Soviet Union fragmented in 1991, the lines of separation turned blurry. Although Crimea emerged as a formal part of the newborn Ukrainian republic, its ethnic Russian inhabitants outnumbered its Ukrainian population nearly three to one.[5] Since then, Russia and Ukraine have floated several mechanisms to fine-tune bilateral relations. At Yalta in 1992, a proportionate split of the Soviet Black Sea Fleet between the Russian and the Ukrainian navies was agreed upon. Two years later at Budapest, Ukraine gave up its massive nuclear stockpile in exchange for Russian acknowledgement of its territorial sovereignty. The 1997 Treaty of Friendship, Cooperation and Partnership bolstered the intent as the Russian Federation accepted Ukrainian dominion over Crimea and Sevastopol. Reciprocating, Ukraine granted four-fifths of the Black Sea Fleet—along with a lease on naval installations in southern Crimea—to Russia. Yet, Crimea continued to be the chief bone of contention in Russo-Ukrainian relations.

As in its days under Ottoman rule, Crimea enjoyed a significant degree of leeway as an autonomous republic within independent Ukraine, complete with its own parliament, the Supreme Council of Crimea. In 1994, while Russia and Ukraine forged the Budapest Agreement, the Supreme Council intrepidly conceived the office of a Crimean president, which was subsequently occupied by the pro-Russia Yuriy Meshkov. The Russophile drift that followed culminated in Crimea's declaration of its own constitution—an invite to the wrath of the overarching Ukrainian parliament. Crimea's fresh constitution and the post of its president were both abrogated as a consequence. Likewise, almost a decade after the Russo-Ukrainian Treaty of Friendship, in 2006, raging popular protests blocked a Ukrainian naval exercise with NATO at Crimea. Visibly, Russian voices inside Ukraine's head never stopped echoing and grew loudest in 2010, when Ukraine got its first markedly pro-Russian head of state, Viktor Yanukovych. Despite initially expressing warmth towards the European Union, he eventually began an eastward tilt. The lease to Russia on military access in and around Sevastopol was quietly extended till 2042. Most controversially, the coveted Ukraine–European Union Association Agreement was shelved in favour of economic bargains from Moscow. The decision did not go down well with most Ukrainians, who favoured integration with Europe. Thereon, the domestic politics of Ukraine was subjected to increasing internationalization.

With agriculture constituting less than a tenth of its GDP—stagnant since 2013—Ukraine is no longer the 'breadbasket of Europe'. By 2014, its reeling economy featured a meagre stock of foreign exchange and a 7.5 per cent unemployment rate.[6] In an interview to the Carnegie Council for Ethics in International Affairs, Anton Shekhovtsov, a London-based expert on eastern Europe, underlined two unassailable benefits that Ukraine saw in a merger with the EU. First, he said, 'the association ... implies modernization of industries and ... of the Ukrainian economy'. Second, since Ukraine was never 'fully independent' from its former Soviet shell, it could 'choose its own political development' as part of the EU.[7] The choice, nonetheless, was not as obvious. In another discussion with the Carnegie Council, Nicolai Petro of the University of Rhode Island noted that Ukraine had sought massive financial bailouts as a precondition for being subsumed by the EU. However, till 2014, a paltry contribution of $1 billion had flowed Kyiv's way, which was 1/140th its external debt. Interestingly, despite being a token sum, the aid did not come from Europe but from Washington. Further assistance was to 'be tied to ... structural and economic reforms, which Ukraine in the past [was unable] to fulfill'.[8] It should also have been clear to anyone familiar with developments within the EU that to join it as a full member state requires painful adjustment, and that given the prevailing financial difficulties in a number of members, the EU was in no position to underwrite a bailout of Ukraine's economy.

Yanukovych's turn towards Putin in the absence of fitting reassurances from the West may be understandable. The EU making financial offers to Kyiv is beyond economic logic. The EU was visibly not in the 'most robust health', preoccupied as it was with its own economic crises. Consequently, German chancellor Angela Merkel—the monetary messiah of the distressed region— sounded 'highly evasive' on the question of bailing out Ukraine if the need arose.[9] Meanwhile, the Russian economy did no better either, as the ruble slipped to an all-time low of 80 rubles to US $1 by the end of 2014.[10] Yet, Yanukovych prepared Ukraine for a Russian-led customs union. On the other hand, the country's pro-integration camp stayed convinced that 'Europe will come up with a very significant figure' as compensation, for it believed that Ukraine played a 'central role' in the West's prevailing aims to contain Russia.[11] While opinions on Ukraine's future split along the Russo-European crevice, both sides misread their options. The EU too failed to 'understand how important for the geopolitical project of Russia Ukraine is'. Installing Kyiv into the West's sphere of influence would be viewed by many as the severing of Russo-Ukrainian ties. Given its complex demographics and history, an 'either/or proposition' mandating a choice 'between ... West or Russia' left Ukraine in a 'strategic limbo', eventually baring its socio-political cracks.[12]

Favouring integration with the EU and censuring corruption in public life, Ukrainians took to the streets in November 2013, assembling at Kyiv's Maidan Nezalezhnosti ('Independence Square'). Stimulated by merciless police crackdowns, the 'Euromaidan' protests escalated into organized rioting, to the extent of spawning dedicated civilian 'self-defence groups'.

Dozens perished in the chaos. The bloodshed prompted the EU to pressure Yanukovych into accepting the opposition's demand for fresh elections, much to Moscow's chagrin. However, the unrest only flared up, with policemen deserting en masse and protesters blockading Yanukovych's estate. Amidst the pandemonium, on 22 February 2014, Yanukovych fled to Russia and the Ukrainian parliament wasted no time in impeaching him. Shrill cries of foul play immediately came from the Russian Federation, which labelled the incident a blatant coup d'état. Alongside, the Russian-speaking southern and eastern stretches of Ukraine launched the 'Anti-Maidan', a counter-revolution to the ongoing Euromaidan, opposing Yanukovych's ouster. With the fuelling of armed vigilantism and even cross-border trespassing from Russia, the vitriolic situation threatened to slip from rival rallying into a civil war along the Russo-Ukrainian ethnic divide. Meanwhile, with clamorous campaigns at Sevastopol on 24 February 2014, Crimea expressed secessionist fervour.[13]

An opinion poll conducted by the International Republican Institute, a Washington-based advocacy group, in early March 2014 indicated that a large number of Russian-speaking Ukrainians supported a Russian military intervention in the crisis.[14] Putin granted the wish before it could be made. On 27 February 2014, militiamen in unmarked green uniforms dotted Crimea and seized key military facilities, along with the Supreme Council of Crimea. The NATO suspected the 'Little Green Men' to be members of the Armed Forces of the Russian Federation (GRU), which already had considerable footmarks on the peninsula.[15] Putin calmly brushed off the events as local mobilizations for 'self-defence' amidst outcries from the West.[16] The same day, surrounded by the Kalashnikov wielders, the Supreme Council elected pro-Kremlin leader Sergey Aksyonov as prime minister of the Autonomous Republic of Crimea. After a quick referendum—the credibility of which was expectedly questioned—and a unilateral declaration of independence, Crimea and Sevastopol became de facto federal subjects of the Russian Federation on 19 March 2014. The West ordered immediate sanctions against the Russians. The G8 suspended Russia, even as the Organization for Economic Cooperation and Development (OECD) stalled its accession as a full member. Days later, a retired Russian admiral, Igor Kasatonov, revealed the armed liberators of Crimea as Russian Special Forces operatives.[17] On 17 April 2014, the Russian president publicly confirmed his military's involvement in the peninsula.[18]

The question that emerges at this point is: where was the UN in all this? As a reminder of 1783, the 2014 secession of Crimea was nothing less than an annexation of it by Russia, justified, no doubt, by the pretext of local will. Surely, the isolation of the peninsula from the Ukrainian mainland by Russian elite troops was an act of unauthorized military intervention, involving the use of means thought necessary. Several notable voices, including those of Hillary Clinton and Czech senate Speaker Milan Stech, compared the Crimean crisis 'to Hitler's annexation of Czechoslovakia in 1938'. For the *Washington Post*, former Georgian president Mikheil Saakashvili observed:

> Watching recent events and the global response, I keep thinking about history repeating itself … Nazi Germany occupied parts of neighbouring Czechoslovakia under the pretext of protecting ethnic Germans. Today, Russia is claiming to protect ethnic Russians … in Crimea … In the West [the] compromise with Russia … smacks of Munich 80 years ago.[19]

Indeed, in 1938, the march of Hitler's forces into Sudetenland to seal it off from the rest of Czechoslovakia was painted as a response to vehement agitations made by the Sudeten Nazis, led by Konrad Heinlein, for a merger of their territory with Germany.

As dire as the realities may have been in Donbass and Crimea, any external intervener ought to have sought the prior permission of the Security Council. Putin's disregard of this convention was another pointer to the eroding sanctity of Westphalian sovereignty. In its own defence, the Security Council may well cite that the upheaval in Ukraine spiralled from civil unrest into military annexation within days, leaving no window open for a concerted international response. It may also be argued that the affiliation of the militiamen sealing the Crimean peninsula remained uncertain till the post-crisis confessions by the Russians, consequently making a ratified intervention untenable. However, such arguments fail to cover the delay of the Security Council's response to Ukraine's conditions. Between the birth of the Anti-Maidan unrest in February and the declaration of Crimean independence on 11 March 2014, the Council issued not even a press statement on the escalating crisis.[20]

The first official response of the Security Council to the Ukrainian crisis came as late as 15 March 2014. Draft Resolution S/2014/189—co-sponsored by the US and its European partners—was tabled to 'reaffirm' Ukraine's territorial integrity and nullify the referendum on Crimean secession. The document cited Article 2 of the UN Charter and echoed humanitarian concerns.[21] China abstained and Russia, as was only to be expected, vetoed it. Seven weeks later, Resolution 68/262 derecognizing Crimea's new status was moved at the UNGA and was adopted with a 59 per cent majority, as 100 members led by the West approved it. The BRICS nations, excluding Russia, were amongst the fifty-eight members that abstained. Eleven members, including Russia, rejected the proposal.[22] In Ukraine, meanwhile, the flames of separatism got invigorated across the Donbass, where a full-blooded conflict erupted between pro-Russian armed outfits and Ukrainian state forces. Yet, the Security Council remained dormant. On 17 July

2014, a civilian aircraft—Malaysian Airlines flight 17 (MH17)—flying from Amsterdam to Kuala Lumpur was shot down by a surface-to-air missile from war-torn eastern Ukraine, killing all 298 individuals aboard. The tragic occurrence became another cause for Russo-Western buck-passing. As the Kremlin instantly held Ukraine guilty,[23] the West—opening a can of evidence, including intelligence snippets—pointed fingers at the separatists of Novorossiya.[24]

The Security Council issued a press statement the next day appealing for 'a full, thorough and independent international investigation into the incident'.[25] By 21 July 2014, however, as part of its Resolution 2166 to condemn the downing of MH17, the Council expressed 'serious concern that armed groups in Ukraine ... impeded immediate, safe, secure and unrestricted access to the crash site ... for investigating authorities'.[26] Till date, no party has been formally held responsible for the incident, with the inquiry into the issue turning inert. Cries of botched investigations and calls for establishing guilt through a dedicated tribunal have remained unheeded.[27]

Likewise, when on 5 September 2014 the Organization for Security and Cooperation in Europe (OSCE) mediated the Minsk Protocol amongst Ukraine, Russia and the cities of Donetsk and Luhansk for a ceasefire in the Donbass, the Security Council made no official move to support it. As the agreement was quick to collapse given the lack of enforcement measures, a multilateral Minsk II agreement to curb the Donbass war was signed on 11 February 2015. It tabled demands on restoration of order, constitutional reforms, amnesty, foregoing of heavy arms and withdrawal of foreign military participants, besides a full ceasefire.[28] Within a week, the Security Council endorsed the 'package of measures' via Resolution 2202 and authorized the OSCE for its facilitation.[29] Four months later, Ukraine's defence minister, Stepan Poltorak, claimed that over 150 lives were lost since Minsk II and that the ceasefire was violated more than 4,000 times.[30]

Present-day Ukraine—with a warring east, a seceded south and a battered economy—serves as a reminder that global politics continues to be largely dominated by big-power interests. Political unrest within a sovereign country, a member state of the UN, spiralled into a flash annexation and then a prolonged conflict with heavy humanitarian costs. The Security Council, by virtue of its veto provisions, remained paralysed. The developments in Ukraine have, thus, revived strategic permutations reminiscent of the Cold War era.

There were also some relatively optimistic voices. Speaking to the Carnegie Council, the managing director of Kissinger Associates, Thomas Graham, summed up the Russo-West deadlock over Ukraine:

> Russia has its own sense of national interests that they believe need to be defended, and they saw some of the steps we [the West] were taking ... in the former Soviet space [as a] threat to their own national security. Since Putin returned to the Kremlin, [a] deterioration [has been] seen in US–Russia relations. Everybody is talking about a new Cold War at this point, and containment policy. I think it is an incorrect assessment. Containment ... is, I think, a lack of imagination in Washington. How do you contain a country like Russia, which is among the top ten economies in the world? How do you isolate a country when its fellow BRICS ... are not in the mood ... to isolate Russia? The problem is that you cannot build [a better] Ukraine unless there is ... cooperation among the United States, Europe and Russia.[31]

In the opinion of a former Indian ambassador M.K. Bhadrakumar, there may be a way forward. However, it relies on multilateral bargains rather than the Security Council:

What is apparent today is that the US' rhetoric on Ukraine has not only tapered off lately, but in a curious U-turn, Washington seems to be quietly nudging Kiev [or Kyiv] to accept the legitimacy of the pro-Russia local authorities in Donetsk and Luhansk. Interestingly, this follows several meetings between top Russian and American diplomats in the recent months and phone conversations between Obama and President Vladimir Putin ... 'Tradeoff' is an ugly word in the diplomatic jargon, but what seems to be shaping up is something close to that: while Washington accommodates Russia's vital interests in Ukraine, it hopes to extract Russia's cooperation on Syria. (The European Union also needs Russia's cooperation to sort out the mess in Libya.)[32]

In essence, Russia's annexation of Crimea was possible because the countries that could have opposed it were preoccupied. The element of surprise, combined with the fact that the Security Council already stood discredited on account of its actions and inaction elsewhere, resulted in a situation where Putin did not even find a referral of the matter to the Council necessary. As has been observed earlier, whilst the Russian overreach, legally speaking, was in clear violation of Ukrainian sovereignty, politically, it was merely justified as serving Russia's strategic interests.

7

SRI LANKA: THE RESPLENDENT ISLE

'Serendipity', the word for making happy and unexpected discoveries by accident, has its origins in 'Serendip', the old name of Sri Lanka. Also, the Persian name for the island was Sarandib, a corruption of the Sanskrit 'Sinhaladvipa', literally 'the island where lions dwell'. Sinhala is also the name of one of Sri Lanka's official languages, the other being Tamil.

Tamil–Sinhalese rivalry is at the heart of the unrest that has plagued the island nation for decades. The rivalry, particularly in Jaffna in northern Sri Lanka and to a lesser extent in Trincomalee and Batticaloa in the eastern part, stemmed largely from middle-class aspirations for government jobs, to which the Tamils, owing to the presence of missionary schools in their provinces, had greater access. This led to resentment among the Sinhalese middle-class youth, who voiced their support for the 'Sinhala Only' cause, hoping to block competition from the Tamils for government jobs. The passing of the Sinhala Only Act in 1956 achieved this to a certain extent. Discrimination against Tamils increased, and their recruitment to the army, police and administrative services declined.[1]

Solomon West Ridgeway Dias Bandaranaike, better known as SWRD, was the prime minister of Sri Lanka, then Ceylon, when the Sinhala Only Act was passed in 1956. Until 1955, however, SWRD had been in favour of making both Sinhala and Tamil the official languages, but by the end of that year, the Sri Lanka Freedom Party (SLFP) led by him resolved at its annual session to anoint only Sinhala as the official language, with a provision for the 'reasonable use of Tamil'. SWRD 'began to exploit the traditional dislike of the Sinhala people for the Tamils to rope in the support of the Sinhalese'.[2] This laid the foundation for majoritarian politics, still in play in Sri Lanka.

In the run-up to his election in 1956, SWRD claimed he drew inspiration from Indian prime minister Jawaharlal Nehru. In justifying the imposition of Sinhala Only, SWRD recalled Nehru's views on his language policy in 1953. Nehru had talked of replacing English with Hindi as the official language of India in twenty-five years. He had said he would do so even though only 42 per cent of the Indian population spoke Hindi. In Ceylon, 72 per cent spoke Sinhala.[3] Bandaranaike concluded that if he 'became prime minister, in twenty-four hours, "Sinhala Only" … will be made [their] official language'.[4]

The Act, when eventually passed, denied Tamils their language rights, resulting in strong protests. SWRD attempted to address the issue of language rights by negotiating with the then main Tamil political party—Federal Party—and offered devolution of power at the district level through the Bandaranaike–Chelvanayakam Pact. Due to political pressure from Sinhalese Buddhist extremists within his party and other right-wing opposition forces, he was forced to retreat even from the limited devolution envisaged. The failure of the pact stirred 'anti-Tamil feelings, which led in 1958 to the first nationwide communal violence in post-independence Sri Lanka'.[5] The political class in New Delhi failed to fully comprehend the implications of the Sinhala Only Act and tended to view it initially as a 'consolidation of anti-imperialist sentiment'; years later, it led to the Tamils being reduced to 'second class citizens' through discrimination that became entrenched in the system.[6]

Nehru could not have anticipated that thirty-five years after the Act, his grandson Rajiv Gandhi, seeking to return to power as prime minister, would be assassinated at the behest of the Liberation Tigers of Tamil Eelam (LTTE), a proscribed terrorist group fighting for the Tamil cause in Sri Lanka. It is ironic that the architect of the bilateral agreement with Sri Lanka that ensured Tamils were granted their legitimate minority rights was assassinated by those struggling for those very rights. As part of the agreement, signed in July 1987 between Rajiv Gandhi and Sri Lankan president J.R. Jayewardene, the LTTE was to lay down arms and pursue its political objectives through peaceful democratic means. Ironically, it was Rajiv Gandhi's mother Indira who as prime minister had commenced the support to Sri Lankan Tamil militants, including the LTTE, ostensibly fighting for Eelam, or a separate homeland, in the 1980s. As prime minister, Rajiv had sought to reverse that policy by seeking a solution to the Tamil issue within the unity and territorial identity of Sri Lanka and ended up paying with his life.

What began around 1956, initially as an effort and then a movement for minority rights, gradually but steadily developed in the face of state repression and military operations into full-blown terrorism. A fratricidal war between the various militant groups—the People's Liberation Organization of Tamil Eelam (PLOTE), the Eelam Revolutionary Organization of Students (EROS) and the LTTE—saw the latter emerge as the most powerful group capable of taking on the might of the Sri Lankan armed forces.

As elsewhere, the distinction between 'good' and 'not so good' and 'bad' rebels has been largely subjective and illusory in Sri Lanka too. The arming of rebels invariably has had unintended consequences. In the 1970s and 1980s, very close relations between New Delhi and Colombo meant that the latter could get the former to give it a free rein in dealing with its Tamil problem. This was certainly the case during the tenure of Sirimavo Bandaranaike, SWRD's wife and prime minister of Sri Lanka after him. When asked how she would deal with the Tamil issue, she would often say in conversation with us in India's high commission in Colombo (where I served from the end of 1984 to March 1988, initially as first secretary and later as counsellor, dealing with political work), 'I will call my sister in New Delhi and ask her to look the other way whilst I sort out this Tamil problem.' The implication was that the incumbent president J.R. Jayewardene was experiencing difficulties on account of strained relations with New Delhi.

Democratically elected governments are reluctant at the best of times to admit that they, or any state agency, have undertaken any funding or arming of rebel groups. When reports started appearing in sections of the Indian press in 1984 that Indian agencies had begun training Tamil militant groups in Dehradun, Indira Gandhi baulked at the suggestion that there were any Tamil militants in the country, saying, 'We have never interfered with the internal developments of any country in the past and we will not do so now.'[7]

Not everyone agreed with this approach. India's high commissioner in Colombo between 1985 and 1989, J.N. (Mani) Dixit, had the following to say in *Assignment Colombo*, an insider's account published in 1998:

> I have always felt that India need not have indulged in the mendacity of denying India's support to Tamil militants. We

should have just kept quiet on the charge. Our response to Sri Lankan accusations in this regard should have been that if there is Tamil militancy, it was due to the discriminatory policies of the Sri Lankan government against the Tamils and that we have no more comments or explanations to offer.[8]

One such militant group that was widely believed to have received training from India and to have undergone a transformation to a 'well-equipped guerilla force'[9] was the LTTE. In 1983, there was a spurt of anti-Tamil violence in Colombo and the simultaneous arming of Tamil militants. An exposé published by *India Today*[10] in March 1984 described in detail how Sri Lankan Tamil rebels not only got sanctuary in Tamil Nadu but also underwent rigorous and complex training in various makeshift camps. The military training (including but not limited to elementary use of firearms) and ideological grounding were given to new recruits in dozens of camps by seasoned guerrillas or retired Indian military officers (some of whom were paid more than what they had earned in the Indian Army).

The fact that Sri Lankan Tamil rebels enjoyed support in Tamil Nadu was clear. Militant rebels set up tactical headquarters in Madras (now Chennai) and operated freely from the city. There were reports that the government was even happy to exempt them from visa and immigration regulations, allowing some of them to travel abroad on Indian passports. The local Tamil political class was visibly sympathetic towards the Sri Lankan Tamils, and the Central government's best option was to support them for fear of stirring up 'a hornet's nest in the ethnically conscious state'.[11] Testimony to this was the Pondy Bazaar incident in Madras in which, on 19 May 1982, PLOTE and LTTE leaders and former associates Uma Maheswaran and Velupillai Prabhakaran opened fire on each other, were later arrested and then released, the case remaining pending till their deaths in 1989 and 2009 respectively. The soft approaches of both the M. Karunanidhi and the M.G.

Ramachandran governments towards the rebels pointed to the sympathy that these militants had gained among Tamils in India.

The pressure on the Central government in New Delhi was visible. Tamil Nadu witnessed widespread protests against the ruling Congress party, with Indira Gandhi, who was widely perceived to have used force to save ethnic Bengalis from persecution in East Pakistan in 1971, now being accused of being silent on and insensitive to Tamil suffering.[12] By this time, the Sri Lankan Tamils had also gained sympathy amongst the Tamil diaspora in countries like Malaysia, Mauritius, the UK, the US, Australia, West Germany and Canada.

The Sri Lankan government was not far behind when it came to receiving international help. While the Tamil rebels were acquiring training from a significant number of retired Indian Army, Indian Navy and Border Security Force (BSF) officers (who had been 'half-heartedly' warned to stay clear by the Indian intelligence agencies), the Sri Lankan forces were gaining access to gunboats from China, armoured cars from Pakistan, American M-16 rifles and training from British Special Air Service (SAS) commandos.[13]

The Sri Lankans were quick to point to India's double standards. President J.R. Jayewardene made the following statement on 3 November 1984 that enraged Rajiv Gandhi:

> In India, some Sikhs are agitating for a separate Khalistan. In Sri Lanka some Tamils are doing the same. Both movements have spawned terrorists. In both countries, the Central governments seek to settle any dispute that may exist constitutionally and peacefully. The Indian and Sri Lankan governments accuse foreign countries of seeking to interfere. In India, the terrorists who committed the assassination were Sikhs. In Sri Lanka they were Tamils. In India the victim was a Hindu. In Sri Lanka twelve of the victims were Buddhist Sinhalese. In India a few enraged Hindus massacred innocent Sikhs. In Sri Lanka a few enraged Sinhalese massacred innocent Tamils.[14]

After the 1983 riots in Colombo following the killing of the mayor of Jaffna, Alfred Duraiappah, by the LTTE, New Delhi had mustered sufficient courage to lead a resolution against Sri Lanka in the Sub-Commission on Prevention of Discrimination and the Protection of Minorities in Geneva. Taking stock of the growing secessionism, the Sri Lankan government that had thus far cried foul about Indian armed intervention had then sought Indira Gandhi's assistance to address the Tamil problem. India had responded by sending G. Parthasarathy, a confidant of the prime minister, to organize tripartite talks involving Jayewardene's United National Party (UNP), Mrs Bandaranaike's SLFP and the Tamil United Liberation Front (TULF). But when the SLFP walked out, Sri Lanka had seemed 'poised on the brink of a prolonged civil strife'.[15]

The Sri Lankan government imposed an economic blockade of the northern Jaffna peninsula and the northern portions of Trincomalee in May 1987. This prevented essential supplies reaching the 200,000 Tamils inhabiting the area. In order to counter this economic blockade, the Indian government—in a show of strength and to preserve Rajiv Gandhi's credibility amongst the Tamils in India—carried out an airdrop of humanitarian supplies on 4 June 1987. By implying that the Indian mission was humanitarian in nature, India demonstrated to the Tamils that 'it was ultimately India on whom the Tamils must depend'.[16] India's alleged humanitarian mission received varying responses from the international community. While several denounced the violation of Sri Lankan airspace, the 'mercy mission' was not condemned as it should have been by the West, and 'was only mildly deplored as it were by the European Parliament'.[17]

As violence and mistrust grew, Rajiv Gandhi sought course correction, with the intent of reversing the previous government's policies of intervention and arming of rebels. This is how Dixit describes the 'course correction':

Rajiv Gandhi indicated to Jayewardene that India would be willing to move away from the partisan role it was playing in dealing with the Sri Lankan situation. He, however, emphasized that a solution would be possible if the legitimate aspirations of Tamils were met by the Sri Lankan government. Otherwise prospects were of conflicts, even dismemberment of the country.[18]

Dixit's assessment was that Rajiv Gandhi, when he assumed power in December 1984:

... maintained continuity in Indian policies but with certain shifts in emphasis and nuances. His assessment was that while Indian mediatory efforts are necessary and useful, India must assume a more impartial stand between the Sinhalese and the Tamils, reducing the pro-Tamil slant in India's approach for them to succeed.[19]

The Sri Lankan government was persuaded to engage in peace talks, which culminated in the Indo-Sri Lanka Peace Accord of 1987. The accord desired 'to preserve the unity, sovereignty and territorial integrity of Sri Lanka'. This preambular provision was strengthened by two specific operational commitments. One, that 'India will take all necessary steps to ensure that Indian territory is not used for activities prejudicial to the unity, integrity and security of Sri Lanka'. Two, '... the Government of India will cooperate by giving to the Government of Sri Lanka such military assistance as and when requested ... to implement these proposals'.[20] The accord was warmly welcomed in Tamil Nadu as well. It represented, at that particular point of time, the best possible deal that India could secure for Sri Lanka's Tamil minority.

India's role in resolving Sri Lanka's Tamil issue, variously described as an 'ethnic crisis' or one essentially concerning minority rights, has never been fully understood nor appreciated. This is not surprising because both parties to the dispute, the Sinhalese government and the Tamils, wanted a solution on their own terms: the Sinhalese government wanted to institutionalize the second-class treatment of the Tamil minority, and the Tamils wanted a separate homeland. Both these extreme propositions were not tenable—not then, not now.

Negotiating a peace agreement is difficult at the best of times. The task is made that much more difficult when levels of distrust are as high as between the Sinhalese and Tamils. Both sides, the Sri Lankan government and the LTTE, reneged on crucial obligations they had assumed, and at different stages of the implementation of the agreement had no compunction about effectively trying to derail the agreement, even sabotaging it. It became increasingly clear that the LTTE had no intention of giving up arms beyond a token surrender, and the Sri Lankan government, for its part, had no desire to merge the northern and eastern provinces and then hold the referendum allowing the inhabitants of the Eastern Province to choose whether or not to remain linked with the Northern Province, stipulated in paragraph 2 of the agreement.[21] The decision to depute the 'Indian Peace Keeping Force' (IPKF) in Sri Lanka, the primary purpose of which was to ensure peace and stability in the wake of the accord, was predicated on certain assessments. These assessments need to be revisited to see if they were anchored in realism or whether they were flawed.

The decision to deploy IPKF in Sri Lanka to implement the accord was, in hindsight, perceived as a high-level policy failure, and rightly so. Why was this misadventure undertaken? There has been considerable criticism, mostly uninformed and unfounded, about Rajiv Gandhi's motivation. His critics have pointed to his domestic difficulties and challenges: the failure of other domestic accords, the pressure generated by the Bofors bribery scandal and so on. Any objective and clinical analysis must, of course, factor some of these domestic preoccupations and their relative importance into the overall decision-making matrix. These so-called preoccupations do not and cannot, however, provide an explanation for the precise reason(s) for sending a peacekeeping force into the territory of a small strife-torn neighbouring country where both parties to the dispute ultimately trace their lineage to India. The search for an explanation needs to commence, in the first instance, with the acknowledgement that Rajiv Gandhi realized he had been dealt a bad hand in the arming of rebels during his mother's tenure—something he wanted to reverse. The fact that he lost his mother in tragic circumstances further motivated and fuelled the desire for course correction.

Dixit, in *Assignment Colombo*, had the following to say:

> I distinctly remember Rajiv Gandhi raising the question as to whether the LTTE would really abide by the agreement, which India was bound to implement as guarantor. Rajiv Gandhi raised this question in the context of doubts and misgivings Prabhakaran expressed when Hardeep Puri provided details of the agreement to him on July 19. Anand K. Verma's [head of India's external intelligence agency] advice to Rajiv Gandhi was: 'If the LTTE was guaranteed an important role in the power structure in the Tamil areas of Sri Lanka, and if the merger of the northern and eastern provinces was somehow made permanent (whatever be the interim provisions proposed) and if the LTTE cadres are absorbed into the administrative set up of the new Province, the LTTE would endorse the agreement, especially as it was being guaranteed by India.' The general sense of his advice was that 'these are boys whom we know and with whom we have been in touch, and so they will listen to us'.[22]

On the possibility of India having to confront the LTTE, Rajiv Gandhi asked his army chief, General K. Sundarji, what his assessment was. The general's reply was that once the LTTE endorsed the agreement, they would not have the wherewithal to go back and confront India or the Sri Lankan government. He went on to say that if the LTTE decided to take on India and Sri Lanka militarily, Indian armed forces would be able to neutralize them militarily within two weeks.[23]

There were too many assumptions in both the assessments and advice provided to the prime minister by Verma and the army chief. Their advice presumed a certain degree of compliance on the part of both the LTTE and the Sri Lankan government. Sincerity and compliance were, however, in short supply on both sides.

Allegations made by LTTE chief Prabhakaran to the IPKF's overall force commander, Lieutenant General Depinder Singh, suggested that the Indian government had authorized the country's intelligence agencies—the Research and Analysis Wing (R&AW) and the Intelligence Bureau (IB)—to not just gather information on the various militant groups but also incite most of them against the LTTE. The IPKF at that time did not take note of it, but Singh admitted this later on:

> Somewhere around August 15, 1987, in one of my meetings with Prabakaran in Jaffna, he mentioned that the LTTE had positive information that the Research and Analysis Wing was inciting other Tamil militant groups, especially the recently created Tri-Star Group, to attack LTTE cadres as the latter became progressively weaker following handing over their weapons. This was a serious allegation and was conveyed to army headquarters that evening for investigation and an early reply. The next day brought a categorical denial which, in turn, was conveyed to Prabakaran, who told me politely that since I was denying it, he believed me, but what Delhi had reported to me was incorrect and therefore he stood by his allegation.[24]

By October 1987, the IPKF was positively working with the Sri Lankan government to pin down the LTTE. When the Sri Lankan navy apprehended seventeen LTTE men and took them to the Sri Lankan army and IPKF bases, their weapons were confiscated. Even as the LTTE screamed foul, claiming it had been granted amnesty by the agreement signed with India, the IPKF units launched attacks in Jaffna.[25]

The IPKF, viewed by Tamils in India and Sri Lanka as having been sent to protect the Tamils, found itself waging a full-scale offensive against those who claimed to represent the Tamils, the LTTE, thereby ratifying the Indian government's claim on 7 October 1987 that it would 'use the strongest measures to deal with all those who seek to undermine the implementation of the Indo-Sri Lankan agreement'.[26] Krishna Chandra Pant, the Indian defence minister, was firmly told by Jayewardene 'to incapacitate the LTTE without further delay'.[27] Karunanidhi's decision not to welcome the returning IPKF forces sent a clear message: he was not pleased with the Indian government's treatment of the Tamils in Sri Lanka. A particularly cynical view was expressed by A.P. Venkateswaran, former secretary to the ministry of foreign affairs:

> We have sown seeds of bitterness for decades even among the people of Tamil ethnic stock in Sri Lanka. Sooner or later the Indian forces will have to withdraw whether peace is restored or not. One can say, definitely, that when this happens, we [would] have left Sri Lanka in [a] worse mess than we [ever] have.[28]

In some respects, the author of the above view misses the point altogether. The IPKF was sent to Sri Lanka to secure the implementation of the accord of July 1987 and not to secure a separate Eelam for the Tamils. The core of the agreement was the desire to secure the best possible deal for the Tamils within the territorial unity of Sri Lanka. India's ability to underwrite the success of the agreement required, in the first instance, the cooperation of both parties to the dispute.

After the assassination of Rajiv Gandhi on 21 May 1991 by an LTTE suicide bomber, India publicly withdrew from the ongoing civil war in its neighbourhood, and the 'Indian intervention ended abruptly when Sri Lanka's democratic process showed the door to the architects of the accord in both countries'.[29] Yet, despite the newly adopted 'hands-off' policy, India continued to extend military support to the Sri Lankan government, which played 'a crucial role in several of the Sri Lankan Air Force's missions aimed at crushing LTTE resistance'.[30]

More recently, journalist Nitin Gokhale had this to say in a book he published in 2009:

> Outwardly, India did adopt a hands-off policy vis-à-vis the Sri Lanka conflict. But that was because of domestic political compulsions born out of the fact that the ruling United Progressive Alliance (UPA) government in New Delhi was dependent upon the DMK party from Tamil Nadu for its survival in the Parliament ... Yet, in early 2006, India quietly gifted five Mi-17 helicopters to the Sri Lankan Air Force. The only Indian condition was: these helicopters would fly under Sri Lankan Air Force colours. New Delhi clearly did not want to annoy UPA's Tamil Nadu allies like the DMK unnecessarily.[31]

India and the international community looked the other way as the Sri Lankan government pushed through with a concerted military strategy and offensive over a 100-day period up to May 2009 when the LTTE was finally crushed militarily.

As these developments were taking place—and even as the humanitarian crisis had escalated over decades—the international community, and more importantly the UN, failed to address the situation in Sri Lanka.

A report pertaining to the crisis in Sri Lanka on the official website of Responsibility to Protect states:

> Although different officials and governments called for the protection of civilians, the UN did not strongly counter the Sri Lankan Government's statements in regards to the number of casualties or strongly condemn the Government for obstructing humanitarian assistance. Also, the UN did not adequately address the Government's attacks on civilians and violations of international humanitarian and human rights law. Furthermore, the UN Secretariat in particular neglected to provide necessary information about the actions of the Sri Lankan Government and LTTE to the Security Council. Hence, not only did the Sri Lankan government fail to protect its civilians from mass atrocities, the international community, particularly the UN, did not take collective action in a timely and decisive manner to prevent and stop mass atrocities.[32]

The experiences of different situations involving mass atrocities have shown that closure becomes possible only if there is a thorough and impartial inquiry, and responsibility is clearly fixed. The OHCHR Investigation on Sri Lanka (OISL), which found that crimes 'amounting' to war crimes were committed in the war between Sri Lankan security forces and the LTTE, could open a new chapter and new opportunities in the island's search for post-war reconciliation between the majority Sinhalese and the Tamils. The report, released on 17 September 2015, blames both the security forces and the LTTE. It, however, rejects the argument of reciprocity. The OISL recognizes:

> ... the complexities inherent in conducting military operations against legitimate military targets in or near densely populated areas. Nevertheless, the presence of LTTE cadres directly

participating in hostilities from within the predominantly civilian population did not change the character of the population, nor did it affect the protection afforded to civilians under international humanitarian law. It is important to recall that the obligations of a party to an armed conflict under international humanitarian law are not conditioned on reciprocity. Violations attributable to one of the parties do not justify lack of compliance on the part of the other.[33]

The report also calls for the setting up of 'a hybrid special court' along the lines of the international criminal courts for Yugoslavia and Rwanda. The Sri Lankan government is asked to adopt specific legislation to set it up by

... integrating international judges, prosecutors, lawyers and investigators mandated to try war crimes and crimes against humanity, with its own independent investigative and prosecuting organ, defense office and witness and victims protection programme, and resource it so that it can promptly and effectively try those responsible.[34]

Welcoming the report that sought to promote reconciliation, accountability and human rights in Sri Lanka, the secretary-general hoped:

that its important recommendations will help support the efforts of the people and the Government of Sri Lanka to carve a durable path toward long-lasting peace and stability and respect for human rights, through a genuine and credible process of accountability and reconciliation that meets international standards. The victims of all communities, their families and the Sri Lankan nation itself demand no less than a full and proper reckoning.[35]

Without closure, experience has shown, the wound will continue to fester and the urgent and overdue task of national reconciliation cannot be achieved. This will require mature handling of both the internal situation within Sri Lanka and a careful calibration by New Delhi, which should work along with the state government of Tamil Nadu to strengthen the hands of Colombo. New Delhi can play such a role only if Colombo itself ensures that the rights of its Tamil citizens are constitutionally guaranteed, and they are shown the respect and dignity all Sri Lankan citizens get. Working at cross purposes, as would appear to have been the case for several decades, will create problems both for Sri Lanka and India. In retrospect, the mistreatment of the Tamil minority was, in the first instance, responsible for outside intervention. A problem that commenced with linguistic rights transformed into one of minority rights and developed into militancy, inviting intervention from across the Palk Strait.

8

DESPERATE MIGRANTS: THE POLICY-INDUCED CRISIS

It's called the pottery store rule: 'you break it, you own it'. But it doesn't just apply to pots and mugs, but to nations. In the build-up to the catastrophic invasion of Iraq, it was invoked by Colin Powell, then US secretary of state. 'You are going to be the proud owner of 25 million people,' he reportedly told George W. Bush. 'You will own all their hopes, aspirations and problems.' But while many of these military interventions have left nations shattered, Western governments have resembled the customer who walks away whistling, hoping no one has noticed the mess left behind. Our media have been all too complicit in allowing them to leave the scene.

—Owen Jones, *Guardian*, 24 March 2014

The year 2015 had a different story to tell about West Asia and North Africa. Both the press and social media drew the world's attention to the humanitarian crisis in the region. A number of tragic developments involving people fleeing the region—such as the sinking of boats with 500 migrants soon after leaving Zuwara in Libya; the discovery of bodies of seventy-one migrants in a truck in Austria and 800 missing in a shipwreck off an Italian island; and numerous instances of physical, psychological, sexual and economic exploitation faced by refugees at the hands of human traffickers—began to stir the conscience of the international community. And who can forget the heartbreaking images of the three-year-old Syrian boy who was washed ashore a Turkish beach?

With violence escalating at home, many Syrians, Iraqis, Libyans and Yemenis have turned refugees and asylum seekers, willing to take the risk of crossing the Mediterranean with people smugglers, perhaps unwillingly becoming part of possibly the biggest refugee exodus this generation has seen. Up to April 2016, the International Organization for Migration reported that 175,797 asylum seekers had arrived in Europe by land and sea routes, most of them landing in Greece (152,461) and Italy (19,322),[1] while more than 737 had perished in the effort between January and April 2016 alone.

The Arab Spring in 2011 was predicated on the hope and expectation that people would have a chance to voice their demands for a better life and economic conditions. It led instead to sustained conflicts and violence that reached unprecedented levels, leaving them only one choice: of fleeing their homes, sometimes with no visible prospects of returning. It is important to take stock of how bad the state of affairs is in these countries and analyse how much has changed since the conflict started.

Syria

During the Ottoman rule, around 1855, there was no 'Syria' in the sense of a nation state; there were only provinces centred around ancient cities. 'The concept of a state, much less a nation state, did not enter into political thought until the end of the nineteenth century. Inhabitants of the various parts of what became Syria could move without feeling or being considered alien from one province of the Ottoman Empire to the next.'[2]

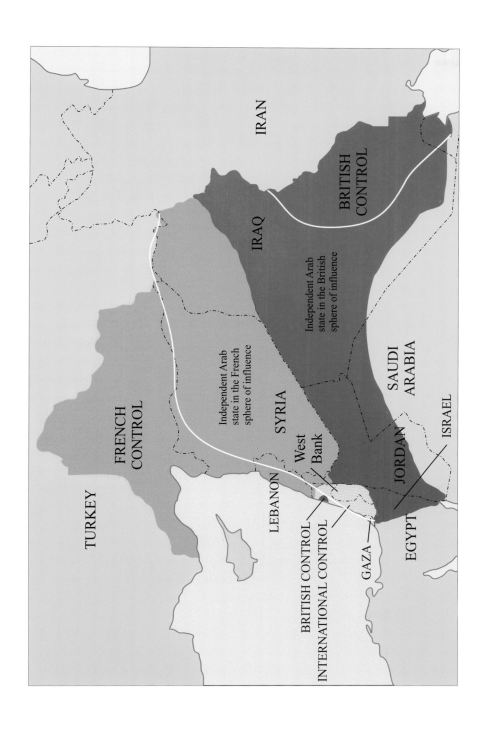

As discussed in the chapter on Syria, the Sykes–Picot Agreement, signed in 1916, involved the French and the British reaching a deal to divide the Middle East, whereby the former came to control the eastern Mediterranean while the latter had territories in the Persian Gulf. Straight lines were drawn across the Middle East, which was now divided into new countries under two spheres of influence:

- Iraq, Transjordan, and Palestine under British influence, and
- Syria and Lebanon under French influence.

The Assad regime, established less than six decades later in 1970, has not been averse to using brutal force, either in 1982 or now in the civil war that commenced in 2011. During the Assad rule, Syria, however, made considerable progress. It had a GDP of $5,000 per capita, which was roughly double that of Pakistan and Yemen and five times that of Afghanistan; nearly 90 per cent of Syrian children attended primary or secondary school; and about 80–90 per cent Syrians achieved literacy. Their approach to governance, however, was clear right from the start, when Hafez al-Assad came to power: help the Syrian people to live better provided only that they not challenge his rule.[3] The political situation under Assad was such that all parties other than the ruling Ba'ath Party were banned and prominent opposition figures were jailed; membership of the Muslim Brotherhood was punishable by death; and Syria was in a state of emergency for forty-eight years.

Bashar al-Assad sought to dampen the unrest of 2011 through attempts such as releasing dozens of political prisoners, lifting the emergency, granting nationality to Syrian Kurds and removing the ban on teachers wearing a niqab. However, these measures did little to curb the growing turmoil. What started as a movement in the small town of Daraa spread throughout the nation, and soon multiple rebel groups emerged (including jihadist groups arguably supported by the West).

Territorial control in Syria has changed several times since the 2011 uprising. Today, there are 'signs the battlefield is transforming, with extremist and Islamist groups establishing a momentum of their own and the forces of Bashar al-Assad under mounting pressure on several fronts'.[4] The ISIS has seized control of significant parts of the country's central corridor. This included the ancient city of Palmyra, with UNESCO world heritage structures nearly 4,000 years old, many of which were tragically and systematically destroyed by the terror group before the Syrian army regained control of the city in March 2016. The al-Nusra Front is making gains by way of garnering people's support. Recognizing the need to have popular support, the latter has been providing essential services such as food, electricity, water and health care, and has also appointed judges with the promise of swift justice. In doing these, al-Nusra has been presenting itself as an alternative government. The advance of the Islamic State has had a particularly significant impact: more than seven million people have been internally displaced while more than four million, out of a national population of twenty-two million, have fled the country, earning Syria the dubious distinction of being the world's largest producer of internally displaced people (IDP) and refugees.

The US, by covertly providing aid to the insurgents,[5] has been justifying the intervention by pointing out that the Syrian government is tyrannical.

By Western standards, it is undoubtedly an authoritarian regime. Whether or not it gassed hundreds of its citizens, it has certainly killed thousands with conventional weapons. (According to the Syrian Observatory for Human Rights, the rebels are known to have killed at least 20,000 and perhaps as many as 30,000 government soldiers, about twice the number of rebel casualties, and both sides have committed documented atrocities).[6]

At the same time, one also needs to note:

> ... the standards Western nations proclaim have been applied in a highly selective way. The EU and the US enjoy cordial and mutually beneficial relations with dozens of tyrannical governments including most of the countries now attempting to regime-change Syria.[7]

The ISIS in Syria has been overpowering the moderate rebels thanks to the funding it has been receiving from the Gulf countries. More significantly, the Syrian government is refusing to target the organization, perhaps in the belief that 'foreign powers like the US may hate Assad but would ultimately prefer him to ISIS'. All of this has helped the jihadist group gain a 'staging ground, territory and battlefield training for its assault'.[8]

Many Syrians have found themselves left with no option but to leave their country. Those in exile in Turkey are also being prompted to migrate to other European countries since returning home is no longer an option, and Syrians cannot settle down in Turkey as it has not legally granted them the right to work.[9] Commenting on the worsening Syrian refugee crisis, Ban Ki-moon admitted that the Security Council had been failing Syria because of 'big power divisions' which have prevented it from taking necessary actions to put an end to a conflict that has resulted in the loss of thousands of lives.[10]

Libya

Another country that has contributed to the desperate migration flows to Europe is Libya. Western military intervention in Libya has been comprehensively covered in Chapter 3. Most Libyans, in the first ever national survey published in February 2012,[11] revealed that they would still prefer a one-man rule over alternatives like democracy. This kind of attitude may be the result of what Gaddafi accomplished when he took over as the leader in 1969 after having deposed King Idris in a military coup. He was twenty-seven when he started governing Libya, one of the poorest nations in Africa. When he died in 2011, Libya was Africa's wealthiest nation with the highest GDP per capita and life expectancy, and with fewer people living below the poverty line than in the Netherlands.[12] Libyans under Gaddafi enjoyed free health care, education and electricity as well as interest-free loans. Women had greater access to rights to education and employment, property, divorce and an income—something that was commended by the United Nations Human Rights Council (UNHRC) in January 2011.[13] On the other hand, those in power since the end of the Gaddafi era, tied to strongly patriarchal traditions, have been clamping down on women's rights to the extent of perceiving gender equality as a Western perversion.[14] The General National Congress (the interim parliament) has criminalized any act of insulting its members; there have been instances of black Libyans being attacked merely on the suspicion of being Gaddafi loyalists; and while thousands have been driven out of their homes to suffer in dreadful conditions in refugee camps, many others have been arbitrarily detained.

Today, Libya is overrun by militia, rebels and mercenaries. The country struggles to deal with a rapidly worsening humanitarian crisis and escalating chaos as it stands on the verge of disintegrating. According to UN experts, Libya has become 'a primary source of illicit weapons', with some of the Russian-made weapons falling into the hands of fundamentalist Islamist rebels in Syria.[15] The country is home to the world's largest 'loose arms cache' and its porous borders are frequently transited by 'heavily armed non-state actors, including the Tuareg rebels and jihadists'.[16]

There are two governments, parliaments and armies—the Toruk-based elected government headed by Abdullah al Thani and the Tripoli-based unelected government headed by Omar al-Hasi—and neither has been able to counter the growing presence of the ISIS, protect civilians, or even ensure the provision of basic amenities. There is little or negligible security outside Tripoli and Benghazi—virtually ghost cities where people have been driven out of their homes and businesses. More than 300,000 in Libya are internally displaced, living off charity in makeshift camps. Libya's health care system is on the verge of collapse as thousands of Filipino workers have fled the country.[17] Thousands of Libyans are migrating to Egypt, Tunisia, the Gulf states and European countries out of fear of arbitrary arrests; many of them have drowned during the hazardous journey. Libya's various groups engaged in conflict have set up bases in different parts of the country, which is gradually heading farther and farther away from the prospects of peace and stability.

Yemen

Yemen, the poorest and most populous corner of the Arabian peninsula, has had internal conflicts ever since the 1990 unification of the North and South. The resentment amongst the Houthis about Saleh, the former leader of North Yemen, getting overall control after the unification caused numerous conflicts. This internal chaos resulted in the al-Qaeda gaining ground in many uncontrolled areas. After the military attacks by the Saudi-led ten-nation coalition against the Houthis, the conflict soon ceased to be merely an internal problem and acquired regional overtones. Already one of the poorest Arab nations, Yemen is now experiencing violence on a daily basis, as aid agencies claim that food, water, fuel and medicines are fast depleting, and the curbs on imports due to an international embargo has not helped the country deal with its cataclysmic conditions.

Picturesque Yemen, full of architectural marvels and beautiful mountains looming in the background, has unfortunately come to be known for the devastation caused by constant warfare between various rebel groups, compounded by the US-backed Saudi intervention. There is now additionally the threat of ISIS setting up base in this country, with the potential of turning it into another Syria. In addition to the rising number of IDPs, Yemen, being a transit country for mixed migration flows, has also had to host hundreds of thousands of registered refugees.[18]

The *New York Tribune* said of Yemen in 1898 that 'order will be supplied from outside', that foreign rule will bring with it peace, and that 'Yemen will no more be the Yemen it has been for forty centuries'.[19] The reality today cannot be further from this claim made more than a hundred years ago. The number of actors involved in the ongoing conflict—the US-backed Saudi-led coalition of ten Arab nations, Iran, Houthis, Saleh, al-Qaeda, ISIS, the Hadi government in exile and the southern movement for secession—have all aggravated the conditions, leaving Yemenis and the international community alike with little or no hope for the country to return to normalcy in the near future.

Iraq

On 18 March 2003, Iraq was stricken with panic. As the country braced itself for the long impending US-led attack, the *Guardian* reported:

> the number of fatal car accidents seemed to surge, with drivers in a panic to get home, or to get out. Chemists sold out of valium. Queues at petrol stations broadened and lengthened in a country where fuel is ridiculously cheap and plentiful. The price of mineral water doubled. Tinned foods and packaged soups disappeared from supermarket shelves. Young couples rushed to get engaged. Workers stored the files and fixtures from Iraqi government office buildings.[20]

The US invaded Iraq in a bid to find and destroy WMDs allegedly stored by the latter, and establish democracy. The WMDs have not been found to this day, but the war did manage to have a long-standing impact on the region. Millions of innocent civilians lost their lives in the bombings, while millions of others have been displaced. This gave room for more internal conflicts to arise later, such as the Shia–Sunni conflict. This too can be traced back to the Sykes–Picot agreement discussed earlier, by which the 'vast Arab Sunni community across the Middle East's center was divided in half by the European-imposed Syria-Iraq border, then lumped in with artificial states with large Shia communities'.[21] This kind of influence on the Arab world that the colonial powers exercised had other ramifications. As Tarek Osman[22] points out:

> ... as these colonial powers, in the 1920s, '30s and '40s, continued to exert immense influence over the Arab world, the thrust of Arab politics—in North Africa and in the eastern Mediterranean—gradually but decisively shifted from building liberal constitutional governance systems (as Egypt, Syria and Iraq had witnessed in the early decades of the 20th century) to assertive nationalism whose main objective was getting rid of the colonialists and the ruling systems that worked with them. This was a key factor behind the rise of the militarist regimes that had come to dominate many Arab countries from the 1950s until the 2011 Arab uprisings.[23]

Yet, Iraq under Saddam Hussein could at least boast of universal healthcare and education systems, sixteen to twenty-four hours' supply of electricity in Baghdad, and a better quality of life and greater respect for women who often occupied government positions. More than a decade later, Iraq is governed by politicians who have been unsuccessful in providing basic rights, such as access to electricity, water, medicine and security. While car bombings, kidnappings and assassinations have become an everyday affair, terrorist groups including ISIS and the al-Qaeda have managed to gain control of large parts of the country. The corruption levels, according to some, have significantly increased.[24] In addition, a survey carried out by local rights-based NGOs suggested that the new government's conservative ideas with respect to women have prevented them from occupying government positions and have resulted in increased levels of unemployment among women.[25]

The de-Ba'athification process that sought to rid the government of any influence from Saddam Hussein's Ba'ath Party played its intended part, only with terrible consequences, as 'large numbers of recently unemployed Iraqi soldiers went and joined insurgent militias, greatly strengthening the anti-government forces while simultaneously stripping the government of its military capabilities'.[26] The ISIS has managed to bring certain territories under its control. Even though it does not directly govern them, it has expelled the government forces. In other areas, it has handed over control to local Sunni groups, while yet others are contested territories with no single group controlling them.

According to HRW, the conditions are not just deplorable but worsening by the day for women, children, activists and journalists. Women 'widowed by the conflict, violence or displacement are vulnerable to trafficking for sexual exploitation and prostitution'.[27]

Ukraine

With the conflict exacerbating amidst the chaos in Europe caused by the destabilization in the Middle East and North Africa, there has also been a severe migration crisis brewing in eastern Europe. Dissatisfaction with public services and the political class, lack of economic opportunities and endemic corruption have resulted in large-scale migration out of Ukraine. The migration flows are of three kinds:[28] forced migration of refugees and IDPs as a result of the Russian annexation of Crimea; migration to avoid military conscription, that is, to escape forceful recruitment by the military; and international migration of individuals seeking employment and education after being pushed into poverty by the war's adverse impact on the economy.

One can take a cue from Franck Düvell's[29] use of the concepts of 'exit strategy' and 'voice strategy', borrowed from economist Albert Hirschman,[30] to understand migration. What began with a voice strategy—an attempt to change dissatisfying conditions by way of protests—has gradually, in most conflict-affected zones today, turned into exit strategies used by many helpless individuals and families to escape the very conditions they attempted to transform. With the worsening of the fighting between Ukrainian troops and pro-Russian separatists, the Ukrainian economy has been severely hit, while less than one-third of the $316 million needed for the UN's humanitarian response has been raised.[31] Yet, the international community has not taken the asylum seekers seriously, insofar as most countries that they have turned to have denied refugee status to large numbers of Ukrainians, arguing that they are not persecuted, nor is there a war back home.

The statistics of refugees originating from Ukraine are staggering. While the number of IDPs has reached almost 1.3 million, the UN reports that the number of Ukrainians to have fled their country stands at an estimated 867,000. Due to deep cultural ties with western Ukraine, Poland is the most preferred destination for these asylum seekers and has received vast numbers of Ukrainians seeking jobs, education and permanent residency. By May 2015, Poland was already playing host to around 400,000 Ukrainians. Other countries that Ukrainians have turned to for asylum include Germany, Italy, Belarus and Russia, with Russia taking in about a million residents from south-eastern Ukraine till May 2015, of whom 330,000 had been granted citizenship. Between 2014 and 2015, more than 100,000 Ukrainians made their way to Belarus, increasing the latter's population by 1 per cent. By employing most of them as agriculture and construction labourers, Belarus has hoped to rescue its agricultural sector.[32]

However, most European countries have not welcomed Ukrainian asylum seekers warmly. Countries already grappling with an influx of refugees from Syria and other countries struck by civil wars have argued that while parts of Ukraine are witnessing violence, the western parts of the country remain largely unaffected by the conflict and are more or less secure, with no life-threatening situations, and have advised Ukrainians to relocate internally.[33] Failing to obtain an asylum or refugee status, many Ukrainians have tried gaining entry into EU states through 'traditional labour migration routes or family routes'.[34]

The Refugee Crisis

The steadily declining conditions in these countries have been driving their citizens to seek safer havens, primarily in Europe, as the world witnesses arguably the biggest refugee crisis since the Second World War. The following figures demonstrate the crisis originating from these countries.

	Syria	Libya	Yemen	Iraq	Ukraine
Refugees	4,194,554	4,317	5,832	377,747	318,786
Asylum Seekers	90,751	5,219	5,618	141,913	20,754
Returned Refugees	0	0	0	3,318	0
Internally Displaced Persons (IDPs)	7,632,500	434,869	1,267,590	3,962,142	1,382,000

Source: UNHCR, as of June 2015.

With the numbers soaring in 2015—as increasing tides of desperate and helpless people, wrapped in blankets and sleeping bags, many carrying small children, braved the treacherous journey to seek asylum in certain European countries—Europe has been faced with the acute challenge of accommodating the asylum seekers and refugees. While Germany has taken in significant numbers of refugees, certain other countries have been reluctant. The EU has struggled to come up with ways to grapple with the situation, with suggestions ranging from setting up a European border force that would manage the external borders, to the need for a joint EU strategy by which each of the twenty-eight member countries would be obliged to accept a certain number of asylum seekers. However, Europe has remained 'bitterly divided over how to cope with the crisis'.[35] Hungary, for instance, which happens to be the main entry point into Europe's borderless Schengen zone for the refugees, has adopted a hard line. Faced with an influx of migrants, Hungary built a controversial 175 km razor-wire fence (with plans to fortify it) to keep the refugees out. David Cameron's announcement in September 2015 about the UK's decision to accept 20,000 refugees in the next five years also disappointed many who expected a larger figure.

The US has also faced a fair amount of criticism for not extending enough help to deal with the crisis. It accepted roughly 1,500 refugees in 2015; Obama ordered his team to admit 10,000 in 2016. Following this, almost 1,300 people in the US signed an online petition calling on the country to lift its limit on Syrian refugees, offering to take some of them into their homes. One of the petitioners, a reverend at a church in Indiana, alluding to the invasion of Iraq in 2003, said: 'We have to share some responsibility for that [war] because of our regime changes in the Middle East. Most of those refugees are a result of that.'[36]

The crisis unfolding in Europe has drawn the attention of the heads of state and common people alike. Many citizens have even come forward offering monetary aid. For the millions of refugees 'stuck in crowded and chronically undersupplied camps where they are subject to cold, hunger and the ravages of disease',[37] money would certainly help them get by at a time when survival itself is the immediate goal. However, increasingly larger numbers of people in the receiving countries are coming out in opposition to the influx of refugees. There have been widely reported cases of Hungarians physically assaulting incoming refugees; massive protests have been witnessed, such as in east Germany, where thousands of people took to the streets protesting the granting of housing in their areas to asylum seekers, terming it the 'Islamization of the West'.[38] Germany's right-wing movement, on 19 October 2015, held an anti-migrant rally that brought to light the 'European backlash towards a massive influx'.[39] This kind of hostility to refugees may prove to be a 'potentially fatal wound'[40] for Merkel and her Christian Democratic Union party. While the EU called for Turkey to 'tighten its border security and help contain the historic influx of Syrians and others escaping conflict, persecution and poverty', Ankara demanded 'greater recognition for its role in hosting more than two million Syrian refugees, an increase in financial help and an acceleration of its stuttering drive for EU membership'.[41]

The fact that protest movements are gaining thousands of followers highlights the vehement opposition to immigrants and Islam in Europe, signalling a possible radicalization of the far right in the continent over the issue of refugees. Incidentally, while Merkel's pro-refugee party has been swiftly losing support in Germany, right-wing parties across Europe have been growing in popularity in 2015. Poland elected one of Europe's most right-wing parliaments in October; the anti-EU, anti-immigration Danish People's Party gained the second largest percentage of Denmark's vote in their national elections in June; and Sweden Democrats, an extreme-right party, ranked as the country's most popular party in a survey in August.[42] Amid the growing refugee crisis, while there has been an outpouring of support for immigrants and refugees from many citizens and political leaders, the popularity of these far-right parties with strong anti-immigration policies is climbing steadily.

For the emigrants who are turned away at the borders, there seems to be nothing to go back to. Adding to the tragedy, according to a UNICEF report, almost 9,000 schools in these war-torn countries are no longer functional, either because they have been destroyed or they are being used as shelters. The number of children who have dropped out of school in Syria, Libya, Iraq, Yemen and Sudan is nearly 13.7 million.[43] An entire generation in parts of the Arab world is therefore going to grow up without proper education or skills, possibly in a completely new environment, which may result in their being stuck in menial jobs and turning bitter and hateful. The internal challenges of the EU nations, combined with the deteriorating humanitarian situation in the conflict-afflicted countries, have wider implications that cannot be ignored, and are crying out for urgent political solutions.

9

THE DOCTRINE OF THE RESPONSIBILITY TO PROTECT

The doctrine of Responsibility to Protect (R2P) arose essentially from the anguished introspection of the international community following the mass atrocities in Rwanda and Srebrenica. The term itself was first used in the report of the International Commission on Intervention and State Sovereignty (ICISS) in 2001 and subsequently adopted by the UN at the 2005 World Summit to prevent genocide, war crimes, ethnic cleansing and crimes against humanity.[1]

The R2P doctrine has three pillars. Pillar one calls on all states to protect their populations from the four mass atrocities mentioned above. It is indeed every state's responsibility to safeguard its population from these. Pillar two concerns states which are failed states or fragile states, those that need assistance in terms of technical capacity building so that they can build the institutions that in turn can save their populations from these atrocities. Clearly, pillars one and two are in the nature of the preventive segment of the doctrine.

What happens in case pillars one and two do not work and there is reasonable evidence to believe that mass atrocities of the kind that the international community witnessed in Rwanda and Srebrenica are likely to recur? What does the international community do then? Clearly, before embarking on action under Chapter VII of the UN Charter and authorizing the use of force, the Security Council would want to satisfy itself that the alleged violations fall within one of the categories of mass atrocity crimes.

During the course of a Security Council retreat in April 2012, there was a discussion on this. How can one know that genocide is going to take place? My response: first, genocide is defined in the 1948 Convention on Genocide.[2] So, there is a threshold. Next question: does the Council wait till genocide actually occurs before it takes action? No, because that is what happened in the case of Rwanda—in breach of the Convention. So, the international community is required to act, and for this the designated forum is the Security Council, which is required to make the determination whether the facts available point in the direction of someone having the intent to commit one or more of the mass atrocities mentioned above.

A caveat is required. The trigger point cannot be human rights violations. Human rights violations can take place everywhere in the world. They can occur in the US, in India, in Sri Lanka and elsewhere. There is already an existing machinery to address such violations. That machinery has been established in Geneva in the form of the Human Rights Council, which reports to the Third Committee of the UN in New York.

Do gross violations of human rights provide a trigger point? If there are persistent and gross violations, is that near enough to the threshold of mass atrocities? That is a subject that requires discussion. And that is where a determination would need to be made whether the requisite threshold (which warrants coercive measures on the part of the international community) has been reached. And then, one has to see whether the use of diplomatic and other humanitarian and peaceful means is possible.

The trigger point has to be the imminent threat of mass atrocities, and that determination can only be made by the Security Council. What is required is a comprehensive and judicious analysis of all possible consequences so that military action does not fuel instability or cause more harm. (Incidentally, that discussion did not take place in the Council in the case of Libya. Many of us asked for it but Gaddafi's poor track record, his threats and the scaremongering got the better of sound judgement.)

Once the determination is made that there is enough evidence in terms of intent, and enough evidence that inaction by the international community will result in large-scale mass atrocities, the international community would obviously have a role to play. Not to assume responsibility in such a scenario would be nothing short of the Council abdicating responsibility in the manner it did in Rwanda in 1994 and in Srebrenica in 1995. Pillar one poses no problem. The international community has agreed that each state has a responsibility to save its own population from the identified mass atrocities. Pillar two envisages that when the states involved are failed or fragile states, the international community has to step in. Under pillar three, if there is a reasonable basis to believe that the state is not shouldering its responsibility or it does not have the capacity to shoulder the responsibility of protection, and the intent to commit mass atrocities is evident, the international community has a definite role to play and a responsibility to assume. However, pillar three is problematic because it has lent itself to strong views and, to an extent, some amount of misuse as well.

The ink was barely dry on the 2005 World Summit Outcome Document when the French foreign minister, Bernard Kouchner, proceeded to characterize it as the 'doctrine of humanitarian intervention'. The urge to disregard notions of Westphalian state sovereignty, to a lesser or greater extent—and to intervene—is invariably more pronounced among the representatives of those countries which were once colonial powers. Their desire to be presumptive, to set norms for everybody that reflect the views only of the West, has always been evident. It is reflected also in the writings of Western commentators.

Kouchner's statement confirmed the worst fears of most developing countries. We viewed the R2P doctrine as providing an opening for the reordering of societies from outside using military force. Most of my colleagues and I, representing developing countries in the multilateral system, have our world views firmly anchored in the framework of Westphalian state sovereignty. This is not surprising. Most of us were born either prior to or just after our countries gained freedom from colonial rule.

Those responsible for the intellectual conditioning for this mindset were Jawaharlal Nehru and Indira Gandhi, Josip Broz Tito of Yugoslavia, Gamal Abdel Nasser of Egypt, Kwame Nkrumah of Ghana and others from Africa in the 1950s, '60s, and '70s. It would, however, be a serious mistake to believe that the colonial experience alone provides an explanation for their inherent suspicion of the doctrine. Their cynicism has been fuelled by the nature of political and economic negotiations in the post-colonial era. Shorn of their complex verbiage, these amounted to nothing more than the strong—those in dominant positions—manipulating the system to their advantage at the expense of the weak and the vulnerable.

During the nineteen or so years that India was away from the Security Council, the intellectual undermining of the concept of Westphalian state sovereignty had increased significantly. Even before India rejoined the Security Council on 1 January 2011, it had become increasingly clear that the work of the Council would largely focus on domestic situations in countries in Africa, particularly North Africa, where authoritarian regimes had decided to employ brutal repression in order to quell growing demands for democratic freedoms.

During India's seventh term on the Security Council as a non-permanent member in 2011–12, I was invited by the Kennedy School at Harvard University, to Columbia and Yale universities, the African Centre for Governance at the Maxwell School at Syracuse University, the International Institute for Strategic Studies, and so on to participate in discussions on this subject. The focus in all these interactions was on how the doctrine was playing out in the work of the Security Council in the evolving situations, first in Libya and then in Syria. The most disturbing feature of these interactions was the barely disguised urge to intervene that was visible among the representatives of some member states, but most worryingly in academia, think tanks and certain sections of civil society as well. This urge was, in fairness to those advocating such intervention, always couched in moralistic terms and the need to protect civilians. This impulse invariably blinded its proponents to the long-term adverse consequences of the use of force.

I was initially tempted to examine the intellectual underpinning of this doctrine and the Security Council's treatment of the theme of protection of civilians, as detailed in earlier Council resolutions, and reflect on how the more recent situations in Ivory Coast, Libya and Syria had been handled. But halfway into our term on the Security Council, it became increasingly clear that the narrative was beginning to change. The brutal assassination of Ambassador Chris Stevens of the US in Benghazi drove home the point to everyone that the ghost of Libya had truly come to haunt the international community. With the situation in Syria deteriorating by the day and—with no end in sight to the sectarian conflict there—threatening to engulf the larger region, it became clear by the middle of 2012 that a study of the doctrine of R2P in the context of Libya would amount to an examination of the doctrine at its lowest point.

As an aside, I would like to mention that I had almost forgotten that I had cautioned against the misuse of R2P as far back as 2009 and was happily reminded of it by Lieutenant General Satish Nambiar, the first commander-in-chief of the UN Protection Force in Zagreb, Croatia, in 1992, when he wrote an article for The Wire on 12 July 2015:

> It is appropriate to conclude this piece by recalling what India's Permanent Representative to the UN said in 2009 during the debate in the General Assembly on the concept of the 'Responsibility to Protect'. 'It has been India's consistent view that the responsibility to protect its population is one of the foremost responsibilities of every State,' said India's Ambassador Hardeep Puri ... 'Willingness to take Chapter VII measures can only be on a case by case basis and in cooperation with relevant regional organisations with a specific proviso that such action should only be taken when peaceful means are inadequate and national authorities manifestly fail in discharging their duty.' In emphasising the need to be realistic he further stated, 'We ... need to be cognisant that creation of new norms should at the same time completely safeguard against their misuse. In this context, responsibility to protect should in no way provide a pretext for humanitarian intervention or unilateral action.
>
> Even a cursory examination of reasons for non-action by the UN, specially the Security Council, reveals that in respect of the tragic events that were witnessed by the entire world, non-action was not due to lack of warning, resources or the barrier of state sovereignty, but because of strategic, political or economic considerations of those on whom the present international architecture had placed the onus to act. The key aspect, therefore, is to address the issue of willingness to act, in which context a necessary ingredient is real reform of the decision making bodies in the UN like the Security Council in its permanent membership.'

To conclude his article, Nambiar observed:

> Six years later, and two decades on from the Srebrenica massacre, those words continue to ring true.[3]

And yet, that is exactly what happened in the case of Libya.

The only summit-level interaction with Libya I recall from the Indian side was when Indira Gandhi visited the country in 1984. Unlike Britain and France, Indian economic entities did not have big contracts in Libya. India had 18,000 workers there, but they had been hired by Western companies. In short, India was not in bed with Gaddafi. Those who *were* in bed with him sent their prime ministers to his desert tent not once or twice; they were selling arms to his regime, over $700 million worth, even in the year prior to the military operation. These are not mere allegations. A head of state/government from western Europe had his election financed by Gaddafi. But by the time of Resolution 1973, there were very few in the international community who wanted to hold a brief for him.

It is entirely correct to say that the international community's anguish about its inaction in Rwanda and Srebrenica was a crucial factor in its Libya decision. The four mass atrocities—genocide, ethnic cleansing, war crimes and crimes against humanity—which the international community witnessed helplessly in the two instances in the 1990s, on a scale of barbarity not seen since the Holocaust and Cambodia, conjured up visions of horror. No one on either side of the R2P argument wanted to have another mass atrocity of this scale on their conscience.

But another factor that was at work was that the apex body of the UN, entrusted with the task of dealing with threats to international peace and security, had been largely politicized. (Our somewhat late realization of this fact was a consequence of India's long absence from the Council.) Consequently, any pursuit of national interest, as perceived at any given point of time, was slowly but surely developing into 'a new doctrine' that was entirely divorced even from the interests of those permanent members of the Security Council espousing intervention and invocation of Article 42 under Chapter VII of the UN Charter. A series of policy-induced mistakes by at least three of the five permanent members of the Security Council led to a complete paralysis of the body in the months ahead when three double vetoes by Russia and China brought the collective action by the Council in relation to events unfolding in Syria to a grinding halt.

In setting the political context for the kind of interventionist policies that the Council attempted, one should recall that very often the definitional distinction between what was contained in the resolutions, based on the ordinary meaning of words, and how the resolutions were finally implemented, was not merely blurred but distorted both in intent and practice. The urge to intervene blinded so many of the dramatis personae that individually and collectively they failed to visualize the damage their actions would cause to their own interests.

There is still little agreement on how the concept of R2P is to be implemented. This is partly because of the closely related concept of Protection of Civilians (PoC) that falls under the UN's peacekeeping operations. Both PoC and R2P share some common elements, particularly with regard to prevention and also in the context of support to national authorities in discharging their responsibilities towards civilians.

Over the last decade, the Security Council has authorized a number of UN peacekeeping missions to use 'all necessary means' under Chapter VII of the UN Charter to act in support or independently of national authorities to protect civilians—in Darfur, the Democratic Republic of the Congo, Ivory Coast,

Liberia, South Sudan, and so on. Also, several sanctions authorized by the Security Council provide for measures against those guilty of violating international humanitarian and human rights law. PoC also finds a mention in a number of thematic resolutions dealing with women, peace and security, sexual violence in armed conflict, children and armed conflict, protection of humanitarian workers, conflict prevention, and so on, such as Resolutions 1325 (on women), 1612 (on children), 1502 (on protection of humanitarian workers), 1625 (on conflict prevention) and 1820 (on sexual exploitation).

The concept cannot, however, be conflated with R2P. PoC is a legal concept deriving from international humanitarian, human rights and refugee laws that are applicable to armed conflict and enjoin combatants to protect civilians/non-combatants. There is little ambiguity about this. On the other hand, R2P is still an evolving concept loaded with politico-legal considerations. All members of the Security Council, particularly the P5, have to be on the same page for authorization of R2P action. The conceptual and legal differences between PoC and R2P get blurred, and it becomes essentially a political call whether and how the international community reacts. The Security Council's handling of Libya—where the death toll was in the low hundreds when it adopted Resolution 1973—and Syria underscores these considerations.

Only the Security Council can take action under Chapter VII, including measures under Article 42. But resorting to 'all necessary means' under Article 42 should have been at the very end of the scale. First, non-coercive measures should have been adopted, including establishment of commissions of inquiry, referral to the ICC, setting up of special tribunals, and so on. Second, non-military coercive measures should have been resorted to, including targeted sanctions (travel ban, asset freeze, etc.).

When a UN mission is given a mandate to protect civilians either in support of a national authority or independently, if the national authority is not in a position to do so, there must be a presumption of neutrality, impartiality and proportionality. On the other hand, when the member states are authorized to protect civilians, there is no mechanism to ensure neutrality, impartiality or proportionality. It is in these situations that Responsibility while Protecting (RwP) assumes great significance. Addressing the sixty-sixth session of the General Assembly in September 2011, President Dilma Rousseff of Brazil first talked about RwP, a concept which has found some resonance.

A mechanism under RwP may include monitoring and review of the implementation of the mandate by the Security Council or even the Department of Peacekeeping Operations (DPKO) as well as strict reporting requirement from member states implementing the mandate. It may also be worthwhile to set up a commission of inquiry to investigate violations. There will, however, be practical difficulties. Since a P5 member is invariably involved in implementing the mandate authorized by the Security Council, it will not be easy to establish a mechanism for RwP. Also, the functioning of any such mechanism will inevitably be conditioned by the interests of P5 members implementing the Council's mandate.

Libya is a textbook example of how the political dynamics of a situation, rather than its actual level status, determine actions by P5 members. Some points of interest in the context of the implementation of Resolutions 1970 and 1973 in the case of Libya need to be enumerated:

- While Resolution 1970 referred the situation in Libya to the ICC and asked the Libyan authorities to cooperate with the ICC, there has been no serious consideration of the status of

Libya's cooperation after the objective of regime change was accomplished. Pro forma debates in the Council have reflected political interests of the Council members rather than Libya's cooperation with the ICC or the ability of Libya's judicial system to guarantee a free and fair trial.

- In spite of the arms embargo imposed under Resolutions 1970 and 1973, weapons were supplied indiscriminately, ostensibly for the protection of civilians. This was done by several states, including the P5 members.

- Arms embargo was used to impose a virtual blockade against the regime and applied across the board to deprive the regime of all goods, not only of military nature. In more than 99 per cent of the cases, the ships inspected by NATO were found not to carry any prohibited goods.

- The no-fly zone was implemented only against the regime's airplanes while those operated by the rebels were allowed.

- Provisions relating to ceasefire and political process (in the context of the African Union's efforts) were completely ignored.

- Military operations ostensibly for PoC continued even after the Gaddafi regime had crumbled and was in no position to pose any threat to civilians. NATO operations stopped only after Gaddafi was killed.

Should the Libyan experience and political considerations deter us from pursuing RwP? I would say, no. The international community needs to act if a mass atrocity seems likely to take place. In my view, if the concept of R2P is to survive and form the basis of action by the Security Council, it must be anchored in the concept of RwP. Then alone will the Security Council members be able to be on the same page to authorize action for R2P. Then alone will the international community have enough confidence to support action under R2P. This also calls for an urgent reform of the Security Council, including expansion in both permanent and non-permanent categories, so that its composition better reflects the politico-economic dynamic of today's world.

AFTERWORD
Imperfect States, Borderless Ills
and Restive Citizenry

This book is a testament to the parlous state of our interconnected but fractured world, where mistrust, injustice,
inequality and violence in many regions seem to be increasing with
each passing day. Politics, leadership and international covenants
that govern state behaviour towards citizens and other states seem
to be fraying in the face of many of the borderless ills confronting
us. More importantly, this book provides an insight into the tragic
legacies of unilateral military interventions by global powers in the
pursuit of un-enlightened national interests, oblivious of lessons
from past misguided adventures.

The great power rivalries that the staunch optimists of the
post-Cold War era had triumphantly written off as a feature of a
bygone era seem to be rising from the dead, except this time in
the shape of a hydra-headed python. The various proxy wars in
the Middle East are examples of what geopolitical rivalries have
wrought in their wake. The ongoing carnage in Yemen and Syria,
as well as the enduring instability in Libya, attest to the havoc that
ill-advised policies of competing regional and global powers have
created. Further, as detailed in several of the preceding chapters,
the Security Council, the custodian of international peace and

security, has either been marginalized or paralysed as a result of this geopolitical competition. The doctrine of Responsibility to Protect instituted for the prevention of mass atrocities unfolding in some of the countries has failed in many cases to live up to its intent, as the book so lucidly illustrates.

Weak states, some long governed by tyrannical rule and convulsed by internal and external crises, are often unable to deliver security and positive public goods to their citizens, consequently edging towards failure, as witnessed in Libya, Yemen, Syria and Iraq. Preventing the collapse of such states, and resuscitating those whose lease of life has all but expired, have become the central preoccupation of global powers and the world community at large. In doing so, and under the pretext of fighting violent extremism, human rights and fundamental freedoms tend to be sacrificed on the altar of pyrrhic state stability. The war on terror over the past decade, now pursued under various guises, has not made our world any safer, as the book amply demonstrates. On the contrary, it has created, in its wake, a bottomless reservoir of humiliation and resentment among sizeable portions of local populations that many of the armed extremist groups, in turn, continue to draw on, attracting recruits to sustain their brutal campaigns. The systematic exclusion of Iraqi Sunnis during the US occupation of the country is a prime example of such policy. It has contributed to the meteoric rise of the theocratic malignancy called the ISIS or Daesh, challenging the nebulous state borders of the region, once etched on a map by the Sykes–Picot pair. This is a phenomenon the book deftly unpacks as part of the disintegration that 'perilous interventions' leave in their wake. Syria, a sui generis case of such disintegration, is the theatre of three simultaneous tragedies: a civil war, a sectarian war and a proxy war. The ongoing attempts to contain the carnage and lay the foundations for a negotiated settlement have proven woefully inadequate. Concerted efforts at the highest levels by Washington and Moscow are needed to pull the country back from an irreparable demise.

Another mark of our troubled times is the securitization of migration, which has hardened borders and transformed hospitality into hostility and xenophobia. As Chapter 8 highlights, those escaping persecution in their countries are often unwelcome in others. The weapon of mass migration has become a bargaining chip of choice in the hands of nations of transit or destination which are no longer prepared to pay for the blunders of the international community that have led to the exodus of refugees. The migration crisis has worsened further following decisions taken by countries in the grip of rising right-wing nationalists, who, heedless of past lessons, believe that building high fences and turning away desperate refugees will make their countries safer. As this book is being prepared for publication, migrants are braving the treacherous Mediterranean in the thousands, undeterred by barriers.

The financial deal struck in March 2016 between Turkey and the European Union to assist the former in stemming the flow of refugees pouring into Europe, tenuous as it is, was not lost on Niger. By May, Niger asked for €1 billion from the European Union in exchange for stopping migrants from Libya and the Mediterranean. In a related development, Kenya's decision of May 2016 to close the world's largest camp and forcibly return nearly half a million refugees to Somalia is not only inhumane but bodes ill for the already haemorrhaging international body of laws protecting refugees. The big powers who are militarily embroiled in the Middle East cauldron—and whose actions, directly or indirectly, account for much of the human displacement and the cortege of miseries in the region—do not seem to be competing to provide asylum to refugees.

In the face of all of these problems that have transnational origins and effects, states, at the local and international levels, do not seem to be coping well with the consequent internal and external pressures. Under stress and poor leadership, many of these states, in the absence of checks and balances, are unleashing destructive capacities on their citizens in ways that surpass those of any other political or social actors. At the same time, expanding information and communication technologies have empowered citizens to document state excesses in unprecedented ways. Many of these citizens feeling marginalized and persecuted become restless and, at times, also destructive.

To address these unhealthy relations, pressure is mounting on states to engage in internal reforms that facilitate greater citizen agency and ensure more responsive and responsible forms of governance. The central driver of this pressure to change is the realization that more people-centric processes are more likely to salvage social contracts in various stages of disrepair, promote pluralistic systems of governance and build the internal resilience needed to manage diversity in the face of the relentless internal vulnerabilities and external dysfunctions that this book so eloquently chronicles.

This book is an important contribution to the debates surrounding international interventions. It compellingly draws the reader's attention to the fact that while many states may not have measured up to their peoples' democratic aspirations, ill-advised military interventions by global and regional powers are not the answer. On the contrary, they have made our world less secure and ushered more uncertain and perilous times for us all.

New York
June 2016
Youssef Mahmoud
Former Special Representative of the UN Secretary-General,
UN Undersecretary-General, and member of the UN High-level
Independent Panel on Peace Operations

NOTES

INTRODUCTION

1. The UNSC, one of the principal organs of the United Nations, consists of five permanent members: China, France, Russia, the UK and the US. Non-permanent members are selected to the Council on a two-year rotational basis. India has served on the Council seven times: 1950–51, 1967–68, 1972–73, 1977–78, 1984–85, 1991–92 and 2011–12.

2. Barbara Tuchman, in her book *The March of Folly* (1985), covers four follies allegedly committed in Western history: letting the wooden horse filled with Greeks into Troy; the refusal of the six Renaissance popes to control the growing corruption in their Church; the British misrule under King George III that resulted in the loss of valuable American colonies; and the American involvement in, and mishandling of, the Vietnam conflict. Barbara W. Tuchman, *The March of Folly: From Troy to Vietnam* (UK: Crux Publishing, 1984).

3. In 1648, delegates from across Europe gathered in Westphalia, Germany, to settle the Thirty Years War (a European war of 1618–48 between the Catholic Holy Roman emperor and some of his German Protestant states) and the Eighty Years War (the Dutch National War of 1568–1648) through diplomatic consensus. The historic Treaty of Westphalia established the concept of preserving a political order based on mutual respect for state sovereignty.

4. IASPS, 'A Clean Break: A New Strategy for Securing the Realm' (Washington: The Institute for Advanced Strategic and Political Studies, 1996), http://www.dougfeith.com/docs/Clean_Break.pdf.

5. Jeffrey Goldberg, 'The Obama Doctrine,' *Atlantic*, April 2016, www.

theatlantic.com/magazine/archive/2016/04/the-obama-doctrine/
471525/.

6. George Washington, 'Clinton Email Shows that Oil and Gold Were
   behind Regime Change in Libya,' *Zero Hedge*, 9 January 2016, http://
   www.zerohedge.com/news/2016-01-09/clinton-email-hints-oil-gold-
   were-behind-regime-change-libya.

7. Dan Sanchez, 'After Me, The Jihad: Gaddafi Tried to Warn the West,
   but Nobody Listened,' *Anti Media*, 15 January 2016, http://
   theantimedia.org/after-me-the-jihad-gaddafi-tried-to-warn-the-west-
   but-nobody-listened/.

8. M.R. Izady is a cartographer who teaches at the US' Joint Special
   Operations University in Florida. A map he produced shows how the
   Persian Gulf's oil is mostly concentrated in Shia-majority areas, which
   forms a basis for the conflicts in the region. Refer: Jon Shwarz, 'One
   Map That Explains the Dangerous Saudi-Iranian Conflict,' The
   Intercept, 7 January 2016, https://theintercept. com/2016/01/06/
   one-map-that-explains-the-dangerous-saudi-iranian-conflict.

9. Ibid.

10. A permanent representative is the head of a diplomatic mission to an
    international organization, such as the UN.

11. Jo Becker and Scott Shane, 'Hillary Clinton, "Smart Power" and a
    Dictator's Fall,' *New York Times*, 27 February 2016, http://www.
    nytimes.com/2016/02/28/us/politics/hillary-clinton-libya.html?_r=0.

12. The NTC was the internationally recognized de facto government of
    Libya for a period of ten months in 2011–12.

13. A no-fly zone (NFZ) is a territory, usually in a military context, over
    which aircraft are not permitted to fly. It is a relatively modern military
    measure and is not the same as traditional coercive assertions into one
    nation's sovereign airspace by another. Though the terms imposed
    by an NFZ vary from one conflict to the other, aircraft defying an NFZ
    may be liable to be shot down. In cases of international interventions,
    as seen since the Gulf War of 1991, intervening powers and coalitions
    often establish an NFZ over the target nation's airspace.

14. Dr Denis Macshane, 'Letter to the Editor,' *Financial Times*, 16
    February 2016.

15. Glenn Greenwald, 'The US Intervention in Libya Was Such a

Smashing Success That a Sequel Is Coming,' *The Intercept*, 27 January 2016, https://theintercept.com/2016/01/27/the-u-s-intervention-in-libya-was-such-a-smashing-success-that-a-sequel-is-coming/.

16. Mohammed Z. Sahloul, Jaber Monla-Hassan, Abdulghani Sankari, Mazen Kherallah, Bassel Atassi, Safwan Badr, Aula Abbara and Annie Sparrow, 'War Is the Enemy of Health,' *American Journal of Respiratory and Critical Care Medicine*, Vol. 13, No. 2 (2016): 147.

17. 'Yemen Crisis: How Bad Is the Humanitarian Situation?' BBC, 15 December 2015, http://www.bbc.com/news/world-middle-east-34011187.

18. The doctrine essentially arose from the anguished introspection of the international community following the atrocities in Rwanda and Srebrenica. It was designed to prevent the recurrence of such mass atrocities. The ink was barely dry when the French politician Bernard Kouchner described it as humanitarian intervention. Subsequent events succeeded in confirming the worst fears of some sceptics.

19. The Brazilian proposal of Responsibility while Protecting is designed to minimize, if not entirely preclude, the collateral damage that the protection of civilians entails.

20. 'Russia Wants to Stop ISIS' Illegal Oil Trade: Churkin,' RT, 2 December 2015, https://www.rt.com/news/324207-churkin-un-oil-isis-turkey/.

1. CHAOS, DESTRUCTION AND DESTABILIZATION

1. While the declared ideology of the ISIS is to establish a caliphate for its Islamic followers the world over, it must be noted that many Islamic clerics and scholars have disclaimed the organization as anything but Islamic.

2. US House of Representatives, 'Conflict with Iraq: An Israeli Perspective' (Washington DC: US Government Printing Office, 12 September 2002), http://www.gpo.gov/fdsys/pkg/CHRG-107hhrg83514/html/CHRG-107hhrg83514.htm.

3. Resolution 1973 was adopted by the UNSC on 17 March 2011 by a vote of ten members approving (Bosnia and Herzegovina, Colombia, France, Gabon, Lebanon, Nigeria, Portugal, South Africa, the UK and

the US) and five abstaining (Brazil, China, Germany, India and Russia). Since there was a widespread apprehension that Gaddafi would attack Benghazi to result in large loss of civilian life, protection of civilians was authorized by the UN by 'all means necessary', which is a euphemism for the use of force.

4. Barack Obama, 'Remarks by President Obama to the United Nations General Assembly' (Washington DC: White House Office of the Press Secretary, 28 September 2015), https://www.whitehouse.gov/the-press-office/2015/09/28/remarks-president-obama-united-nations-general-assembly.

5. In March 2003, a US-led coalition undertook militarily action in Iraq without UNSC authorization to 'free the Iraqi people' and 'disarm' Saddam Hussein from weapons of mass destruction (WMDs), the presence of which could never be formally established.

6. 'Iraqi Deaths from Violence, 2003–2011,' Iraq Body Count, 2 January 2012, http://www.iraqbodycount.org/analysis/numbers/2011.

7. Barack Obama, 'Remarks by the President in Address to the Nation on the End of Combat Operations in Iraq' (Washington, DC: White House Office of the Press Secretary, 31 August 2010), www.whitehouse.gov/the-press-office/2010/08/31/remarks-president-address-nation-end-combat-operations-iraq.

8. Michael Weiss and Hassan Hassan, *ISIS: Inside the Army of Terror* (New York: Regan Arts, 2015).

9. Eric Schmitt and David D. Kirkpatrick, 'Islamic State Sprouting Limbs beyond Its Base,' *New York Times*, 14 February 2014, http://www.nytimes.com/2015/02/15/world/middleeast/islamic-state-sprouting-limbs-beyond-mideast.html?_r=2.

10. Nick Robins-Early, 'Here's What We Know about How the Islamic State Is Run,' Huffington Post, 27 September 2014, http://www.huffingtonpost.com/2014/09/26/isis-leadership_n_5870334.html?1411746242&ir=India&adsSiteOverride=in.

11. Ben Winsor, 'How Muslims Are Using Sharia Law to Condemn ISIS,' *Business Insider*, 8 October 2014, http://www.businessinsider.in/How-Muslims-Are-Using-Sharia-Law-To-Condemn-ISIS/articleshow/44719110.cms.

12. Eline Gordts, 'This Is How ISIS Makes $3 Million A Day,'

Huffington Post, 23 September 2014, http://www.
huffingtonpost.com/2014/09/22/isis-funding_n_5850286.
html?1411416847&ir=India&adsSiteOverride=in.

13. 'As ISIS Routs the Iraqi Army, Here's a Look at What the Jihadists
Have in Their Arsenal,' *Business Insider*, http://www.businessinsider.
in/As-ISIS-Routs-The-Iraqi-Army-Heres-A-Look-At-What-
The-Jihadists-Have-In-Their-Arsenal/FIM-92-Stinger-MANPAD/
slideshow/38029324.cms.

14. Paul Jackson, 'Warlords as Alternative Forms of Governance,' *Small
Wars and Insurgencies*, Vol. 14, No. 2 (2003): 131–50.

15. Robert G. Rabil, 'The ISIS Chronicles: A History,' National Interest,
17 July 2014, http://nationalinterest.org/feature/the-isis-chronicles-
history-10895.

16. Max Boot, 'We Can't Afford to Let ISIS Run Wild in Iraq,' *Spectator*,
16 August 2014, http://www.spectator.co.uk/features/9287832/
defeat-isis-yes-we-can/.

17. Seymour M. Hersh, 'The Redirection,' *New Yorker*, 5 March 2007,
http://www.newyorker.com/magazine/2007/03/05/the-redirection.

18. Barbara Plett Usher, 'Joe Biden Apologised over IS Remarks, but Was
He Right?' BBC, 7 October 2014, http://www.bbc.com/news/world-
us-canada-29528482.

19. Rebecca Shabad, 'Paul: ISIS Emboldened after US Armed Its
Allies in Syria,' The Hill, 22 June 2014, http://thehill.com/policy/
international/210168-us-has-been-arming-isis-in-syria-sen-paul-
claims.

20. 'ISIL "Completely Fabricated Enemy by US",' Press TV, 28 August
2014, http://www.presstv.in/detail/2014/08/28/376913/isil-
completely-fabricated-enemy-by-us/.

21. 'DOD Release, 2015.04.10,' Judicial Watch (uploads, official website),
http://www.judicialwatch.org/wp-content/uploads/2015/05/Pg.-291-
Pgs.-287-293-JW-v-DOD-and-State-14-812-DOD-Release-2015-
04-10-final-version11.pdf.

22. Jacob Siegel, 'The ISIS Conspiracy that Ate the Web,' *Daily Beast*, 6
June 2015, http://www.thedailybeast.com/articles/2015/06/06/the-
isis-conspiracy-that-ate-the-web.html.

23. Brad Hoff, 'Former Defense Intelligence Agency Chief Says Rise of

Islamic State Was "a Willful Decision",' Information Clearing House, 7 August 2015, http://www.informationclearinghouse.info/article42567.htm.

24. Rami G. Khouri, 'Why Obama Has Picked the Worst Allies for His War on ISIS,' Huffington Post, 11 November 2014, http://www.huffingtonpost.com/rami-g-khouri/obama-isis-war-allies_b_5800244.html?ir=India&adsSiteOverride=in.

25. Martin Chulov, 'ISIS: The Inside Story,' *Guardian*, 11 December 2014, http://www.theguardian.com/world/2014/dec/11/-sp-isis-the-inside-story.

26. Rami G. Khouri, 'Why Obama Has Picked the Worst Allies for His War on ISIS,' Huffington Post, 11 November 2014, http://www.huffingtonpost.com/rami-g-khouri/obama-isis-war-allies_b_5800244.html?ir=India&adsSiteOverride=in.

27. Mark Thompson, 'How Disbanding the Iraqi Army Fuelled ISIS,' *Time*, 28 May 2015, http://time.com/3900753/isis-iraq-syria-army-united-states-military/.

28. Associated Press and Tom Wyke, 'The Secret to ISIS's Success: Over 100 Former Saddam Hussein-era Officers Run Jihadi Group's Military and Intelligence Operations in Iraq and Syria,' Mail Online, 8 August 2015, http://www.dailymail.co.uk/news/article-3190314/The-secret-ISIS-s-success-100-former-Saddam-Hussein-era-officers-run-jihadi-group-s-military-intelligence-operations-Iraq-Syria.html.

29. Even an 'achiever' within a given society may find himself/herself 'frustrated' upon comparisons with the relative well-being of fellow 'achievers'. See: Carol Graham and Steffano Pettinato, 'Frustrated Achievers: Winners, Losers and Subjective Well-Being in New Market Economies,' *Journal of Development Studies,* Vol. 606 (2006): 128–53.

30. Richard Barrett, 'Foreign Fighters in Syria' (New York: Carnegie Council for Ethics in International Affairs, 23 September 2014).

31. David Paul, 'Is ISIS a Religious Group? Of course It Is,' Huffington Post, 24 April 2015, http://www.huffingtonpost.com/david-paul/is-isis-a-religious-group_b_6730968.html?ir=India&adsSiteOverride=in.

32. Erin Banco, 'Why Do People Join ISIS? The Psychology of a Terrorist,' *International Business Times,* 5 September 2014, www.ibtimes.com/why-do-people-join-ISIS-psychology-terrorist-1680444.

33. 'Al-Qaeda in Syria Forms Female Brigades,' Al Arabiya News, 2 February 2014, http://english.alarabiya.net/en/News/middle-east/2014/02/02/Syria-jihadist-group-ISIS-forms-women-only-battalions.html.

34. Arthur Brown, 'Why Do Young People Join ISIS?' The Institute of Middle East Studies, 2 April 2015, https://imeslebanon.wordpress.com/2015/04/02/why-do-young-people-join-isis/.

35. 'What are jus ad bellum and jus in bello?' ICRC Resource Center, 1 January 2004, www.icrc.org/eng/resources/documents/misc/5kzjjd.htm.

36. David Held, *Global Transformations: Politics, Economics and Culture* (Stanford: Stanford University Press, 1999), 37–38.

37. In September 2011, under the chairmanship of India, the UN Counter-terrorism Committee, while commemorating the adoption of Resolution 1373 in 2001, introduced the 'zero-tolerance paradigm into the international community's fight against terrorism'. See http://www.un.org/en/sc/ctc/specialmeetings/2011/docs/rapporteurs_summary.pdf.

38. Kofi Annan, 'Secretary-General's statement to the Commission on Human Rights' (Geneva: Office of the UN Secretary-General, 24 April 2003), http://www.un.org/sg/STATEMENTS/index.asp?nid=322.

2. UNDERSTANDING THE ARAB SPRING

1. Warren Hoge's speaking notes made available to the author.

2. Popular uprisings across Eastern Europe in 1989, which were rooted in economic crises, led to the overthrow of the communist rule as they wanted the Western style of governance.

3. Alain Juppe, 'Arab Spring: Closing Speech to the Arab World Institute' (Paris: Embassy of France in the UK, 16 April 2011), http://www.ambafrance-uk.org/Arab-spring-symposium-closing.

4. Lisa Bryant, 'Sarkozy: Critical That G8 Support Arab "Spring",' Voice of America, 25 May 2011, http://m.voanews.com/a/sarkozy-critical-that-g8-support-arab-spring-122687034/139951.html.

5. Andrew Porter, 'Arab Spring Will Add to Extremism if We Do Not Help, Says David Cameron,' *Telegraph*, 27 May 2011, http://www.

telegraph.co.uk/news/politics/david-cameron/8539420/Arab-Spring-will-add-to-extremism-if-we-do-not-help-says-David- Cameron.html, accessed 27 April 2015.

6. Barack Obama, 'Remarks by the President on the Middle East and North Africa' (Washington, DC: White House Office of the Press Secretary, 19 May 2011), https://www.whitehouse.gov/the-press-office/2011/05/19/remarks-president-middle-east-and-north-africa.

7. Patrick Weidinger, '10 Horrifying Acts of Self Immolation,' Listverse, 10 March 2011, http://listverse.com/2011/03/10/10-horrifying-acts-of-self-immolation/.

8. '2 in Egypt torch themselves; 1 dead,' CNN, 18 January 2011, http://edition.cnn.com/2011/WORLD/africa/01/18/egypt.self.immolation/index.html.

9. Patrick Weidinger, '10 Horrifying Acts of Self Immolation,' Listverse, 10 March 2011, http://listverse.com/2011/03/10/10-horrifying-acts-of-self-immolation/.

10. Ibid.

11. 'Algerian Dies from Self-immolation,' Al Jazeera, 17 January 2011, http://www.aljazeera.com/news/africa/2011/01/20111162363063915.html.

12. Josh Levs, 'Self-immolation Reports Spread through North Africa,' CNN, 17 January 2011, http://edition.cnn.com/2011/WORLD/africa/01/17/tunisia.self.immolation/.

13. Ibid.

14. Nada Bakri, 'Self-Immolation Is on the Rise in the Arab World,' *New York Times*, 20 January 2012, http://www.nytimes.com/2012/01/21/world/africa/self-immolation-on-the-rise-in-the-arab-world.html?_r=0.

15. Deutsche Welle, 'Death by Fire: Self-immolation in the Arab World,' Deutsche Welle, 9 March 2011, http://www.dw.de/death-by-fire-self-immolation-in-the-arab-world/a-14898706.

16. Tarek Masoud, Jason Brownlee and Andrew Reynolds, *The Arab Spring: Pathways of Repression and Reform* (London: Oxford University Press, 2015), 221.

17. Sandeep Dixit, 'India Welcomes Mubarak's Decision,' *Hindu*, 13 February 2011.

18. Ibid.

19. Sandeep Dixit, 'India Can Help Build Democracy in Arab World,' *Hindu*, 27 February 2011.

20. Henry Kissinger, *World Order* (New York: Penguin, 2014), 123.

21. Ayatollah Khamenei, 'Leader's Speech at Inauguration of Islamic Awakening and Ulama Conference' (29 April 2013), http://english. khamenei.ir/news/1772/Leader-s-Speech-at-Inauguration-of-Islamic-Awakening-and-Ulama.

22. Professor Gareth Evans currently co-chairs the International Advisory Board of the New York-based Global Centre for the Responsibility to Protect.

23. Michael Ignatieff, 'Libya, Syria and R2P' (Third Annual Gareth Evans Lecture, 12 September 2013), http://www.globalr2p.org/ publications/255.

24. Barack Obama, 'Remarks by the President on the Middle East and North Africa' (White House Office of the Press Secretary).

3. LIBYA: THE UNRAVELLING OF A COUNTRY

1. 'S/2003/818' (New York: United Nations Security Council), https:// documents-dds-ny.un.org/doc/UNDOC/GEN/N03/467/60/PDF/ N0346760.pdf?OpenElement.

2. Alasdair Soussi, 'Controversy remains 25 years after Lockerbie,' Al Jazeera, 21 December 2013, http://www.aljazeera.com/indepth/ features/2013/12/controversy-remains-25-years-after-lockerbie-2013122184326527724.html.

3. Ali Treki, the foreign minister of Libya between 1976 and 1982, and the permanent representative of Libya to the UN between 2003 and 2009, passed away in October 2015.

4. Roula Khalaf, 'West's Policy Exposed as Mad Dog Finds Bite,' *Financial Times*, 21 February 2011, http://www.ft.com/intl/cms/s/0/ f068d70e-3ddd-11e0-99ac-00144feabdc0.html#axzz3Ui1FStHq.

5. 'The Arab Revolt Comes to Tripoli,' *Financial Times*, 21 February 2011, http://www.ft.com/intl/cms/s/0/29c9bfba-3df5-11e0-99ac-00144feabdc0.html#axzz3Ui1FStHq.

6. Ian Black, 'Muammar Gaddafi Lashes Out as Power Slips Away,'

Guardian, 21 February 2011, http://www.theguardian.com/world/2011/feb/21/libya-protests-bloodiest-yet-Qadhafi.

7. 'The Middle East: People, Power, Politics,' *Guardian*, 21 February 2011, http://www.theguardian.com/commentisfree/2011/feb/21/middle-east-obama-policy.

8. Ben Macintyre, 'Gaddafi's Model Dictatorship Is Turning to Dust,' *Times*, 22 February 2011, http://www.thetimes.co.uk/tto/opinion/columnists/benmacintyre/article2921517.ece.

9. 'Time to Muzzle Libya's Mad Dog,' *Financial Times*, 24 February 2011, http://www.ft.com/intl/cms/s/0/ea52af7a-4053-11e0-9140-00144feabdc0.html#axzz3Ui1FStHq.

10. Adopted at the United Nations Diplomatic Conference on 12 July 1998, the Rome Statute is the treaty that established the International Criminal Court. 'Among other things, it sets out the crimes falling within the jurisdiction of the ICC, the rules of procedure and the mechanisms for States to cooperate with the ICC.' See https://www.icc-cpi.int/en_menus/icc/about%20the%20court/frequently%20asked%20questions/Pages/3.aspx.

11. Article 41 of the UN Charter states: 'The Security Council may decide what measures not involving the use of armed force are to be employed to give effect to its decisions, and it may call upon the Members of the United Nations to apply such measures. These may include complete or partial interruption of economic relations and of rail, sea, air, postal, telegraphic, radio, and other means of communication, and the severance of diplomatic relations.' See http://www.un.org/en/sections/un-charter/chapter-vii/.

12. Article 42 of the UN Charter states: 'Should the Security Council consider that measures provided for in Article 41 would be inadequate or have proved to be inadequate, it may take such action by air, sea, or land forces as may be necessary to maintain or restore international peace and security. Such action may include demonstrations, blockade, and other operations by air, sea, or land forces of Members of the United Nations.' See http://www.un.org/en/sections/un-charter/chapter-vii/.

13. A highly respected and much admired professional, he passed away on 22 July 2015. In a befitting and moving tribute to him, Samantha

Power, the permanent representative of the United States, said on 27 July 2015: 'It is a testament to the largeness of Roble's personality, the boundlessness of his energy, and the breadth of his ambition—for Djibouti but also for Africa as a whole—that his colleagues and friends in both New York and Washington felt him as a full-time presence.' See http://usun.state.gov/remarks/6775.

14. Zagat is a survey established by Tim and Nina Zagat in 1979 to collect and compare ratings of restaurants given by diners.

15. Steven Erlanger, 'By His Own Reckoning, One Man Made Libya a French Cause,' New York Times, 1 April 2011, http://www.nytimes.com/2011/04/02/world/africa/02levy.html?_r=0.

16. Cristopher Dickey, 'Why Sarkozy Went to War,' Newsweek, 3 April 2011, http://www.newsweek.com/why-sarkozy-went-war-66463.

17. Steven Erlanger, 'By His Own Reckoning, One Man Made Libya a French Cause,' New York Times, 1 April 2011, http://www.nytimes.com/2011/04/02/world/africa/02levy.html?_r=0.

18. Ibid.

19. As widely reported in the press, the Arab League, on 12 March, called on the UN to impose a no-fly zone over Libya in order to protect civilians from the aerial attacks against Gaddafi. This was reiterated by the Lebanese PR, Nawaf Salam, in the Security Council.

20. Cristopher Dickey, 'Why Sarkozy Went to War,' Newsweek, 3 April 2011, http://www.newsweek.com/why-sarkozy-went-war-66463.

21. Ibid.

22. Jonathan Alter, 'Woman of the World,' Vanity Fair News, June 2011, http://www.vanityfair.com/news/2011/06/hillary-clinton-201106.

23. 'Following a major earthquake, a 15-metre tsunami disabled the power supply and cooling of three Fukushima Daiichi reactors, causing a nuclear accident on 11 March 2011. All three cores largely melted in the first three days … [and there were] high radioactive releases over days 4 to 6.' 'Fukushima Accident,' World Nuclear Association, http://www.world-nuclear.org/information-library/safety-and-security/safety-of-plants/fukushima-accident.aspx.

24. Robert Fisk, 'The Historical Narrative that Lies beneath the Gaddafi Rebellion,' Independent, 3 March 2011, http://www.independent.co.uk/voices/commentators/fisk/robert-fisk-the-historical-narrative-that-lies-beneath-the-Qadhafi-rebellion-2230654.html.

25. Catrina Stewart, 'Gaddafi Says Libya Could Be "Another Vietnam",' *Independent*, 3 March 2011, http://www.independent.co.uk/news/ world/africa/Qadhafi-says-libya-could-be-another-vietnam-2230653. html.

26. Ben Macintyre, 'Britain's Dogs of War Must Be on a Tighter Leash,' *Times*, 8 March 2011, http://www.thetimes.co.uk/tto/opinion/ columnists/benmacintyre/article2937598.ece.

27. Ibid.

28. Niholas Watt and Ian Traynor, 'Libya No-Fly Zone Setback for David Cameron,' *Guardian*, 11 March 2011, http://www.theguardian.com/ world/2011/mar/11/libya-no-fly-zone-david-cameron.

29. Chris McGreal, 'Gaddafi's Army Will Kill Half a Million, Warn Libyan Rebels,' *Guardian*, 12 March 2011, http://www.theguardian. com/world/2011/mar/12/gaddafi-army-kill-half-million.

30. 'The World Cannot Afford to Let Gaddafi Crush the Rebels,' *Financial Times*, 18 March 2011, http://www.ft.com/intl/cms/s/0/b596b46a-5198-11e0-888e-00144feab49a.html#axzz3Ui1FStHq.

31. 'Kadhafi: Discours "effrayant" (Merkel),' *Le Figaro*, 22 February 2011, http://www.lefigaro.fr/flash-actu/2011/02/22/97001-20110222FILWWW00684-kadhafi-discours-tres-effrayant-merkel. php.

32. 'Libye: Rome craint "un exode biblique",' *Le Figaro*, 23 February 2011, http://www.lefigaro.fr/flash-actu/2011/02/23/97001-20110223FILWWW00410-libye-rome-craint-un-exode-biblique. php.

33. 'Libye/UE: Sarkozy veut des "sanctions",' *Le Figaro*, 23 February 2011, http://www.lefigaro.fr/flash-eco/2011/02/23/97002-20110223FILWWW00428-libyeue-sarkozy-veut-des-sanctions.php.

34. 'Libye: Kadhafi promet l'"enfer",' *Le Figaro*, 18 March 2011, http://www. lefigaro.fr/flash-actu/2011/03/18/97001-20110318FILWWW00430-libye-kadhafi-promet-l-enfer.php.

35. Romeo Dallaire, *Shake Hands with the Devil: The Failure of Humanity in Rwanda* (New York: Random House, 2008).

36. The imposition of a no-fly zone over Bosnia and Herzegovina as part of Operation Deny Flight between 1993 and 1995 amidst the Bosnian War was to mark a cornerstone in NATO-UN coordination. Although

it significantly helped change the conflict conditions, the NFZ also led to tensions. On the ground, UN peacekeepers were held hostage as a response to the NFZ's establishment. In the air, due to a disconcerted dual command structure, the participating air forces failed to deliver in key missions.

37. Andreas Rinke, 'Srebrenica or Afghanistan? Why Germany Abstained on the Libya Vote—Tracing the History of a Decision' (German Council on Foreign Relations, 14 June 2011), https://dgap.org/en/article/18473/print.

38. Ibid.

39. Richard Brody, 'Did Bernard-Henri Levy Take NATO to War?' *New Yorker*, 25 March 2011, http://www.newyorker.com/culture/richard-brody/did-bernard-henri-lvy-take-nato-to-war.

40. A 'black swan' moment metaphorically refers to an event that first comes as a surprise, but is then rationalized in hindsight. It follows the old parable that black swans were presumed to be nonexistent before they were actually discovered. See Nassim Nicholas Taleb, *The Black Swan* (New York: Random House, 2007).

41. Ben Quinn and Jonathan Haynes, 'Gaddafi Speech and Libya Unrest—As It Happened,' *Guardian*, 22 February 2011, http://www.theguardian.com/world/blog/2011/feb/22/libya-gaddafi-speech-reaction-live-updates.

42. David Swanson, 'Top 45 Lies in Obama's Speech at UN,' *Global Research*, 25 September 2013, http://www.globalresearch.ca/top-45-lies-in-obamas-speech-at-un/5351432.

43. David D. Kirkpatrick and Kareem Fahim, 'Qaddafi Warns of Assault on Benghazi as UN Vote Nears,' *New York Times*, 17 March 2011, http://www.nytimes.com/2011/03/18/world/africa/18libya.html?pagewanted=all&_r=0.

44. Muammar Gaddafi, 'Muammar Gaddafi Speech Translated,' YouTube, 23 February 2011, https://www.youtube.com/watch?v=69wBG6 ULNzQ.

45. Ibid.

46. Alan J. Kuperman, 'A Model Humanitarian Intervention? Reassessing NATO's Libya Campaign,' *International Security*, Vol. 38, No. 1 (2013): 105–36.

47. Ibid.

48. Ibid.

49. 'Defiant Gaddafi Threatens Europe,' Al Jazeera, 2 July 2011, http://www.aljazeera.com/news/africa/2011/07/201171181812716313.html.

50. Muammar Gaddafi, 'Gaddafi Speech Translated 2011-4-30,' YouTube, 30 April 2011, https://www.youtube.com/watch?v=a2MgzOoCBME.

51. Not to be confused with the British art historian, Sir Hugh Ashley Roberts.

52. The Srebrenica massacre of July 1995 involved the slaughtering of over 8,000 Muslim Bosniaks by the Bosnian Serb Army (VRS) led by General Ratko Mladić.

53. Hugh Roberts, 'Who Said Gaddafi Had to Go?' *London Review of Books,* Vol. 33, No. 22 (2011): 8–18.

54. Roula Khalaf, 'West's Policy Exposed as Mad Dog Finds Bite,' *Financial Times*, 21 February 2011, http://www.ft.com/intl/cms/s/0/f068d70e-3ddd-11e0-99ac-00144feabdc0.html#axzz3Ui1FStHq.

55. Gideon Rachman, 'A grubby Libyan Lesson in Realpolitik,' *Financial Times*, 21 February 2011, http://www.ft.com/intl/cms/s/0/adb0edd2-3e07-11e0-99ac-00144feabdc0.html.

56. 'The Arab Revolt Comes to Tripoli,' *Financial Times*, 21 February 2011, http://www.ft.com/intl/cms/s/0/29c9bfba-3df5-11e0-99ac-00144feabdc0.html#axzz3Ui1FStHq.

57. 'Libya: Gaddafi's Destructive Path,' *Guardian*, 22 February 2011, http://www.theguardian.com/commentisfree/2011/feb/22/libya-gaddafi-destructive-path-editorial.

58. In the case of Rwanda, there was reliable and accurate information on the impending genocide, and the international community failed to act. Likewise was the case in Darfur and the Balkans. In Libya, on the other hand, scaremongering based on Gaddafi's track-record and the likelihood of civilian deaths prompted action by the international community.

59. In a conversation with the author on 22 March 2011.

60. Peter Ferrara, 'Benghazi: Obama's Actions Amount to a Shameful Dereliction of Duty,' *Forbes*, 25 October 2012, http://www.forbes.com/sites/peterferrara/2012/10/25/benghazi-obamas-actions-amount-to-a-shameful-dereliction-of-duty/#61acd7e27977.

61. Ibid.

4. SYRIA: THE MULTI-LAYERED AND STILL UNFOLDING TRAGEDIES

1. Ian Black, 'Report on Syria Conflict Finds 11.5% of Population Killed or Injured,' *Guardian*, 11 February 2016, http://www.theguardian.com/world/2016/feb/11/report-on-syria-conflict-finds-115-of-population-killed-or-injured.

2. Charles Glass, 'In the Syrian Deadlands,' *New York Review of Books*, 22 October 2015, http://www.nybooks.com/articles/2015/10/22/syrian-deadlands.

3. Russia's growing closeness with Middle Eastern sheikhdoms is a fairly recent phenomenon. In Syria, Russia has harnessed interests since its Soviet days, notably including a naval base in Tartus. In fact, Russia's alliance with Syria has been an important driver of its policy in the region, an explanation for which may lie in Syria's ties with Iran.

4. David W. Lesch, 'Prudence Suggests Staying Out of Syria,' *Current History*, Vol. 111, No. 748 (2012), http://www.currenthistory.com/Article.php?ID=1009.

5. Barack Obama, 'Press Conference by the President' (Washington, DC: White House Office of the Press Secretary, 6 March 2012), https://www.whitehouse.gov/the-press-office/2012/03/06/press-conference-president.

6. Macon Phillips, 'President Obama: The Future of Syria Must Be Determined by Its People, but President Bashar al-Assad Is Standing in Their Way' (White House Blog, 18 August 2011), https://www.whitehouse.gov/blog/2011/08/18/president-obama-future-syria-must-be-determined-its-people-president-bashar-al-assad.

7. 'Putin Rips "Medieval Crusade' in Libya,' *Moscow Times*, 22 March 2011, http://www.themoscowtimes.com/news/article/putin-rips-medieval-crusade-in-libya/433447.html.

8. Dmitry Medvedev, 'Statement by Dmitry Medvedev on the Situation in Libya' (21 March 2011), http://en.kremlin.ru/events/president/news/10701.

9. David J. Kramer and Christopher Walker, 'The Kremlin's Big Gamble,' *Foreign Policy*, 1 March 2012, http://foreignpolicy.com/2012/03/01/the-kremlins-big-gamble/.

10. Thomas J. Christensen, *The China Challenge: Shaping the Choices of a Rising Power* (New York: WW Norton, 2015).

11. James Barr, *A Line in the Sand: The Anglo-French Struggle for the Middle East, 1914-1948* (New York: WW Norton).

12. Ibid, 3–8.

13. Ken Grossi, Maren Milligan and Ted Waddelow, 'Restoring Lost Voices of Self-Determination' (King-Crane Commission Digital Collection, August 2011), http://www.oberlin.edu/library/digital/king-crane/intro.html.

14. 'The Balfour Declaration' (Balfour Project, 8 November 2013), http://www.balfourproject.org/the-balfour-declaration/.

15. David W. Lesch, 'Will Syria War Mean End of Sykes-Picot?' Al Monitor, 12 August 2013, http://www.al-monitor.com/pulse/en/originals/2013/08/syria-sykes-picot-ottoman-borders-breakup-levant-mandates.html#.

16. Basma Atassi, 'Breaking the Silence over Hama Atrocities,' Al Jazeera, 2 February 2012, http://www.aljazeera.com/indepth/features/2012/02/20122232155715210.html.

17. Wendell Steavenson, 'Assad's Hama Rules, Again,' *New Yorker*, 4 February 2012, http://www.newyorker.com/news/wendell-steavenson/assads-hama-rules-again.

18. Neil MacFarquhar, 'Hafez al-Assad, Who Turned Syria into a Power in the Middle East, Dies at 69,' *New York Times*, 11 June 2000, http://www.nytimes.com/2000/06/11/world/hafez-al-assad-who-turned-syria-into-a-power-in-the-middle-east-dies-at-69.html?pagewanted=all.

19. 'Bashar's World,' *Economist*, 15 June 2000, http://www.economist.com/node/81745.

20. Jean Shaoul and Chris Marsden, 'The Bitter Legacy of Syria's Hafez al-Assad,' World Socialist Web Site, 16 June 2000, https://www.wsws.org/en/articles/2000/06/assa-j16.html.

21. Subhi Hadidi, 'The Hama Massacre and the Syrian "Experience" in Fighting Terrorism,' MEMRI, 11 January 2002, www.memri.org/report/en/print590.htm.

22. Wendell Steavenson, 'Assad's Hama Rules, Again,' *New Yorker*, 4 February 2012, http://www.newyorker.com/news/wendell-steavenson/assads-hama-rules-again.

23. 'A Wasted Decade: Human Rights in Syria during Bashar al-Assad's First Ten Years in Power' (New York: Human Rights Watch, 2010).

24. 'Spring Reaches Damascus,' *Times*, 26 March 2011, http://www.thetimes.co.uk/tto/opinion/leaders/article2961859.ece.

25. Rana Kabbani, 'From the Turks to Assad: To us Syrians It Is All Brutal Colonialism,' *Guardian*, 30 March 2011, http://www.theguardian.com/commentisfree/2011/mar/30/turks-assad-colonialism-family-mafia.

26. Nicholas Blanford, 'Assad Unleashes Tanks to Crush Protesters in Syria,' *Times*, 25 April 2011, http://www.thetimes.co.uk/tto/news/world/middleeast/article2997797.ece.

27. Hugh Macleod and Annasofie Flamand, 'Assad's Regime of Torture,' Al Jazeera, 15 May 2011, http://www.aljazeera.com/indepth/features/2011/05/2011515113431187136.html.

28. 'Genocide and Mass Atrocities Alert: Syria,' Genocide Watch, February 2012, http://www.genocidewatch.org/syria.html.

29. Rannie Amiri, 'The Shia Crescent Revisited,' Counter Punch, 19 February 2010, http://www.counterpunch.org/2010/02/19/the-shia-crescent-revisited/.

30. Robin Wright and Peter Baker, 'Iraq, Jordan See Threat to Election from Iran,' *Washington Post*, 8 December 2004, http://www.washingtonpost.com/wp-dyn/articles/A43980-2004Dec7.html.

31. Edward Wong, 'Top Iraqis Assail Egyptian Leader's Talk of Civil War,' *New York Times*, 9 April 2006, http://www.nytimes.com/2006/04/09/world/middleeast/09cnd-iraq.html?_r=0.

32. Rannie Amiri, 'The Shia Crescent Revisited,' Counter Punch, 19 February 2010, http://www.counterpunch.org/2010/02/19/the-shia-crescent-revisited/.

33. Islam recognizes eight schools of thought, four Sunni (Hanafi, Maliki, Shafii and Hanbali), two Shia (Jafari and Zaidi), one Ibadi and one Zahiri. The fifth amongst them is Jafari, which is the school of jurisprudence accepted by a majority of Shias.

34. Loraine Sievers and Sam Daws, *The Procedure of the UN Security Council* (New York: Oxford University Press, 2014), 340, 399.

35. 'Israeli Defense Official: "Syria is Gone",' Reuters, 30 June 2015, http://www.reuters.com/article/us-mideast-crisis-syria-israel-idUSKCN0PA0UQ20150630.

36. Barack Obama. 'Remarks by President Obama to the United Nations General Assembly.' (New York, White House Office of the Press Secretary, 28 September 2015). https://www.whitehouse.gov/the-press-office/2015/09/28/remarks-president-obama-united-nations-general-assembly.

37. 'US-trained Syria rebels Gave Ammo, Equipment to Al Qaeda Group, Pentagon Confirms,' ABC, 26 September 2015, http://www.abc.net.au/news/2015-09-26/us-trained-syria-rebels-gave-ammo-equipment-to-qaeda-group/6807274.

38. 'Russian PM Says Defending "National Interests" in Syria, Not Bashar Al-Assad,' NDTV, 17 October 2015, http://www.ndtv.com/world-news/russian-pm-says-defending-national-interests-in-syria-not-bashar-al-assad-1233339.

39. Ibid.

40. Hassan Mneimneh, 'Will Assad Create a Useful Syria?' Middle East Institute, 19 November 2015, http://www.mei.edu/content/at/will-assad-create-useful-syria.

41. Gardiner Harris and Somini Sengupta, 'Obama and Putin Play Diplomatic Poker over Syria,' *New York Times*, 28 September 2015, http://www.nytimes.com/2015/09/29/world/middleeast/un-general-assembly-syria-isis-refugees.html.

42. Henry Kissinger, 'A Path Out of the Middle East Collapse,' *Wall Street Journal*, 16 October 2015, http://www.wsj.com/articles/a-path-out-of-the-middle-east-collapse-1445037513.

43. Patrick Cockburn, 'Too Weak, Too Strong,' *London Review of Books*, Vol. 37, No. 21 (2015): 3–6.

44. Patrick Cockburn, 'Russia in Syria: Air Strikes Pose Twin Threat to Turkey by Keeping Assad in Power and Strengthening Kurdish Threat,' *Independent*, 29 October 2015, http://www.independent.co.uk/news/world/middle-east/russia-in-syria-air-strikes-pose-twin-threat-to-turkey-by-keeping-assad-in-power-and-strengthening-a6712626.html.

45. David E. Sanger, David D. Kirkpatrick and Somini Sengupta, 'Rancor between Saudi Arabia and Iran Threatens Talks on Syria,' *New York Times*, 29 October 2015, http://www.nytimes.com/2015/10/30/world/middleeast/syria-saudi-arabia-iran-peace-talks.html?_r=0.

46. Michael D. Shear and Nick Cumming-Bruce, 'Obama Calls on Putin to Help Reduce Violence in Syria after Peace Talks Stall,' *New York Times*, 18 April 2016, http://www.nytimes.com/2016/04/19/world/middleeast/syria-talks-stall-as-opposition-negotiators-withdraw.html?_r=1.

5. YEMEN AND THE OTHER ELEPHANT IN THE TENT

1. Bernard Haykel, 'Crisis in Yemen: Instability on the Arabian Peninsula,' Carnegie Council for Ethics in International Affairs (2015).
2. Damien McElroy, 'Large Protests Staged against Yemen President,' *Telegraph*, 27 January 2011, http://www.telegraph.co.uk/news/worldnews/middleeast/yemen/8286412/Large-protests-staged-against-Yemen-president.html.
3. 'The National Dialogue Conference,' Islamopedia Online, 1 March 2014, http://www.islamopediaonline.org/country-profile/yemen/political-landscape/national-dialogue-conference.
4. The Article stipulates that the Security Council may decide on additional measures not including the use of force to effect its decisions.
5. Bernard Haykel, 'Crisis in Yemen: Instability on the Arabian Peninsula,' Carnegie Council for Ethics in International Affairs (2015).
6. Ibid.
7. Hamid Alizadeh, 'Saudi War on Yemen: Rising Tensions in the Middle East and the Crisis of Imperialism,' In Defence of Marxism, 31 March 2015, http://www.marxist.com/saudi-war-on-yemen-rising-tensions-in-the-middle-east-and-the-crisis-of-imperialism.htm.
8. Shuaib Almosawa and Ben Hubbard, 'Saudi Bombing Only Fans Yemen's Flames,' *New York Times*, 24 June 2015, http://www.nytimes.com/2015/06/25/world/middleeast/yemen-saudi-arabia-houthis.html?_r=0.
9. Hamid Alizadeh, 'Saudi War on Yemen: Rising Tensions in the Middle East and the Crisis of Imperialism,' In Defence of Marxism, 31 March 2015, http://www.marxist.com/saudi-war-on-yemen-rising-tensions-in-the-middle-east-and-the-crisis-of-imperialism.htm.
10. As told to the Washington Press by Mustafa Alani, quoted in ibid.

11. Amal Mudallali, 'The Iranian Sphere of Influence Expands into Yemen,' *Foreign Policy*, 8 October 2014, http://foreignpolicy.com/2014/10/08/the-iranian-sphere-of-influence-expands-into-yemen/.

12. Hamid Alizadeh, 'Saudi War on Yemen: Rising Tensions in the Middle East and the Crisis of Imperialism,' In Defence of Marxism, 31 March 2015, http://www.marxist.com/saudi-war-on-yemen-rising-tensions-in-the-middle-east-and-the-crisis-of-imperialism.htm.

13. Bruce Riedel, 'Gulf Pulse,' Al Monitor, 22 May 2015, http://www.al-monitor.com/pulse/originals/2015/05/yemen-war-escalates-stakes-raise-saudi-princes.html.

14. 'Yemen Crisis: Who Is Fighting Whom?' BBC, 26 March 2015, http://www.bbc.com/news/world-middle-east-29319423.

15. Article 51, Chapter VII, of the UN Charter states: 'Nothing in the present Charter shall impair the inherent right of individual or collective self-defence if an armed attack occurs against a Member of the United Nations, until the Security Council has taken measures necessary to maintain international peace and security. Measures taken by Members in the exercise of this right of self-defence shall be immediately reported to the Security Council and shall not in any way affect the authority and responsibility of the Security Council under the present Charter to take at any time such action as it deems necessary in order to maintain or restore international peace and security." See http://www.un.org/en/sections/un-charter/chapter-vii/.

16. Joe Dyke, 'Is the Saudi War on Yemen Legal?' IRIN, 3 April 2015, http://www.irinnews.org/analysis/2015/04/03/saudi-war-yemen-legal.

17. Medeleine Rees, 'Military Intervention in Yemen: The International System in Crisis,' Inclusive Democracy, 9 April 2015, https://www.opendemocracy.net/5050/madeleine-rees/military-intervention-in-yemen-international-system-in-crisis.

18. Majid Kianinejad, 'Legal Analysis of the Legitimacy of Saudi Military Intervention in Yemen,' Iran Review, 16 May 2015, http://www.iranreview.org/content/Documents/Legal-Analysis-of-the-Legitimacy-of-Saudi-Military-Intervention-in-Yemen.htm.

19. Shuaib Almosawa and Ben Hubbard, 'Saudi Bombing Only Fans Yemen's Flames,' *New York Times*, 24 June 2015, http://www.nytimes.com/2015/06/25/world/middleeast/yemen-saudi-arabia-houthis.html?_r=0.

20. Bruce Riedel, 'Gulf Pulse,' Al Monitor, 22 May 2015, http://www.al-monitor.com/pulse/originals/2015/05/yemen-war-escalates-stakes-raise-saudi-princes.html.

21. Ibid.

22. Bernard Haykel, 'Crisis in Yemen: Instability on the Arabian Peninsula,' Carnegie Council for Ethics in International Affairs (2015).

23. Ibid.

24. Bruce Riedel, 'Gulf Pulse,' Al Monitor, 22 May 2015, http://www.al-monitor.com/pulse/originals/2015/05/yemen-war-escalates-stakes-raise-saudi-princes.html.

25. Ibid.

26. Shuaib Almosawa and Ben Hubbard, 'Saudi Bombing Only Fans Yemen's Flames,' *New York Times*, 24 June 2015, http://www.nytimes.com/2015/06/25/world/middleeast/yemen-saudi-arabia-houthis.html?_r=0.

27. Asher Orkaby, 'Houthi Who? A History of Unlikely Alliances in an Uncertain Yemen,' *Foreign Affairs*, 25 March 2015, https://www.foreignaffairs.com/articles/middle-east/2015-03-25/houthi-who.

28. Bernard Haykel, 'Crisis in Yemen: Instability on the Arabian Peninsula,' Carnegie Council for Ethics in International Affairs (2015).

29. Jamal al-Jabiri and Fawaz al-Haidari, 'Yemen's Hadi Says "No Negotiations" with Rebels in Geneva,' Yahoo News, 8 June 2015, http://news.yahoo.com/yemen-president-says-un-talks-not-reconciliation-090613459.html.

30. Hamid Alizadeh, 'Saudi War on Yemen: Rising Tensions in the Middle East and the Crisis of Imperialism,' In Defence of Marxism, 31 March 2015, http://www.marxist.com/saudi-war-on-yemen-rising-tensions-in-the-middle-east-and-the-crisis-of-imperialism.htm.

31. Ibid.

32. Ibid.

33. 'Ban Appoints "Veteran UN Senior Leader" Benomar as His Special Adviser,' UN News Centre, 9 November 2015, http://www.un.org/apps/news/story.asp?NewsID=52502#.Vxcp9DB97IU.

34. Tik Root and Peter Salisbury, 'Jamal Benomar and the Fine Art of Making Peace in Yemen,' Atlantic Council, 17 June 2014, www.atlanticcouncil.org/blogs/menasource/jamal-benomar-and-the-fine-art-of-making-peace-in-yemen.

35. 'UN Documents for Yemen: Security Council Presidential Statements' (Security Council Report), http://www.securitycouncilreport.org/un-documents/yemen/.

36. 'UN Declares Highest-level Aid Emergency in Yemen,' *Daily Star*, 1 July 2015, http://www.dailystar.com.lb/News/World/2015/Jul-01/304682-un-declares-highest-level-aid-emergency-in-yemen.ashx.

37. Jamal al-Jabiri and Fawaz al-Haidari, 'Yemen's Hadi Says "No Negotiations" with Rebels in Geneva,' Yahoo News, 8 June 2015, http://news.yahoo.com/yemen-president-says-un-talks-not-reconciliation-090613459.html.

38. Ibid.

39. 'Report of the Security Council Mission to Yemen' (United Nations Security Council, 27 January 2013).

40. Article 41 of the UN Charter allows the Security Council to decide what measures, not involving the use of armed force, are to be employed to give effect to its decisions. Ibid.

41. Hamid Alizadeh, 'Saudi War on Yemen: Rising Tensions in the Middle East and the Crisis of Imperialism,' In Defence of Marxism, 31 March 2015, http://www.marxist.com/saudi-war-on-yemen-rising-tensions-in-the-middle-east-and-the-crisis-of-imperialism.htm.

42. 'UN Declares Highest-level Aid Emergency in Yemen,' *Daily Star*, 1 July 2015, http://www.dailystar.com.lb/News/World/2015/Jul-01/304682-un-declares-highest-level-aid-emergency-in-yemen.ashx.

43. 'UN Condemns Saudi Attacks on Yemen,' Deutsche Welle, 4 May 2015, http://www.dw.com/en/un-condemns-saudi-attacks-on-yemen/a-18428486.

44. 'Saudi Arabia Bombs Yemen, Launches Coalition Op against Houthi Rebels,' RT Network, 25 March 2015, https://www.rt.com/news/244117-saudi-arabia-bombs-yemen-houthis/.

45. Ibid.

46. Thomas Gaist, 'US Threatens Military Intervention as UN Warns of "Disintegration" in Yemen,' World Socialist Web Site, 14 February 2015, https://www.wsws.org/en/articles/2015/02/14/yeme-f14.html.

47. 'UN Condemns Saudi Attacks on Yemen,' Deutsche Welle, 4 May 2015, http://www.dw.com/en/un-condemns-saudi-attacks-on-yemen/a-18428486.

48. 'Condemning Houthi Actions, Spiralling Violence, Security Council, in Statement on Yemen, Urges Non-State Actors to Withdraw from Government Facilities' (United Nations Security Council, 22 March 2015), http://www.un.org/press/en/2015/sc11828.doc.htm.

49. Bernard Haykel, 'Crisis in Yemen: Instability on the Arabian Peninsula,' Carnegie Council for Ethics in International Affairs (2015).

50. Jamal al-Jabiri and Fawaz al-Haidari, 'Yemen's Hadi Says "No Negotiations" with Rebels in Geneva,' Yahoo News, 8 June 2015, http://news.yahoo.com/yemen-president-says-un-talks-not-reconciliation-090613459.html.

51. Samuel Oakford, 'Saudi Arabia Used the UN to Brag about Helping Yemen while Still Bombing Yemen,' Vice News, 27 October 2015, https://news.vice.com/article/saudi-arabia-used-the-un-to-brag-about-helping-yemen-while-still-bombing-yemen.

52. 'Preamble of the United Nations,' United Nations, http://www.un.org/en/sections/un-charter/preamble/.

53. 'Yemen: Bombing of MSF Hospital May Amount to a War Crime,' Amnesty International, 27 October 2015, https://www.amnesty.org/en/press-releases/2015/10/yemen-bombing-of-msf-hospital-may-amount-to-a-war-crime/.

54. 'Yemen: MSF Hospital Destroyed by Airstrikes,' Médecins sans Frontières, 27 October 2015, http://www.doctorswithoutborders.org/article/yemen-msf-hospital-destroyed-airstrikes.

6. CRIMEA/UKRAINE: 'LEGITIMATE' RUSSIAN INTERESTS?

1. 'Russia Has Legitimate Interests in Ukraine: Shivshankar Menon, NSA,' *Economic Times*, 6 March 2014, http://articles.economictimes.indiatimes.com/2014-03-06/news/47971186_1_crimea-ukraine-black-sea-fleet.

2. 'Address by President of the Russian Federation,' (Kremlin, 18 March 2014), http://en.kremlin.ru/events/president/news/20603.

3. Ibid.

4. Adam Taylor, 'Is It Time for the West to Stop Calling It "Kiev" and Start Calling It "Kyiv"?' *Business Insider*, 25 January 2014, http://www.businessinsider.in/Is-It-Time-For-The-West-To-Stop-Calling-It-Kiev-And-Start-Calling-It-Kyiv/articleshow/29326098.cms.

5. John Herbst, 'Russia Would Lose a Fair Crimea Vote,' National Interest, 15 March 2014, http://nationalinterest.org/commentary/russia-would-lose-fair-crimea-vote-10054.

6. Meagan Clark, '10 Things You Need to Know about Ukraine's Economy,' International Business Times, 19 February 2014, http://www.ibtimes.com/10-things-you-need-know-about-ukraines-economy-1556651.

7. Anton Shekhovtsov and David C. Speedie, 'Crisis in Ukraine: The Role and Responsibility of the West' (New York: Carnegie Council Security Bulletin, 7 February 2014).

8. Nicolai Petro and David C. Speedie, 'Crisis in Ukraine: Crimean Stand-off' (New York: Carnegie Council Security Bulletin, 4 March 2014).

9. Ibid.

10. Peter Spence, 'Russian Economic Crisis: As It Happened,' Telegraph, 16 December 2014, http://www.telegraph.co.uk/finance/economics/11296233/Russian-economic-crisis-live.html.

11. Nicolai Petro and David C. Speedie, 'Crisis in Ukraine: Crimean Stand-off' (New York: Carnegie Council Security Bulletin, 4 March 2014).

12. Anton Shekhovtsov and David C. Speedie, 'Crisis in Ukraine: The Role and Responsibility of the West' (New York: Carnegie Council Security Bulletin, 7 February 2014).

13. Tom Parfitt, 'Crimea, One Year On: The Night Wolves Howl for Putin,' Telegraph, 17 March 2015, http://www.telegraph.co.uk/news/worldnews/europe/ukraine/11478456/Crimea-one-year-on-the-Night-Wolves-howl-for-Putin.html.

14. 'Public Opinion Survey: Residents of Ukraine' (International Republican Institute, 14-26 March 2014), http://www.iri.org/sites/default/files/2014%20April%205%20IRI%20Public%20Opinion%20Survey%20of%20Ukraine,%20March%2014-26,%202014.pdf.

15. 'Top NATO Commander Concerned about "Little Green Men" in Moldova,' Atlantic Council, 17 September 2014, http://www.atlanticcouncil.org/blogs/natosource/top-nato-commander-concerned-about-little-green-men-in-moldova.

16. Bill Chappell and Mark Memmott, 'Putin Says Those Aren't Russian Forces in Crimea,' NPR, 4 March 2014, http://www.npr.org/sections/

thetwo-way/2014/03/04/285653335/putin-says-those-arent-russian-forces-in-crimea.

17. 'NATO Recon Missed Everything: Admiral Reveals Details of Crimea Operation,' Sputnik News, 13 March 2015, http://sputniknews.com/russia/20150313/1019448901.html.

18. Alessandra Prentice, 'Putin Admits Russian Forces Were Deployed to Crimea,' Reuters, 17 April 2014, http://uk.reuters.com/article/2014/04/17/russia-putin-crimea-idUKL6N0N921H20140417.

19. Simona Kralova, 'Crimea Seen as "Hitler-style" Land Grab,' BBC, 7 March 2014, http://www.bbc.com/news/world-europe-26488652.

20. 'Statements Made to the Press by the President of the Security Council in 2014,' http://www.un.org/en/sc/documents/press/2014.shtml.

21. 'S/2014/189' (United Nations, 15 March 2014), http://www.securitycouncilreport.org/atf/cf/%7B65BFCF9B-6D27-4E9C-8CD3-CF6E4FF96FF9%7D/s_2014_189.pdf.

22. 'General Assembly Adopts Resolution Calling upon States Not to Recognize Changes in Status of Crimea Region' (27 March 2014), http://www.un.org/press/en/2014/ga11493.doc.htm.

23. 'Russia Again Claims Ukraine Shot Down MH17,' Guardian, 25 December 2014, http://www.theguardian.com/world/2014/dec/25/mh17-russia-claims-to-have-airfield-witness-who-blames-ukrainian-pilot.

24. Hubert Gude and Fidelius Schmid, 'Deadly Ukraine Crash: German Intelligence Claims Pro-Russian Separatists Downed MH17,' Spiegel, 19 October 2014, http://www.spiegel.de/international/europe/german-intelligence-blames-pro-russian-separatists-for-mh17-downing-a-997972.html.

25. 'Security Council Press Statement on Malaysian Plane Crash' (18 July 2014), http://www.un.org/press/en/2014/sc11480.doc.htm.

26. 'S/RES/2166(2014)' (21 July 2014), http://www.securitycouncilreport.org/atf/cf/%7B65BFCF9B-6D27-4E9C-8CD3-CF6E4FF96FF9%7D/s_res_2166.pdf.

27. 'MH17 tribunal would create "new hotbed of intl confrontation"–Russian UN envoy,' RT, 28 July 2015, https://www.rt.com/news/310910-mh17-tribunal-un-russia/.

28. 'Minsk Agreement on Ukraine Crisis: Text in Full,' Telegraph, 12

February 2015, http://www.telegraph.co.uk/news/worldnews/europe/ukraine/11408266/Minsk-agreement-on-Ukraine-crisis-text-in-full.html.

29. 'S/RES/2202(2015)' (17 February 2015), http://www.securitycouncilreport.org/atf/ cf/%7B65BFCF9B-6D27-4E9C-8CD3-CF6E4FF96FF9%7D/s_ res_2202.pdf.

30. 'Over 100 Ukrainian Troops, 50 Civilians Killed during Ceasefire: DM,' Xinhua, 8 June 2016, http://news.xinhuanet.com/english/2015-06/08/c_134308193.htm.

31. Thomas Graham and David C. Speedie, 'Ukraine and US-Russia Relations' (New York: Carnegie Council Security Bulletin, 21 April 2014).

32. M.K. Bhadrakumar, 'US Takes Russia's Help on Syria, Eases Pressure on Ukraine,' Rediff, 4 August 2015, http://blogs.rediff.com/mkbhadrakumar/2015/08/04/us-takes-russias-help-on-syria-eases-pressure-on-ukraine/.

7. SRI LANKA: THE RESPLENDENT ISLE

1. S.K. Senthivel, 'The Sri Lankan National Question' (Summary of talk intended to be delivered by Comrade Senthivel, the general secretary of New Democratic Marxist Leninist Party, Sri Lanka, on 2 February 2014), http://www.cpiml.in/home/index.php?view=article&id=1320:the-sri-lankan-national-question--sk-senthivel&Itemid=112&option=com_content.

2. K.T. Rajasingham, 'Sri Lanka: The Untold Story,' Asia Times Online, Chapter 16, 24 November 2001, http://atimes.com/ind-pak/CK24Df05.html.

3. T.D.S.A. Dissanayake, War or Peace in Sri Lanka (Delhi: Popular Prakashan, 2004) 16.

4. Ibid.

5. S.K. Senthivel, 'The Sri Lankan National Question' (Summary of talk intended to be delivered by Comrade Senthivel, the general secretary of New Democratic Marxist Leninist Party, Sri Lanka, on 2 February 2014), http://www.cpiml.in/home/index.php?view=article&id=1320:the-sri-lankan-national-question--sk-senthivel&Itemid=112&option=com_content.

6. Hardeep Singh Puri, 'Why India Is Right on Sri Lanka,' *Hindu*, 9 April 2013.

7. 'India's Sordid Record in Sri Lanka,' *Sunday Times*, 1 March 2015, http://www.sundaytimes.lk/150301/sunday-times-2/indias-sordid-record-in-lanka-138177.html.

8. J.N. Dixit, *Assignment Colombo* (Delhi: Konark Publishers, 1998), 24.

9. Ibid.

10. Shekhar Gupta, 'Large Number of Sri Lankan Tamil Rebels Acquires Training in Obscure Parts of Tamil Nadu,' *India Today*, 31 March 1984.

11. Ibid.

12. Ibid.

13. Ibid.

14. 'India's Sordid Record in Sri Lanka,' *Sunday Times*, 1 March 2015, http://www.sundaytimes.lk/150301/sunday-times-2/indias-sordid-record-in-lanka-138177.html.

15. Shekhar Gupta, 'Large Number of Sri Lankan Tamil Rebels Acquires Training in Obscure Parts of Tamil Nadu,' *India Today*, 31 March 1984.

16. 'The Broken Palmyra,' University Teachers for Human Rights, Jaffna, http://www.uthr.org/BP/volume1/Chapter8.htm.

17. Ibid.

18. J.N. Dixit, *Assignment Colombo* (Delhi: Konark Publishers, 1998), 24.

19. Ibid, 331

20. 'Indo-Sri Lanka Agreement to Establish Peace and Normalcy in Sri Lanka,' South Asia Terrorism Portal, http://www.satp.org/satporgtp/countries/shrilanka/document/papers/indo_srilanks_agreement.htm.

21. 'Indo-Lanka Accord' (United Nations, 29 July 1987), http://peacemaker.un.org/sites/peacemaker.un.org/files/IN%20LK_870729_Indo-Lanka%20Accord.pdf.

22. Ibid, 155.

23. Ibid, 156.

24. Depinder Singh, *Indian Peacekeeping Force in Sri Lanka* (Delhi: Natraj Publishers, 2001).

25. K.T. Rajasingham, 'Sri Lanka: The Untold Story,' Asia Times Online, Chapter 35, 24 November 2001, http://atimes.com/ind-pak/CK24Df05.html.

26. Ibid.

27. Ibid.

28. K.T. Rajasingham, 'Sri Lanka: The Untold Story,' Asia Times Online, Chapter 35, 24 November 2001, http://atimes.com/ind-pak/CK24Df05.html.

29. Ibid.

30. Pratyush, 'India and Sri Lanka's Civil War,' *Diplomat*, 29 December 2012, http://thediplomat.com/2012/12/india-and-sri-lankas-civil-war/.

31. Nitin A. Gokhale, *Sri Lanka: From War to Peace* (New Delhi: Har-Anand Publications, 2009).

32. 'Crisis in Sri Lanka,' International Coalition for the Responsibility to Protect, http://www.responsibilitytoprotect.org/index.php/crises/crisis-in-sri-lanka#UN.

33. Nirupama Subramanian, 'Sri Lanka's Moment of Truth,' *Indian Express*, 18 September 2015, http://indianexpress.com/article/explained/sri-lankas-moment-of-truth/.

34. Ibid.

35. 'Statement Attributable to the Spokesman for the Secretary-General on the Release of the Report of the Office of the Human Rights Commissioner's Investigation on Sri Lanka' (17 September 2015), http://www.un.org/sg/statements/index.asp?nid=8984.

8. DESPERATE MIGRANTS: THE POLICY-INDUCED CRISIS

1. 'Europe/Mediterranean Migration Response,' International Organization for Migration, 7 April 2016, http://www.iom.int/sites/default/files/situation_reports/file/Europe-Med-Migration-Response_Sitrep18-7April2016.pdf.

2. William R. Polk, 'Understanding Syria: From Pre-Civil War to Post-Assad,' *Atlantic*, 10 December 2013, http://www.theatlantic.com/international/archive/2013/12/understanding-syria-from-pre-civil-war-to-post-assad/281989/.

3. Ibid.

4. 'Syria: Mapping the Conflict,' BBC, 10 July 2015, http://www.bbc.com/news/world-middle-east-22798391.

5. Joel Gehrke, 'Obama Waives Ban on Arming Terrorists to Allow Aid to Syrian Opposition,' *Washington Examiner*, 15 September 2013, http://www.washingtonexaminer.com/updated-obama-waives-ban-on-arming-terrorists-to-allow-aid-to-syrian-opposition/article/2535885.

6. William R. Polk, 'Understanding Syria: From Pre-Civil War to Post-Assad,' *Atlantic*, 10 December 2013, http://www.theatlantic.com/international/archive/2013/12/understanding-syria-from-pre-civil-war-to-post-assad/281989/.

7. Ibid.

8. Zack Beauchamp, Max Fisher and Dylan Matthews, '27 Maps That Explain the Crisis in Iraq,' Vox, 8 August 2014, http://www.vox.com/a/maps-explain-crisis-iraq.

9. Patrick Kingsley, Mark Rice-Oxley and Alberto Nadelli, 'Syrian Refugee Crisis: Why Has It Become So Bad?' *Guardian*, 4 September 2015, http://www.theguardian.com/world/2015/sep/04/syrian-refugee-crisis-why-has-it-become-so-bad.

10. Chris McGreal, 'UN Security Council Is Failing Syria, Ban Ki-moon Admits,' *Guardian*, 7 September 2015, http://www.theguardian.com/world/2015/sep/07/un-security-council-is-failing-syria-ban-ki-moon.

11. A face-to-face survey conducted amongst a representative sample of the Libyan population between December 2011 and January 2012 in a joint research project by the Institute of Human Sciences at the University of Oxford and Oxford Research International.

12. Garikai Chengu, 'Libya: From Africa's Richest State under Gaddafi to Failed State after NATO Intervention,' Global Research, 22 February 2015, www.globalresearch.ca/libya-from-africas-richest-state-under-gaddafi-to-failed-state-after-nato-intervention/5408740.

13. 'Report of the Working Group on the Universal Periodic Review: Libya Arab Jamahiriya' (United Nations Human Rights Council, 4 January 2011).

14. Garikai Chengu, 'Libya: From Africa's Richest State under Gaddafi to Failed State after NATO Intervention,' Global Research, 22 February 2015, www.globalresearch.ca/libya-from-africas-richest-state-under-gaddafi-to-failed-state-after-nato-intervention/5408740.

15. Owen Jones, 'Libya Is a Disaster We Helped Create. The West

Must Take Responsibility,' *Guardian*, 24 March 2014, www.
theguardian.com/commentisfree/2014/mar/24/libya-disaster-shames-
western-interventionists.

16. Giorgio Cafiero and Daniel Wagner, 'Four Years after Gaddafi, Libya
Is a Failed State,' Foreign Policy in Focus, 6 April 2015, www.fpif.
org/four-years-after-gaddafi-libya-is-a-failed-state.

17. Garikai Chengu, 'Libya: From Africa's Richest State under Gaddafi to
Failed State after NATO Intervention,' Global Research, 22 February
2015, www.globalresearch.ca/libya-from-africas-richest-state-under-
gaddafi-to-failed-state-after-nato-intervention/5408740.

18. 'Worldwide Displacement Hits All-time High as War and Persecution
Increase' (United Nations High Commissioner for Refugees, 18 June
2015), www.unhcr.org/558193896.html.

19. Paul Mutter, 'The Fight for Yemen, Then and Now,' The Arabist. 28
April 2015, http://arabist.net/blog/2015/4/28/the-fight-for-yemen-
then-and-now.

20. Suzanne Goldenberg, 'From the Archive, 19 March 2003: Suddenly,
the Iraq War Is Very Real,' *Guardian*, 19 March 2013, http://www.
theguardian.com/theguardian/2013/mar/19/iraq-war-saddam-bush-
starts-2003.

21. Zack Beauchamp, Max Fisher and Dylan Matthews, '27 Maps That
Explain the Crisis in Iraq,' Vox, 8 August 2014, http://www.vox.
com/a/maps-explain-crisis-iraq.

22. Tarek Osman is a political economist, author and broadcaster. He
is the author of international bestseller *Egypt on the Brink* (New Haven:
Yale University Press, 2010), which appeared weeks before Egypt's
2011 uprising.

23. Tarek Osman, 'Why Border Lines Drawn with a Ruler in WW1 Still
Rock the Middle East,' BBC, 14 December 2013, http://www.
bbc.com/news/world-middle-east-25299553.

24. 'Iraq 10 Years On: In Numbers,' BBC, 20 March 2013, www.bbc.
com/news/world-middle-east-21752819.

25. 'Women Were More Respected under Saddam, Say Women's Groups,'
IRIN News, 13 April 2006, http://www.irinnews.org/report/26289/
iraq-women-were-more-respected-under-saddam-say-women-s-
groups.

26. Zack Beauchamp, Max Fisher and Dylan Matthews, '27 Maps That

Explain the Crisis in Iraq,' Vox, 8 August 2014, http://www.vox.com/a/maps-explain-crisis-iraq.

27. 'Iraq 10 Years On: In Numbers,' BBC, 20 March 2013, www.bbc.com/news/world-middle-east-21752819.

28. Franck Düvell and Irina Lapshyna, 'The EuroMaidan Protests, Corruption, and War in Ukraine: Migration Trends and Ambitions,' Migration Policy Institute, 15 July 2015, www.migrationpolicy.org/article/euromaidan-protests-corruption-and-war-ukraine-migration-trends-and-ambitions.

29. Franck Düvell is Senior Researcher, Centre on Migration, Policy, and Society (COMPAS), at the University of Oxford.

30. Albert O. Hirschman, 'Exit, Voice, and the State,' *World Politics,* Vol. 28, No. 1 (1978): 90–107, http://homepages.wmich.edu/~plambert/comp/hirschman.pdf.

31. Patrick Boehler and Sergio Peçanha, 'The Global Refugee Crisis, Region by Region,' *New York Times,* 26 August 2015, http://www.nytimes.com/interactive/2015/06/09/world/migrants-global-refugee-crisis-mediterranean-ukraine-syria-rohingya-malaysia-iraq.html.

32. Ryhor Astapenia, 'Migrants from Eastern Ukraine Put Pressure on Belarus,' *Belarus Digest,* 3 August 2015, www.belarusdigest.com/story/migrants-eastern-ukraine-put-pressure-belarus-22949.

33. Rick Lyman, 'Ukrainian Migrants Fleeing Conflict Get a Cool Reception in Europe,' *New York Times,* 30 May 2015, www.nytimes.com/2015/05/31/world/europe/ukrainian-migrants-fleeing-conflict-get-a-cool-reception-in-europe.html?_r=0.

34. 'Russian Migration Service: Inflow of Ukrainians Proof of Humanitarian Disaster in Ukraine,' Russia Beyond the Headlines, 25 May 2015, www.rbth.com/news/2015/05/25/russian_migration_service_inflow_of_ukrainians_proof_of_humanitarian_dis_46336.html.

35. 'US to Accept 10,000 Syrian Refugees: White House,' *Hindu,* 11 September 2015.

36. Ian Simpson, 'Hundreds of Americans Sign Petition Offering to House Syrian Refugees,' Reuters, 7 September 2015, http://uk.reuters.com/article/2015/09/07/uk-europe-migrants-usa-petition-idUKKCN0R72CL20150907.

37. Amanda Taub, 'We Know How to Solve the Refugee Crisis but It

Will Take More Than Money,' Vox, 9 September 2015, http://www. vox.com/2015/9/9/9293139/refugee-crisis-europe-syria-solution.

38. Melissa Eddy, 'Violent Backlash against Migrants in Germany as Asylum-Seekers Pour In,' *New York Times*, 13 August 2015, http:// www.nytimes.com/2015/08/14/world/europe/germany-migrants-attacks-asylum-seekers-backlash.html?_r=0.

39. 'German Anti-Migrant Rally Highlights European Backlash,' *Times of India*, 19 October 2015, http://timesofindia.indiatimes.com/ world/europe/German-anti-migrant-rally-highlights- European-backlash/articleshow/49449310.cms.

40. Philip Stephens, 'If Angela Merkel Is Ousted, Europe Will Unravel,' *Financial Times*, 29 October 2015, http://www.ft.com/intl/cms/s/0/ e986df5c-7d80-11e5-98fb-5a6d4728f74e.html.

41. Ibid.

42. Nick Robins-Early, 'How the Refugee Crisis Is Fueling the Rise of Europe's Right,' Huffington Post, 28 October 2015, http://www.huffingtonpost.com/entry/europe-right-wing-refugees_562e9e64e4b06317990f1922?section= india&adsSiteOverride=in.

43. 'Middle East Wars Deprive 13m Children of Education: UN,' BBC, 3 September 2015, http://www.bbc.com/news/world-middle-east-34136074.

9. THE DOCTRINE OF THE RESPONSIBILITY TO PROTECT

1. The etymology of the term has been thoroughly researched in Gareth Evans, *The Responsibility to Protect* (Washington, DC: Brookings Institution, 2008).

2. The Convention on the Prevention and Punishment of the Crime of Genocide (CPPCG) was adopted by the United Nations General Assembly on 9 December 1948 as General Assembly Resolution 260. The convention entered into force on 12 January 1951. All participating countries are required to prevent and punish actions of genocide, whether carried out in war or in peacetime. The number of states that have ratified the convention is currently 147.

3. Satish Nambiar, 'An Indian General Recalls How the World Failed Srebrenica 20 Years Ago,' The Wire, 12 July 2015, http://thewire. in/2015/07/12/an-indian-general-recalls-how-the-world-failed-srebrenica-20-years-ago-6051/.

INDEX

ACKNOWLEDGEMENTS

This book is about the use of force, the arming of rebels, and the unravelling of countries brought about by perilous interventions. By this, I neither mean to imply that all interventions are bad nor am I arguing that there is a notion of 'immaculate conception' in the affairs of countries when it comes to intervention by outside powers. I developed the idea of this book as an eyewitness to how the Security Council dealt with the question of intervention in specific contexts. It could not, therefore, have been written if I had not been posted to New York as India's Permanent Representative in 2009 for the privilege of representing India on the Security Council in 2011–12. The timing of my being assigned to New York becomes important because this was when we sought election to the Security Council after a gap of seventeen years and won the election overwhelmingly.

I must, therefore, start by acknowledging the role of those who delayed my appointment to New York and those whose efforts finally resulted in it materializing.

The team that assisted me on the Council included the Foreign Service's best and brightest: Manjeev Puri, Vinay Kumar, Manish Gupta, Prakash Gupta and, earlier, Anupam Ray and Vikram Doraiswamy. Countries have traditionally sent their finest diplomats to New York, and this group was a case in point.

Our delegation stood out both for its small size and exceptional professionalism. An intelligent and hard-working set of colleagues is indispensable, particularly during a stint on the Council.

After leaving the Indian Mission to the UN on retirement, I was invited to join the International Peace Institute (IPI), a non-profit think tank headquartered in New York with offices in Vienna and Manama. I would like to thank its President, Terje Rod-Larsen, for the hospitality shown by the IPI. As its Vice-President and Secretary General of the Independent Commission on Multilateralism (ICM) chaired by former Prime Minister of Australia Kevin Rudd, I had the unique privilege of interacting with a number of highly intelligent, intellectually sophisticated and experienced people.

Two of them, Omar El Okdah and Youssef Mahmoud, need to be singled out because they were particularly helpful. The brilliant Omar, all of twenty-six years of age when this book was written, has an academic record that would be the envy of any academic: 43 points in IB, a first from Oxford and an MA from Columbia. He packs in a punch, particularly in terms of his knowledge of the parts of the world this book covers. He guided me to the latest literature and pointed me in directions which I had not thought of. This was especially valuable because I have never served in the Middle East. Youssef Mahmoud, on the other hand, has an unmatched wealth of experience as a former SRSG and USG in the UN. Engaging with him is an education not only in contemporary developments in the Middle East and North Africa, but also the likely evolution of the state-citizen compact and its fault lines, on which his understanding is of a true master. He also very graciously agreed to write the afterword.

I also benefited immensely from long discussions with Rami Shehadeh, who looks after the Syria file in the Department of

Political Affairs in the UN. Conversations with him invariably served as a reality check and a safeguard against the exuberance expressed in other quarters.

This book would not have seen the light of day had it not been for the painstaking and diligent research of my exceptionally bright and outstanding young researchers, Madhulika Narasimhan and Anubhav Roy, policy analysts in my New Delhi Office. Writing becomes so much easier when you can leave the endnotes and citations to someone else. They immersed themselves wholeheartedly in this project. In several respects, it was a joint voyage of discovery.

To my younger colleagues on the IPI/ICM team, Rodrigo Saad, my executive assistant, Anette Ringnes and Ariun Enkhsaikhan, a special word of thanks. Also to Marie Michelle Artur and Patricia Cortes, my wife Lakshmi's colleagues, for their many acts of kindness.

I owe big thanks to Krishan Chopra, Publisher and Chief Editor at HarperCollins. He met me and encouraged me to write a book. Here it is. He and the other book doctors on his team— Siddhesh Inamdar, Shreya Punj and Bonita Vaz-Shimray—were ever so courteous and helpful.

As young language students in Tokyo, Lakshmi and I came across a colloquial Japanese expression, really a question: 'Anatano my wife desu ka?' which translates as, 'Is she your "my wife"?' I have been married forty-two years. She is my best friend, companion and soulmate. She is probably the most accomplished wordsmith I have encountered in a long professional life. She has been a great source of strength and support on this journey, my first attempt at a book. I did, however, have a little difficulty. I had to once or twice remind her not to re-write my draft. Somewhat reluctantly she agreed, but only after I had reassured her that several members of Krishan's team were busy trying to do the same. Playing around with someone else's draft is not easy when the writer has strong views and a ready willingness to own up and acknowledge his mistakes, the most rigorous peer review notwithstanding.

A special round of thanks to my lovely daughters Himayani and Tilottama, and to my wonderful son-in-law Hari, for continuing to be sources of strength and inspiration. And last but not the least, a special word of thanks to my young friend Mahesh Chawla. He had to bear the brunt of my being technologically challenged and preferring the traditional way of putting pen to paper.

I place on record my eternal gratitude to all those who helped. The views expressed and responsibilities for any errors that still remain are entirely mine.

ABOUT THE AUTHOR

HARDEEP SINGH PURI is a former Indian Foreign Service officer who served as the Permanent Representative of India to the United Nations in Geneva from 2002 to 2005 and in New York from 2009 to 2013, coinciding with the period in 2011–12 when India was a non-permanent member of the Security Council. He was president of the Council in August 2011 and November 2012, and chairman of its Counter-terrorism Committee from January 2011 to February 2013. He was previously stationed at important diplomatic posts in Brazil, Japan, Sri Lanka and the UK.